TWILIGHT IN HAZARD

Twilight
in Hazard

AN APPALACHIAN RECKONING

ALAN MAIMON

MELVILLE HOUSE
BROOKLYN · LONDON

Twilight in Hazard: An Appalachian Reckoning
First published in 2021 by Melville House

First Melville House Printing: June 2021

Melville House Publishing
46 John Street
Brooklyn, NY 11201

and

Melville House UK
Suite 2000
16/18 Woodford Road
London E7 0HA

mhpbooks.com
@melvillehouse

ISBN: 978-1-61219-997-9
ISBN: 978-1-61219-886-6 (eBook)

Library of Congress Control Number 2021932767

Designed by Euan Monaghan

Printed in the United States of America

1 3 5 7 9 10 8 6 4 2

A catalog record for this book is available
from the Library of Congress

For my children

"And what we students of history always learn is that the human being is a very complicated contraption and that they are not good or bad but are good and bad and the good comes out of the bad and the bad out of the good, and the devil take the hindmost."

—Robert Penn Warren, *All the King's Men*

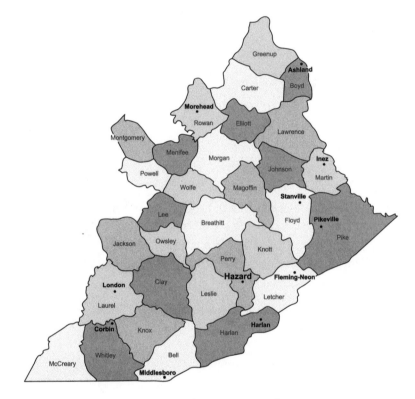

Counties of Eastern Kentucky

Contents

TWILIGHT IN HAZARD

Preface

By every socioeconomic measurement, the area of Eastern Kentucky that I covered for the *Louisville Courier-Journal* in the 2000s is Appalachia at its most compelling and extreme. I was the last major metropolitan newspaper reporter based in those coalfields, and I wanted to write this book to provide what I believe is the most complete account to date of one of the most mythologized and least understood places in the country.

It took me five years of chronicling Eastern Kentucky as a reporter and another fifteen years of thinking about and returning to those stories, in my dual role as a writer and the husband of a Harlan County coal miner's daughter, to understand why we still don't understand Appalachia.

There was hope after the 2016 presidential election that we might be moving toward a more nuanced view of Eastern Kentucky when, for a moment in time, the country's scholars and storytellers begrudgingly moved past looking at the region merely as an object of perverse curiosity. All of the credit for this hint of progress went to one man: Donald Trump. In the wake of Trump's improbable ascendancy to the White House, writers and commentators, almost exclusively from Blue State America, set their gaze on Appalachia to ask variations of the same question: *How could you have let this happen?* Forget that Pennsylvania, Michigan, and Wisconsin were the states that swung the election to Trump. Forget that most Eastern Kentucky counties gave previous Republican presidential candidates John McCain and Mitt Romney roughly the same level of support that they gave Trump. And forget that Bernie Sanders trounced Hillary Clinton by a two-to-one margin in most parts of Eastern

Kentucky in the 2016 Democratic primary. The experts pronounced that Appalachia held the key to explaining Trump and Trumpism. For the first time, Appalachians and what they thought actually mattered to the country at large. Or that was the premise, at least.

This wave of national interest in Eastern Kentucky was predicated on a misinterpretation of voter registration figures. It is true that registered Democrats far outnumber registered Republicans in many counties in the region, but those numbers are a vestige of mid-twentieth-century social dynamics that do not represent the political leanings of today. If reporters left their bubbles in the hopes of discovering large clusters of people who voted for Barack Obama in 2008 and 2012 and Donald Trump in 2016, they simply went to the wrong place. Of the 206 counties nationwide that fit that description, 31 are in Iowa and 23 are in Wisconsin. Only one, Elliott County, is in Kentucky.[1] The results there were indeed notable because Elliott County had voted for the Democratic candidate in every presidential election since the county was established in 1869.[2] In 2020, Elliott County again came out in force for Trump, who carried every Kentucky county but two, Jefferson and Fayette.

In the absence of anything more broadly applicable to a dissection of electoral politics, most of the resulting Eastern Kentucky–set stories relied on tired old tropes about alienation from government and parochial worldviews. Welcome to Trump Country, everyone. Nothing more to see here. Time to catch that flight back. Left unchallenged, that bogus narrative has persisted, with national publications ruminating on a "split partisan identity" in Eastern Kentucky that doesn't exist.

Unlike after the 2016 election, no one in 2020 flocked to Eastern Kentucky seeking insight or votes. Only parts of Central Appalachia in key battleground states received any attention at all from the presidential candidates. Moon Township, Pennsylvania, became a regular campaign stop. For all the attention it was paid, Appalachian Kentucky might as well have been a region on the moon. The future of Central Appalachian coal jobs, a major theme of the '16 campaign, hardly got mentioned, mainly because Trump failed to deliver on his promise to revive the coal industry. So, instead, he tried to use Democratic opposition to fracking as a new Republican rallying point.

Yet there remains an undeniable symbolism to Eastern Kentucky, and it is one that both captures and transcends the troubled political climate of the day. But to grasp it, we need to get better at viewing the region in the framework of a larger American story about income inequality, generational poverty, and the lack of upward mobility. Only then will we start the demystification process.

When I think about the things I saw and documented in Appalachian Kentucky, I realize that this small swath of America with a population of around 700,000 offers tremendous insight into who we are and what we value as a nation. You cannot tell the story of a place as complex and contradictory as Eastern Kentucky in 800- or 1,200-word chunks written in inverted pyramid style, as I was once tasked with doing. That was a whiplash-inducing and at times overwhelming assignment. Coal mining could have been its own beat. The same applies to prescription drugs, poverty, religion, and culture. This book is my attempt to pull all of the strands together, to journey beyond the hundreds of newspaper bylines I accumulated, to capture the essence of a place that I observed for years and continue to revisit and reevaluate. The major events I chronicled for the *Courier-Journal* frame the narrative, but it is the material that didn't make it into the paper that I believe makes this more than just another crack at explaining Appalachia.

The book examines the economic and social experiment that created the power structure of modern-day Eastern Kentucky, a proxy for struggling regions everywhere, and traces how the dramatic events of the early years of this century impacted the region and influenced the soul of the nation as a whole. It also highlights the essential role of the journalist in writing the first rough drafts of history, especially now that newspapers have left Eastern Kentucky and places like it, leaving no one to tell some very essential stories.

The result is a story about drug epidemics, political violence, environmental degradation, and morality debates, but also about a seemingly laid-back rural culture where a large segment of the population is clinically depressed, about an area of natural beauty where the land has been stripped and the forests torched for amusement, and about a defining push and pull between fierce pride and a nagging sense of inferiority. Ultimately it is a story about how America and its institutions have failed Eastern Kentucky, but for better and for worse, how the people of the region have remained loyal to their idea of Americanism.

Do Us Right

In the fall of 2000, I had a decision to make: stay in Europe, where I had been working and living since graduating from college five years earlier, or put an end to my overseas adventure and move back to the United States to continue my burgeoning journalism career. I had a job as the news assistant in *The New York Times*'s Berlin bureau where, between making coffee runs and trips to the post office for the bureau chief, I had managed to carve out a niche for myself as a reporter, mostly covering the European sports scene. Eventually I moved on to weightier subject matter, including a story about the shattered lives of female swimmers in East Germany who were force-fed a daily regimen of steroids as young girls and sent out to compete in championship meets.[1] The sources I developed while writing a number of smaller pieces on the subject helped me build rapport with these former athletes. I was proud of the story. I felt it mattered. And I wanted to do more like it.

But after half a decade in Europe, I felt on the brink of becoming an "expat," that breed of individual who achieves an advanced level of comfort abroad and starts to question the virtues of returning home. The year 2000 seemed as favorable a time as any to start a new chapter. Earlier that year, I had declined admission to an international studies program at Georgetown. The thought of sitting in a classroom for two years didn't appeal to me. Relocating to my native Philadelphia or another East Coast city also didn't grab me. The editors I worked with at the *Times* felt I could use more seasoning, and a job at a different big-city newspaper would have likely meant a few years of dues-paying on the suburban desk covering zoning and school board meetings—not a bad gig, but not the kind of beat that excited me.

Based on a somewhat vague notion, I came to the conclusion that my transition to life back in the United States would go more smoothly if I went to a place where I had no connections or familiarity, where the newness would challenge and consume me. If possible, I wanted to work in a region that would feel as foreign to me as a different country. It wasn't long after I formulated that idea that I ran across an ad for an opening in the *Louisville Courier-Journal*'s Eastern Kentucky bureau. Based in the town of Hazard, it seemed to fit the bill. I read up a bit on the *Courier-Journal* and learned that the Hazard office had recently been vacated by a reporter who won a prestigious national award for a series called *Dust, Deception and Death* about coal mining industry manipulation of coal-dust tests in underground mines. That was the high-impact type of project I wanted to work on.

Up until that point, I don't think that I had ever really known anyone from Appalachian Kentucky. On family car trips in my youth, we had nipped the corners of West Virginia and passed through some of the other more well-traveled parts of the region, but Eastern Kentucky, as I soon learned, isn't a place you pass through on the way to anywhere else. If you end up there, it's because that's where you intended to go. And not many people from outside the area have that intention.

Other than it being poor and poorly depicted in movies, particularly John Boorman's 1972 Academy Award–nominated film, *Deliverance* (tagline: "Where does the camping trip end . . . and the nightmare begin?"), I knew little about Appalachia. But its reputation intrigued me. One of my strongest mental connections to the area came from a short-story anthology that my father cowrote in the 1970s. One of the stories is about a man who enters into a conversation with a stranger while riding a metropolitan subway to his high school reunion. We only hear one side of the conversation as the man talks about his eagerness to reconnect with old friends, but also about his deep regret over how he and his classmates tormented a newly arrived kid from Appalachia to the point where his parents pulled him out of the school. I had thought a lot over the years about people's tendency to stereotype and how dehumanizing a habit it is. Few areas in the US have been as subject to stereotype as Appalachia.

I applied for the Hazard job, which entailed covering an area roughly the size of Vermont and New Hampshire put together and included eight of the poorest twenty counties in the country. The federal government has a name for places where more than 20 percent of the population has lived in poverty for the past twenty-five years: persistent poverty counties. The entire eastern part of Kentucky falls into that category. A US map highlighting the nation's most economically distressed areas shows clusters of extreme poverty in certain urban areas, American Indian communities, and the Deep South. But no other part of the country has as concentrated a pocket of distress as Eastern Kentucky.[2]

The editors at the *Courier-Journal* flew me in for an interview. It was a long day of meetings in a newsroom full of clicking keyboards and harried-looking journalists. My only distinct memory of the visit was something that regional editor Gideon Gil said to me as I made the rounds:

"Most people in Louisville have never been to Eastern Kentucky and have no idea what's happening there," he said. "We would want you to cover the area like a foreign correspondent would."

That confirmed what had been running through my head. I could live in the United States and still heed Stephen Dedalus's words about "fly[ing] by those nets" of nationality, language, and religion. I could be a foreigner in my own country. A few months later, I accepted an offer to become the newspaper's Eastern Kentucky correspondent. My planned relocation to Kentucky invited the expected jokes. "Have fun in Kentucky working on your still in between articles on squirrel brain delicacies and coon huntin' contests," one friend emailed. Another suggested I could get a luxury box at the local cockfighting arena. And of course there were the *Dukes of Hazzard* quips. I'll get to that subject in a moment.

*

In late December 2000, I packed up all of my worldly possessions, most of which fit in an oversized blue duffel bag and the rest of which I had shipped to the nearest airline hub in Cincinnati. My orientation at the *Courier-Journal* lasted two days. The paper put me up at the historic Brown Hotel, the birthplace of the Hot Brown sandwich, a riff on the classic Welsh rarebit. I tried one and learned I'm not a fan of turkey sandwiches smothered in brownish cheese sauce. I took a tour of the Louisville Slugger baseball bat museum and factory and got to know the city a little bit, concluding that its sensibilities weren't totally Southern, but not quite Midwestern or Northern, either. I met new colleagues, including former 1970s-era Hazard correspondent David Hawpe, who had recently been displaced as editor-in-chief of the paper and moved over to run the op-ed department. Hawpe's new office sat on the third floor of the building, but it felt miles away from the rattle and hum of the cubicle-filled fourth-floor newsroom. A smiling woman sat at a reception desk, the air didn't smell of burnt coffee, and plush leather and mahogany furnishings filled the area.

Hawpe was known as a vigorous supporter of aggressive coverage of the Kentucky coalfields. Born in the Eastern Kentucky town of Pikeville, Hawpe expressed clear affection for the people of the region, but he had a far less favorable view of the institutions that controlled them. He had no love for the coal industry. He believed it had done far more harm than good to Appalachian Kentucky. In December 1970, Hawpe covered the Hurricane Creek mine disaster, which took place on the one-year anniversary of the historic passage of the federal Coal Mine Health and Safety Act. Hawpe was eating lunch that day when he heard about the explosion at the Leslie County mine. He drove to the scene through a foot of snow and got there even before the rescue teams did. Only one of the thirty-eight miners working that shift survived. Hawpe saw the makeshift morgue that was set up near the local high school to temporarily house the disfigured bodies. A subsequent investigation of the blast revealed egregious safety failures at the mine, including the use of illegal explosives. Elburt Osborn, the head of the US Bureau of Mines, downplayed the incident by saying the disaster "was not unexpected" and that the coal industry had had "two good years" since an explosion at a West Virginia mine killed seventy-eight people. "I think we can almost expect one of these a year," Osborn said.[3]

Hawpe said he vowed after Hurricane Creek to do what he could as a journalist to bring attention to and advocate for mine safety. During our first meeting, he told me that he would quit the paper if it or Gannett, the Arlington, Virginia–based company that owned it, ever decided to retreat from Eastern Kentucky. He also spoke proudly about his 1975 Nieman Fellowship at Harvard.

Hawpe, like many of the old-timers at the paper, viewed the corporate overlords with suspicion. Gannett, whose biggest asset was and remains *USA Today*, had spent years snapping up family-owned metropolitan dailies around the country. Along the way, the company had gained a reputation for streamlining operations in the name of increasing profit margins. This type of business model was anathema to old-school journalists at the *Courier-Journal* who came to the paper prior to its sale to Gannett in the 1980s, when it was still locally and family owned. When I was deciding whether to take the job in Kentucky, I sought the advice of veteran journalists across the country, all of whom lauded the paper's former longtime owners, the Bingham family. The five Pulitzer Prizes that the *Courier-Journal* earned during the Bingham era suggested that the praise was deserved. One of those prizes, for international reporting from Cambodia in 1980, stood out to me. No papers of similar size would have dreamed of sending a reporter to cover the fall of Pol Pot's Khmer Rouge, but Joel Brinkley, later of *The New York Times*, got the assignment and did stellar work with it. The paper received another of its Pulitzers in 1967 for a series of stories about the environmental toll of strip mining. More than a few people inside the

Courier-Journal building spoke wistfully of those days, realizing they were likely never to return on Gannett's watch.

I had reason for hope, however, that my coverage of Eastern Kentucky would get prominent play in the paper. Having Hawpe in charge of editorials helped ensure that my news stories would generate a significant number of topics for the opinions page, which, along with sports and the comics pages, was the most popular section of the paper. On the flip side, I learned there was a contingent of metro editors and reporters who felt a Louisville newspaper should stick to Louisville, even though we were considered the state's paper of record. In addition to Hazard, the paper had a state capital bureau in Frankfort, as well as a south central Kentucky bureau in Bowling Green, a western Kentucky bureau in Paducah, and a central Kentucky bureau in Elizabethtown. It also had a Washington correspondent. The responsibility fell to Gideon Gil and his successors on the regional desk to fight for space in the daily paper for stories from outside of Louisville.

I was excited to dive into the new job. Following my brief orientation, I threw my duffel in the back of a company-owned Ford Explorer, alongside a box containing a chunky laptop computer, reporters' notebooks, an *AP Stylebook*, and copies of James Still's classic Appalachian novel *River of Earth* and Harry Caudill's seminal work about the region, *Night Comes to the Cumberlands*. I kept my cell and satellite phones in the front seat with me. From Louisville, I headed due east on Interstate 64 for about seventy-five miles to the Bluegrass area around Lexington, a land of thoroughbred farms, stately manors, and the state's flagship university. I then pivoted south past the "Winchester Wall," a figurative geographical divide between Central and Eastern Kentucky, where major highways end. I continued past the Red River Gorge area and onto Route 15, the kudzu-lined hills providing a clue that I was entering a new land. The Louisville-to-Hazard trip takes between three and four hours depending on fog and other weather conditions on 15, not to mention how many coal trucks you get stuck behind on that last stretch of mostly two-lane blacktop. There are a lot fewer coal trucks pounding those roads these days.

I got to Hazard—population 5,000 and dropping—on Friday, December 22, 2000, about a week after Florida stopped studying hanging chads and Al Gore conceded the election to George W. Bush. I spent my first weeks in a room in a motel that was at the time the only real motel in Hazard. This was before the Hampton Inn, the Holiday Inn Express, and the Applebee's moved in, giving the town not only name-brand hotels, but a full-service chain restaurant. The motel I stayed in overlooked the well-traveled Route 80, a stretch of road that connected to the Daniel Boone Parkway, and an impressive row of fast-food restaurants. It was up on a hill alongside a nightclub called T. J.'s Hillbilly Palace Bar, which eventually shut down and became the Gospel Light Baptist Church. Based on the lack of cars in the motel parking lot, I concluded that I might be one of maybe ten guests in the entire establishment.

During those first days in Hazard—among the coldest and shortest of the year—I tried to get a sense of place as I sat holed up in my room. I started with the recent election results. Most Eastern Kentucky counties had swung for Gore, in some cases by wide margins. In the House of Representatives, however, the area once again backed Republican Hal Rogers, who defeated his Democratic opponent by a three-to-one landslide to win his eleventh term in Congress. Over the next few years, I would write a lot about Rogers's various efforts to bring federal money to Kentucky's Fifth Congressional District. One story I didn't write but wish I had was about a state transportation agency decision in 2003 to rename the aforementioned Daniel Boone Parkway after Rogers, in recognition of his success in securing funding to make the roadway toll-free. A handful of Boone descendants complained about the name change, but a resolution seeking to give Boone and Rogers equal billing on the parkway failed to pass the Kentucky House of Representatives. History be damned, Rogers had made it so motorists no longer had to fish around for quarters while driving the roadway. Such voter-friendly maneuvers help explain why Rogers returned to Congress for a twenty-first term in 2021.

I also leafed through the local phone book, which was more of a phone booklet, really, combining both the white and yellow pages. I noticed that certain surnames dominated the former: Combs, Fugate, Neace, Maggard, and Noble, among them. A friend had mentioned a Hazard-born theater director she had worked with in Chicago by the name of Napier. The director told my friend that Napiers comprised 80 percent of the local population. He was exaggerating, but sure enough, the Napier section of the phone booklet ran almost an entire page.

To avoid too strong a case of cabin fever, I spent some time driving around the area, sticking to Route 80 between Hazard and Prestonsburg, another town on my beat. Out on the road, it was mostly just me, the coal trucks, and the entertaining road signs pointing travelers toward little mountain hamlets with names like Dwarf, Rowdy, Soft Shell, Mousie, Fisty, and Pippa Passes. Back then, there wasn't much activity, commercial or otherwise, along that road. Today, it's dotted with drug treatment clinics, a belated response to an epidemic that I would soon become very familiar with.

My coverage area was expansive, and I wanted to figure out Hazard's place in the larger framework of both Eastern Kentucky and the coal-producing counties of southeastern Kentucky. Twenty miles up the road in Hindman was the Hindman Settlement School and the Appalachian Artisan Center. Paintsville, located in the home county of Loretta Lynn, Crystal Gayle, and Chris Stapleton billed itself as the music capital of Eastern Kentucky. Whitesburg, home to the arts collective Appalshop, laid claim to being the cultural capital of Eastern Kentucky. Harlan, through film and television, probably ranked as the region's most infamous county. Prestonsburg was known for its courageous group of public interest lawyers and for the East Kentucky Science Center and Planetarium. There was also the part of Eastern Kentucky that had more in common with the Deep South. The town of Corbin, which is best known as the birthplace of Colonel Harland Sanders of fried-chicken fame, was the site of a 1919 race riot that culminated in a white mob rounding up hundreds of Black railroad workers and, at gunpoint, putting them on freight trains bound for Knoxville, Tennessee, an act prompted by reports that a white man had been mugged by two Black men. Corbin had remained a largely segregated "sundown town" ever since.

As far as I could tell, it was the "population centers" of Hazard and Pikeville that ranked as the true capitals of southeastern Kentucky, with an edge in the early 2000s going to Pikeville because it was the hometown of incumbent Democratic governor, Paul Patton. Pikeville, like Hazard, was one of the few "wet" cities in the region at the time, giving these towns what passed in Eastern Kentucky as a cosmopolitan vibe. In recent years, more areas have voted to end Prohibition-era conditions by allowing alcohol service in restaurants, sales in stores, or both. But in places like Pike County, where everywhere but Pikeville is dry, anyone who buys alcohol in town and drives it back to a more rural part of the county faces a possible charge for illegally transporting it.

I was delighted when the assistant regional editor called to assign my first story: five hundred words on a new US Office of Surface Mining rule that made it easier for companies with financial ties to polluting mines to open new mines.

It wasn't the meatiest of stories, but it was a story, and that was all that mattered. Not knowing much of anything about surface mining at this point, I had the simple goal of writing an error-free article that conveyed the needed information and made sense. I did the story by phone. After a few calls, I learned that the Kentucky Coal Association, the mining industry's advocacy group, welcomed the new rule, and that environmental groups viewed it with suspicion. Looking back at the unremarkable story, I'm struck by a quote from then-Coal Association President Bill Caylor. "There are enough safety nets to find out who the outlaws are," Caylor said of the new rule. "It takes away the unneeded bureaucracy and administrative nightmares."[4] In my coverage of the coal industry, I would hear similar words from Caylor time and again in the coming years.

A day or two later, my second story took me out in the field for the first time, chasing a tip from the *Courier-Journal*'s sports desk that a man named Vernon Cooper was involved in a brewing scandal over a five-hundred-dollar donation he thought he had made to the University of Kentucky football program. But rather than landing in the athletic department's coffers, the check was cashed by an assistant football coach who then funneled the money to a high school coach with several sought-after recruits on his team. It was the kind of situation that made NCAA compliance officers salivate.

The seventy-seven-year-old Cooper lived in a sprawling ranch-style home situated on the incongruously named La Citadelle Mountain, one of the highest points of Hazard, not far from the site of a shuttered resort hotel that Cooper had co-owned for forty years. Most people in town knew Cooper by one of two nicknames: "Bruiser," which he picked up as a Navy gunner in World War II, or "Mr. Bulldog," which he earned for his decades-long moral and financial support of the local high school's athletics program. Cooper had accumulated considerable wealth during a career in banking and insurance, and an Internet search, or what passed for one in the year 2000, indicated that he was very much the giving type. His civic-mindedness is what brought me to his doorstep that December morning.

We spoke for over an hour, but only in the last five minutes did we get to the topic that I came to discuss. He spent the rest of the time regaling me with stories about his lifetime of adventure. He gave me a tour of the impressive astronomical observatory that sat next to his house. He pulled out a jacket from his closet identifying him as an honorary colonel in the Argentine army. He told me that he had climbed many of the world's tallest peaks. To prove it, he showed me a framed photo on his wall of four smiling Nepalese Sherpas who he said had escorted him up Mount Everest. I wanted to ask why he wasn't pictured but thought better of it if I wanted to stick around long enough to talk about the five-hundred-dollar check.

Cooper had other friends in high places who helped him cultivate his persona. Four years after I met Cooper, Senator Mitch McConnell read the following into the congressional record: "Mr. Cooper has fought in Asia in World War II, skinned seals with Eskimos in the Arctic, and climbed mountains in the Andes. But after all those vast experiences, his Perry County home in Eastern Kentucky holds a prime place in his heart, and he expresses this through great generosity."[5]

And the check to the athletic department? He wrote it, documented it in his ledger, and later asked for confirmation from the university that it was received. But instead of a receipt, he got back a five-hundred-dollar money order from the assistant coach at the center of the controversy who, by this time, knew he was in trouble. That coach's improprieties, the university discovered, went far beyond trying to lure recruits with cash. And that is how Cooper became a minor player in major sanctions against a college football program that he helped support in exchange for sideline access at games.

As a result of the front-page story about Cooper's ill-fated donation, Hazard City Hall was put on notice of my arrival. Cooper's first cousin Bill Gorman also inhabited high standing—as Hazard's longtime mayor. Mayor Gorman saw the article and phoned the *Courier-Journal*'s main office to ask how to get in touch with me. His call was routed to another of my predecessors in the Hazard bureau, Ralph Dunlop, who had gone on to become a standout reporter on the paper's investigative unit. He had played a lead role in the paper's series about bogus coal-mine dust tests. Ralph passed along Gorman's message and, with a hint of irony in his voice, told me that an audience with the mayor was a mandatory part of my orientation to Eastern Kentucky. Ralph was well acquainted with Hazard mayors, having married a daughter of Gorman's predecessor. He knew Eastern Kentucky as well as anybody at the paper and liked to check in on me from time to time, which I appreciated. On his first visit, we went to see the Tom Hanks movie *Cast Away* at a local theater. At the time, it felt very relatable.

*

I went to visit Gorman at his downtown office. I had viewed aerial photos of Main Street as part of my research of Hazard, but this was my first in-person visit. From above, the town center had an undeniable charm. Flanked by mountains and the North Fork of the Kentucky River, century-old buildings stood alongside a few newer structures. A ground-level view offered a bleaker account of the town's fortunes. On the edge of town was a sign welcoming everyone to "The Queen City of the Mountains." The county court-house and several law offices comprised most of the downtown area. Beyond that, there was a bank, a bridal shop, an optometrist's office, a family drug store, a radio station, a bar called The Broke Spoke, and several empty storefronts. Tattered posters for the "Black Gold Festival" of years past hung on store windows and telephone poles.

When I entered his office, Gorman, a squat, well-put-together man who spoke like he had a lungful of sausage gravy and cigar smoke, had a copy of the *Courier-Journal* splayed out across his desk.

"My Cousin Vernon sure is a character, ain't he?" Gorman asked me with a hearty laugh.

Oh, yes, Vernon was a character all right, but I wasn't sure I should say as much.

The mayor asked me about my background and how I came to take the Hazard job. I said I grew up in Philadelphia, and he told me that he had traveled nearly everywhere in the country but had liked few places as well as Philadelphia. He and I bonded over the fact that we had both attended what many people consider the greatest college basketball game ever, the 1992 NCAA tournament clash in Philadelphia between Kentucky and Duke. Christian Laettner, who earlier in the game had enraged Kentucky fans by purposely stepping on a downed Wildcat player, won the game for Duke on an overtime buzzer-beating shot. As we talked, Gorman visibly winced at the memory of the finish to the game. All of these years later, Kentucky's antipathy for the Blue Devils remains strong, even among people who don't follow basketball or are too young to remember the heartbreaking 1992 loss. In the absence of a 2020 NCAA men's basketball tournament because of the COVID-19 pandemic, CBS replayed the game on a Saturday afternoon that otherwise would have featured live March Madness games. It was required viewing for many Kentucky parents who wanted their children to know why Mommy and Daddy can't stand Duke.

Prominently displayed in Gorman's office was a framed photo of him with former president Bill Clinton, who had visited Hazard a year earlier as part of a tour of impoverished America. While in Hazard, Clinton spoke of the need to defeat poverty by encouraging private investment in the distressed region. There was also a photo of Gorman with Robert F. Kennedy, who famously came to the area in 1968 for the same reason. In the thirty-two years between those visits, poverty appeared to be keeping the upper hand. Also in Gorman's office was a picture of the mayor with country singer Glen "Rhinestone Cowboy" Campbell, who had befriended the mayor's coal operator brother after performing a free concert in Hazard in the early 1980s.

Gorman got down to business. He stood up and pointed to a map of Kentucky that hung on one of his wood-paneled walls. On it were thumbtacks showing the location of all of the state's four-year, public universities.

"See that?" he asked.

I quickly studied the map and noticed there was a conspicuous lack of tacks in the southeastern corner. There was Morehead State University in the northeastern part of the state. And there was a school called Eastern Kentucky University, but that was a misnomer, because it sat smack dab in the middle of the map in Richmond, more than two hours away from Hazard and any of the counties I would be covering. He didn't place a tack there, but a few miles south of Richmond was Berea College, one of the best and most innovative liberal arts colleges in the country. Gorman saw that I got his point and went on to deliver a sermon about how the lack of educational opportunities in the mountains had disadvantaged the region and contributed to "brain drain." Gorman was also a realist, pointing out that the region's rough terrain limited its development opportunities. He supported mountaintop removal mining because it forcibly flattened the land.

I had done my due diligence by reading a couple of articles about the mayor before my visit. He had his hands in every pot: banking, insurance, coal, real estate, and media, the last of which he took an interest in after seeing one too many negative portrayals of Eastern Kentucky in the national news. The way that the legendary Charles Kuralt depicted Eastern Kentucky in the 1964 CBS special *Christmas in Appalachia* upset Gorman. By the time of the airing of the 1968 public television documentary *Appalachia: Rich Land, Poor People*, Gorman could no longer countenance seeing only helpless, jobless, toothless Eastern Kentuckians flashing across his screen. He wanted to help control the narrative, so, in 1969, he lobbied the Federal Communications Commission to establish a network affiliate in Hazard. That station eventually became WYMT, We're Your Mountain Television, a CBS affiliate that still features local news broadcasts throughout the day.

Gorman was one of Hazard and Eastern Kentucky's most vocal cheerleaders. And he had his pitch down to a science: the photos of him with Clinton and Kennedy, the thumbtacked map, and most ingenious of all, the tradition of bestowing "duke" or "duchess" status upon visitors to Hazard, an honor that came with a certificate, a white marble paperweight, and an oversized key to the city. I'm guessing that there are enough dukes and duchesses out there to fill Madison Square Garden, and I am proud to be one of them.

I got asked time and again by people who heard that I had relocated to Hazard, Kentucky, whether Hazard was the setting for the popular CBS action-comedy series *The Dukes of Hazzard*. The difference in spelling between the locations didn't provide a conclusive answer, so I decided to conduct a little research on the subject, meaning the next time I was in a town with a Borders, I leafed through the pages of a book called *The Dukes of Hazzard: The Unofficial Companion*. There I learned that the show's creators saw Hazard, Kentucky, on a map, took a liking to the name, but decided a show about the exploits of cousins Bo and Luke Duke and their beloved Confederate flag–adorned car, the General Lee, would work better in a Deep South milieu.[6] There also happened to be a Hazard in North Georgia, so they slapped an extra "z" onto the name and made that part of the country the setting for the show. The Hazard in Kentucky, the one that is the county seat of Perry County, was named after Commodore Oliver Hazard Perry, the hero of the Battle of Lake Erie during the War of 1812. But Gorman didn't mind the confusion over the name. Years earlier, he had even invited the *Dukes* stars to spend a weekend at La Citadelle resort as his guest.

The mayor ended our meeting on a positive note, telling me to keep an eye out for what he expected would be an influx of new business to the area. He mentioned Sykes Enterprises as one of the companies that had answered Bill Clinton's call to action by setting up two technical-assistance call centers in the region.

"Do us right," Gorman said shortly before our meeting ended. I didn't know whether to interpret it as an order or a threat. Coming from the mouth of the affable Gorman, the words didn't sound at all malevolent. As it turned out, I would hear this phrase, or some variation of it, many times in the coming years, from people of all walks of life. And I came to understand it not as a warning, but as a plea. *Do right by us because we have been wronged too many times before.*

I found an apartment in Hazard that suited my home-office needs and moved out of the motel. The apartment complex sat in a part of town that had become developable after a mining company blew off the top of a mountain. After the coal got extracted, the new tract of land was repurposed and became home to businesses, a regional hospital, and, above the building where I lived, a garish set of new homes in all imaginable architectural styles. In my two-story apartment building lived the few transplants in town, which included a number of foreign-born doctors, who had obtained work visas by agreeing to practice in this distressed rural enclave.

Soon after moving in, Mayor Gorman invited me to dinner at his house. I had been living off of fast food since my arrival and couldn't pass up a home-cooked meal. When I arrived at the Gorman home, which sat a few hundred yards down Gorman Ridge Road from Vernon Cooper's observatory, a light snowfall was starting to blanket the hills. That night, I met the mayor's wife, Nan, an artist who had studied at New York's Parsons School of Design and had traveled much of the world before returning home to Kentucky to put her training to work. I don't recall what was on the menu that night. It wasn't a local favorite like chili buns or soup beans, though I wouldn't have minded if it had been. What I do remember is that everyone at the table drank considerable amounts of bourbon and wine before dinner was served. Mindful that the snow had become heavier and I had a slippery mountain road to descend, I put the brakes on my alcohol consumption. Mayor Gorman could see I was getting nervous and assured me I would be fine. A couple of hours later, when I walked outside, I saw the flashing lights of two police cars. The mayor had called in a police escort for me. I realized that this put me on shaky ethical ground, but I couldn't think of a way out of it. So down the mountain I drove, one police cruiser in front of me and one behind me.

In meeting Cooper and Gorman early on, I caught a glimpse of a different side of Eastern Kentucky than most people hear about—a prosperous one. There are plenty of wealthy people and not all of them are mustache-twirling barons of industry with sinister laughs. Some have hearts and positive intentions, but something, maybe it is the fierce pride I mentioned earlier, keeps them from really seeing the causes of the struggles all around them.

The more representative side of the region awaited me, and I would soon find out just how badly many of the people of the area were hurting. The economic reality of Eastern Kentucky—the persistent poverty—serves as a backdrop to almost every issue and anecdote featured in this book.

*

We should root for the underdogs and outsiders in these stories. The original settlers of Eastern Kentucky came to this country not for religious reasons, but for the express purpose of bettering their lives. Shunted off to inhospitable land with limited agricultural and commercial potential, their struggles began almost from day one.

Appalachian Kentuckians saw their land occupied and fought over by both sides in the Civil War. Out of that discord grew the legendary Hatfield-McCoy feud. The majority of Eastern Kentucky tacitly supported the Union in the hopes that the Northern states would buy their tobacco. The agrarian wealth of the South and the industrial prosperity of the North remained beyond their reach, leaving Appalachian Kentuckians economically and geographically stuck. The first resource to be exploited in the area was timber, which was taken and removed from the region via the Kentucky River. There were no railroads or roads to transport resources back then, just waterways. That changed in the late nineteenth century when the Cincinnati Southern Railway company built a rail line through Eastern Kentucky. Soon after that, in 1900, the first Eastern Kentucky coal mine opened.

A 2014 article in *The Week* pointedly summed up Eastern Kentucky, calling it "the last redoubt of the Scots-Irish working class that picked up where African slave labor left off, mining and cropping and sawing the raw materials for a modern American economy that would soon run out of profitable uses for the class of people who 500 years ago would have been known, without any derogation, as peasants."[7]

Let's be clear: white Eastern Kentuckians have not been victimized by the deeply ingrained systemic and institutional inequality, racism, and discrimination that have defined the African-American experience in this country. Even my late father-in-law, a sixth-generation Appalachian whose ancestors were among the first white settlers of Harlan County, didn't shy away from teaching his children about the realities of racism. This was impressive considering that his own father was a KKK sympathizer who believed the Holocaust was a myth. Robert Fee told his children about when he returned from the Vietnam War and traveled the country, bunking at the homes of family, friends, and fellow vets. To earn money to fund his barnstorming, he found work washing dishes at diners across America. At one of the restaurants he worked at in the Southwestern United States, the manager put up a help-wanted notice for a second dishwasher. When a Black man came in one day to see about the job, the manager lied and said it had already been filled. My father-in-law never forgot that experience and used it to illustrate how white people, even those who live up "hollers," those narrow and remote Eastern Kentucky roads nestled between mountains, enjoy a certain privilege that isn't granted to Black Americans.

No, white Appalachians do not face the same systemic obstacles as Black Americans. Nor do they have some of the historic disadvantages of the Cherokee Indians and other indigenous Americans that once called the mountains home. But I would argue that Appalachians are part of a troubling American caste system that seems to be becoming more extreme.

No one has rushed to honor Appalachian culture (which is often dismissed as the *absence* of culture for not conforming with mainstream white America) unless it's to attend a theme party where guests are asked to "mullet it up" and dress like "a real backwoods redneck." That's not cultural appropriation. It's cultural abnegation. And it's a subject worth contemplating. Imagine a culture that holds such an unexalted place in the collective consciousness that everyone from the entertainment industry to the federal government lines up to take shots, some subtle, some less so.

In our eagerness to comprehend Appalachia, we have gravitated toward works of nonfiction whose creators might not be the most reliable messengers. I am not here to take shots at J. D. Vance's *Hillbilly Elegy*. Enough people have done that already. But to be fair, far more readers have heaped praise on Vance's 2016 memoir about his hardships and triumphs. The book has sold millions of copies, was adapted into a movie directed by Ron Howard, and turned Vance into a de facto spokesman for Appalachia. It has shaped many people's impressions of Appalachia today.

I read *Hillbilly Elegy* with interest a few years after it came out. And I did so with an open mind, suspecting that the book's most vocal detractors, many who resided in Appalachia, may simply have been bristling at a harsh but largely true depiction of the region and its people. I found it to be a gripping personal narrative of

Vance's childhood and adolescence in Middletown, Ohio, an industrial town located between Cincinnati and Dayton. A key hook to
Vance's story is that his family has Eastern Kentucky roots. We
know Breathitt County, Kentucky, is his ancestral home because he
writes at length about his God-fearing but foul-mouthed mamaw
and his alcoholic but sage papaw. Mamaw and Papaw are from
Eastern Kentucky. J. D. Vance is not, and only possesses vague
memories of spending weekends and summer vacations there as a
kid. That is to say that almost none of the book actually takes place
in Kentucky. It is largely set in the Appalachian diaspora, a fascinating place, to be sure, but not Appalachia itself. The message: He
made it out. Why can't the rest of you lazy Appalachians? When we
ask this question we misunderstand the region's problems.

*

In fact, many people misunderstand the region geographically. The
2,200-mile Appalachian Trail that runs from Georgia to Maine
does not mirror the borders of Appalachia. The official definition
of the region comes from the Appalachian Regional Commission,
a federal agency formed by Congress in 1965 to help coordinate
economic development initiatives in an area that had lagged behind
the rest of the country. In 2017, Donald Trump put federal funding
for the commission on the chopping block, but legislators, including
Mitch McConnell, lobbied to keep it going. West Virginia is the only
state that Congress defined as 100 percent Appalachian. Portions of
twelve other states, as far south as Macon County, Alabama, and
as far north as Otsego County, New York, make up the federally
designated area of Appalachia.

Appalachian State University is in Boone, North Carolina, a
town near the Tennessee and Virginia borders. Occasionally people
associate "Appalachia," correctly pronounced "Appa-latch-uh,"
with Asheville, North Carolina. More than a few of these people
drive Subarus with OBX (Outer Banks) stickers affixed to them.
About ninety miles south of Boone, Asheville is an Appalachian

town with high name recognition among Northeasterners because of its distinctive architecture, thriving arts scene, and flourishing tourism industry. Asheville has several legs up on any town in Eastern Kentucky. With a population of close to 100,000, Asheville is more of a city, really, the so-called "Paris of the South," with all of the amenities one would associate with a popular getaway destination. It is also easy to get to, located off of two major interstates and with a regional airport that has direct flights from cities including New York, Chicago, Atlanta, and Philadelphia. Asheville's minor league baseball team is named the Tourists. Novelist Thomas Wolfe, an Asheville native, probably couldn't go home again because of all of the out-of-towners who were crowding the streets. Asheville has embraced progressivism like few other places in the country. In July 2020, the Asheville City Council apologized for the city's culpability for slavery and racial prejudice and voted to offer reparations to Black residents. The more representative Central Appalachia, which includes West Virginia and parts of Kentucky, Tennessee, Virginia, and North Carolina, is the most impoverished part of the region. Fifty-four of Kentucky's counties are considered Appalachian. Eastern Kentucky's Appalachian counties as a group—the main focus of this book—comprise the most distressed part of Central Appalachia.

In 2014, *The New York Times Magazine* published an article entitled "What's the Matter with Eastern Kentucky?" that featured an illustration of a Kentucky license plate with the words HELP ME on it. The first paragraph of the article reads, "There are many tough places in this country: the ghost cities of Detroit, Camden and Gary, the sunbaked misery of inland California and the isolated reservations where Native American communities were left to struggle. But in its persistent poverty, Eastern Kentucky—land of storybook hills and drawls—just might be the hardest place to live in the United States. Statistically speaking."[8]

We knew that already. The more compelling subjects are how this came to be and whether there is a possibility for a brighter future.

What gives me the right to take a crack at explaining this troubled region? I know I'm treading on dangerous ground by attempting to do so. Eastern Kentuckians like to tell their own stories, and they tend to do so quite effectively. To some who pick up this book, I will be pegged as the dreaded outsider seeking to continue the long tradition of exploiting people of the region through overgeneralization and stereotype. I don't take on the task lightly. I got to know Eastern Kentucky at a pivotal time. What I saw confirmed some of my biases and challenged others.

Two stories dominated my first year in the region: a prescription drug epidemic that hit Appalachia first and continues to impact the entire nation, and a devastating coal sludge spill that remains the region's dirty little secret. These are the subjects of the first chapter, and the founding events in a drama that has had profound political, economic, and social consequences for a struggling region that typifies an America that has been left behind. I then explore the ongoing challenges of trying to move Eastern Kentucky beyond a coal-based economy. Despite diversification efforts, King Coal casts a large shadow that permeates every aspect of the region's existence. The decline of coal and the hold of OxyContin and other drugs have made for desperate times.

The next section chronicles drug-motivated murders tied to county sheriff's races in two counties, a wave of violence that can only happen when the pillars of civil society collapse or don't exist in the first place. A vote-buying scandal in another county that year brought down a large swath of local government.

From there, I explore the struggle to keep communities together and faith intact amid a crumbling social order. I'll introduce you to the people I met on a 2001 bus ride with an Eastern Kentucky church to attend a Rev. Billy Graham rally in Louisville. I look at their lives then and twenty years later in the context of a region that has increasingly embraced antigovernmental views and social and political conservatism despite having one of the highest rates of reliance on federal benefits.

A discussion of the region isn't complete without an examination of its well-above-average rates of anxiety and depression. One

Eastern Kentucky disability lawyer's plot to enrich himself at the expense of thousands of residents helps tell that story.

Throughout, I'll explore the mysteries and complexities of the region's electoral politics, a subject area that the hordes of reporters who came to Eastern Kentucky after the election of Donald Trump badly whiffed on.

*

I didn't stop covering Eastern Kentucky by choice. In 2005, the *Courier-Journal* closed all of its regional bureaus except for the one in the state capital. The move came at a time when metropolitan newspapers around the country, almost always on a mandate from their corporate bosses, started focusing on quick-hit, "local-local" news reporting. This meant that the *C-J* would not only be covering local Louisville bake sales, but covering those bake sales while they were in progress and posting a story online about the popularity of the blueberry scones. It was a misguided strategy to address the existential threat that newspapers faced, and still face now. For Eastern Kentucky, the closure meant an end to day-to-day coverage and the loss of a crucial voice.

Since I left, not a day has passed when I haven't thought of Eastern Kentucky. When I return to the area, I see many of the same problems I chronicled, but also signs of a more promising future. Within Eastern Kentucky, there is significant variance in outlook and performance. Some towns are enduring, if not quite thriving. Others are simply dying out.

This book might not solve the region's long-standing challenges, but I hope it will help us contemplate issues of class and regionalism in a new way.

CHAPTER 1

The Dams Break

In the early 2000s, CBS, which was enjoying ratings success with a string of new reality television shows including *Survivor*, decided that Americans might like an unscripted show about hillbillies. The idea was inspired by the network's classic situation comedy of the 1960s and 1970s, *The Beverly Hillbillies*, a show about a family from the Ozarks that ends up striking oil and moving to a posh California mansion. Out West, the Clampett family's circumstances change, but it just can't shed the backward ways of home. The popularity of the sitcom spawned other CBS shows with stereotypical rural American characters like *Green Acres* and *Hee Haw*.

The concept for the reality show, tentatively titled *The Real Beverly Hillbillies*, involved plucking a sheltered, multigenerational Appalachian family from its mountain home and relocating them to Hollywood, where they would live in luxury and wealth for as long as the cameras rolled. CBS sent producers to Eastern Kentucky and other locales to scout for the ideal clan for the gig. Amid criticism, network executives defended the premise by arguing that Beverly Hills, and not the Appalachians who relocated there, would be the butt of most of the show's jokes.

Appalachians protested. But what could they do to stop a corporate giant like CBS from airing anything it wanted? That had always been a losing fight. But timing worked in their favor this time. A newly formed Eastern Kentucky–based group called the Center for Rural Strategies was looking for causes and decided to make a confrontation with CBS its first major initiative. Dee Davis, the group's leader, launched a $1 million campaign against the proposed show, running ads in papers including *The New York Times* and *The Washington Post* and threatening a boycott of the network if the show went forward.

The protest got the attention of Kentucky Congressman Hal Rogers. In a letter to then-CBS president Les Moonves, Rogers condemned the premise of the show, writing that "many people, including you, continue to believe the long-since outdated and erroneous stereotype that Appalachians are lazy, uneducated, barefooted hicks."[1]

CBS blinked. The show went into developmental limbo and subsequently died. In the years since, it has never been resurrected.

Davis's group won the battle against CBS, but that doesn't mean Appalachia has come close to winning the war against negative media representations. A few years later, another major network swooped in and gave the deep dark hills of Eastern Kentucky the kind of journalistic beatdown that can influence a whole generation's impressions of a place.

The ABC News 20/20 special "A Hidden America: Children of the Mountains" was two years in the making and pulled in the show's largest viewership numbers in years. Hosted by veteran journalist Diane Sawyer, who was a few months away from becoming ABC's lead news anchor, the hour-long show had all of the appearances of serious investigative reporting.

With her trademark gravitas, Sawyer, a native of a non-Appalachian part of Kentucky, introduced viewers to a thirty-six-year-old woman with eight grandchildren, a recovering drug addict who walked sixteen miles round trip to attend a court-ordered GED class, and a high school football star living out of his truck.

For the appearance of balance, but also to highlight the notoriously poor health of Appalachian Kentuckians, the program featured legendary activist Eula Hall. Born in 1927, Hall did as much as anyone to ensure that even the area's poorest people received quality medical care. In the proud tradition of the Frontier Nursing Service, Hall in 1973 established the Mud Creek Clinic, a practice that drew patients from hundreds of miles away. The clinic that Hall ran out of her house thrived and, after it burned to the ground in an unsolved arson incident in 1982, Hall, the community, and the federal Appalachian Regional Commission banded together to build an expansive new clinic that has remained in operation ever since.

Many people's lasting memory of the special, my own included, centered on Sawyer's exploration of Eastern Kentucky's dental woes. If viewers tuned in expecting to see toothless Appalachians, they were not left wanting. Sawyer's report noted that it wasn't just poor eating habits and a lack of dental care that made Eastern Kentucky one of the tooth decay capitals of the country. She breathlessly introduced us to another culprit, a fizzy green one called Mountain Dew.

Forget the tragically mishandled opioid epidemic unfolding across the region. The real story, according to Sawyer, was that Appalachians were becoming addicted to Mountain Dew at a tender age. Young kids were swilling it by the twelve-pack. Teenagers were struggling to go cold turkey on it lest they lose all of their teeth. Babies might even be drinking it from bottles. As a petrified-looking teenage girl sat in a dentist chair about to have the living hell drilled out of her teeth, Sawyer leaned over and cooed, "I think the doctor is going to tell you that Mountain Dew isn't your best friend."[2]

Much to the dismay of PepsiCo, Mountain Dew's parent company, the 20/20 episode led to the coining of the term "Mountain Dew Mouth." PepsiCo called the report "old, irresponsible news." By that time, the area's soda-drinking habits had become something of legend. A 1980 *Courier-Journal* article about aluminum can recycling stated that Eastern Kentuckians were the world's largest consumers of Pepsi. In a blow to tradition and the local economy, PepsiCo, in 2017, closed a bottling facility in Hazard that had operated for sixty years. The Mountain Dew narrative gained new life in 2020 when, amid the COVID-19 pandemic, a Kentucky couple tried to buy a Louisville grocery store's entire canned inventory of the soft drink, some twenty-three cases. An angry confrontation ensued when a store manager told them they couldn't make the purchase.

Does it really matter if television networks continue to produce shows that depict Appalachia in a harsh light? Maybe, after all, there is some truth to what they're showing. Saying Eastern

Kentucky is poor is not a generalization. It is a fact-based statement. Saying *all* Eastern Kentuckians are poor is the generalization.
In reality, some are incredibly wealthy, and that is important to
portray, because it is impossible to understand the struggles of the
region without acknowledging the socioeconomic inequities that
arise from having a regional ruling class. The people at the top
of the Eastern Kentucky financial ladder, everyone from the late
mayor of Hazard to the coal executives who live in mansions and
vacation in exotic locales, are integral to the story of how power has
been gained and exerted in the region. But that type of investigation
wouldn't make for entertaining prime-time television. It would only
feed fears of class warfare.

But what happens when unflattering associations with a certain
group start affecting public policy?

A 2017 journal article about opioid abuse endorsed by the
National Institutes of Health website codified the idea of Central
Appalachia's otherness. Citing a twenty-seven-year-old article,
the report compared rural Appalachians to the Amish and other
minority groups that have "self-contained cultures."

"Such groups may resist Western medicine approaches," the report
said. "However, unlike the subcultures of Native Americans and
Amish people, the distinct ways of life and belief systems of Appalachians are less readily acknowledged . . . Similarities between
normative Americans and rural Appalachians may work against
Appalachians in that less emphasis is placed on awareness and
specialized training to facilitate understanding of local beliefs that
could lead to better patient experiences and improved treatment
outcomes."[3]

Let's put that into plain language, the kind that even poor Appalachians would understand: They might look like normal white
people, but beneath the surface, they are different and need to
be treated as such. Their rejection of what is "normative" might
explain why it is so difficult to keep them off of drugs.

No one would describe blue-collar communities in Wisconsin or
Ohio in such alien terms. It is true that Appalachian Kentucky isn't

your typical "working class" region. Taking into account the percentage of the population that depends on government assistance, it
can easily be argued that the region is predominantly "non-working
class." But we should use history and data, not a strange form of
exoticism, to examine health care disparities and other social challenges. If we had taken that approach in the late 1990s and early
2000s, I believe we would have saved a lot of lives in Appalachia
and the rest of the country. Instead, a pair of dams broke wide
open, one literally, the other figuratively. The coal mining disaster
and the opioid crisis that ensued highlight how corporate greed and
institutional neglect can more easily rule the day in a place never
thought of as normal.

*

One February morning in 2001, the fax machine in my home office
spit out a single-page press release from the US attorney's office in
Lexington notifying reporters that a major announcement was due
the next day. All I could get from a spokesperson was that it had
something to do with drugs. I figured that I should get myself to
Lexington.

During the entire previous year, the *Courier-Journal* had published only a single story that mentioned the powerful prescription
painkiller OxyContin. The story, which carried an Associated Press
byline, told of the indictments of ten people who operated a multi-
million-dollar drug ring out of an Eastern Kentucky home. It is difficult to read the story now without cringing. In making the arrests,
police in Clay County noted that they observed nearly *sixty thousand* cars come and go from the home during a five-month period.
That comes out to about four hundred vehicles a day. Clay County
is a rural, thinly populated county, making the volume of business
at the house all the more staggering. The dealers at the drug house
were selling marijuana and a variety of painkillers including Tylox
and Percocet, but none fetched a higher price than OxyContin,
according to the article.

The press conference in Lexington served as a primer on Oxy-Contin, the brand name of a form of oxycodone originally designed for cancer patients and other chronic and severe pain sufferers. Over the previous year, Oxy, as it was known, had deluged the streets of every community in Eastern Kentucky and become the most abused drug in the region. Abusers were stealing it from pharmacies or from people who had received legitimate prescriptions. Dealers were seeking it any way they could, recognizing the extraordinary demand and potential for profit. And people were dying. Officially, around sixty people had fatally overdosed on OxyContin in the previous thirteen months, many of them under twenty-five years of age and from Eastern Kentucky. But as I would soon learn from my reporting, that number was likely much higher because county coroners often didn't list "drug overdose" as a cause of death.

OxyContin, which first hit the market in 1997, came in several dosage amounts, all the way up to a 160-milligram pill that was more than 30 times stronger than most other painkillers. Oxy was selling on the street for about a dollar per milligram. When taken properly, a pill was supposed to be swallowed whole. But abusers of the drug figured out that they could bypass OxyContin's time-release mechanism and get a more intense, heroin-like high by removing a pill's exterior coating, crushing it, and then snorting the powder. Other abusers heated the powder, turning it into an injectable liquid.

Hazard Police Chief Rod Maggard took the microphone at the news conference to explain the disastrous impact the drug was having in his town.

"If this had been diphtheria or smallpox, we would have been quarantined from the rest of the state," Maggard said. "You would have a hard time mentioning five families in Hazard who haven't somehow been touched by this."[4]

The irony of Maggard's statement is that the region has always existed under a type of quarantine, its struggles visible to the outside world only through the occasional book, documentary, network television special, or overdue government response.

The "hillbilly heroin" problem was allowed to fester and spread. Over the border in southwestern Virginia, the situation was no better.

"It's like vitamins—they take 'em once a day," the police chief of Grundy, Virginia, told the *Courier-Journal*. "Addicts would sell their soul to get it."[5]

The morning of the press conference, the US attorney's office announced that a law enforcement initiative dubbed Oxyfest 2001 had yielded more than two hundred indictments, mostly of dealers but also of a Harlan County doctor who was charged with illegally prescribing the drug. US Attorney Joseph Famularo proclaimed that the investigation was the largest in state history dealing with illegal drug activity and referred to the OxyContin problem as "an epidemic, like some sort of locust plague rolling through southeastern Kentucky."[6] He said the people getting hooked on the drug ranged from "the young to 50-year-olds and from the upper echelon to welfare recipients." It turned out to be a major news day in Lexington. As Famularo spoke, Kentucky head football coach Hal Mumme was across town tendering his resignation following an NCAA investigation into the recruiting violations I had written about two months earlier.

The abuse of narcotic painkillers, even those with oxycodone, was nothing new in Eastern Kentucky. They were among the recreational drugs of choice in the area, not surprising considering the well-documented link between workplace injuries and prescription drug abuse. Every year in every county, people got arrested for trafficking and illegally possessing Lortab, Lorcet, Vicodin, and other drugs. But these were the types of drugs that a coal miner could take over the weekend and be back at work on Monday. People weren't fatally overdosing, the few drug treatment facilities in the area could keep up with demand, jails didn't dangerously exceed capacity, and struggling communities were able to carry on without additional social disruption.

The arrival of OxyContin dramatically changed all of that. For the purposes of data collection, the federal government classifies every drug in the oxycodone class together. Early in 2001, the National Drug Intelligence Center released statistics showing a 93 percent increase in oxycodone-related deaths between 1997 and 1998, the first full year that OxyContin was on the market.[7] That bulletin, like many responses to the problem, came a few years too late. By the time the US attorney's office summoned reporters to Lexington in February 2001, the OxyContin emergency was beyond containment.

Having received a crash course on OxyContin, I returned to Hazard to get a closer look at the impact the drug was having on the community. The previous times I had driven past Perry County Park, I didn't think twice about all of the human activity I saw there. It was a park after all. But others in town knew exactly what was drawing the crowds. Yvon Allen, the principal of the county high school, had had a prime view of the park for years. Every day after the final bell rang, he saw the park fill up with students and adults whose interactions with each other appeared transactional in nature. Allen alerted the police department about his concerns. Maggard told him he was preaching to the choir, that the area was packed at all hours of the day, and despite its best efforts, his under-resourced police department had lost control of the park that had become known as "Pillville." The realization that he and other local police chiefs were out of their depth with OxyContin prompted Maggard to ask federal authorities to intervene.

As availability of OxyContin continued to increase, more and more people in the region joined the ranks of the addicted. I also saw the first wave of Eastern Kentuckians who realized they needed help after being strung out on the drug for years. But addicts, especially ones still in denial about their problem, need a place to get help. And Eastern Kentucky didn't have anywhere close to the drug treatment resources it needed to provide that care. A psychotherapist in Hazard told me that he had no choice but to refer his Oxy-Contin-hooked clients to facilities in Nashville, Tennessee, which was three hundred miles away, because inpatient clinics closer to home were nearly nonexistent. The burden of helping addicts fell largely on emergency rooms, methadone clinics, and drug counselors at one of the few outpatient facilities in the area. These patients were often in the throes of withdrawal.

Back then, I spoke to Daniel Mongiardo, a Hazard ear, nose, and throat surgeon who had recently been elected to the Kentucky state Senate. He said family physicians, especially, were being put in a difficult spot with OxyContin. They didn't want to be accused of undertreating pain, and if a patient reported experiencing a nine or ten on the smiley-face pain scale, the doctors weren't about to administer a polygraph test to see if the patient was being truthful. Mongiardo saw the pharmaceutical salespeople making the rounds of hospitals and doctor's offices, pitching OxyContin's ability to provide steady pain relief over a long period of time. He had mostly pediatric patients, so OxyContin wasn't a part of his daily practice. But in a recent conversation, he told me about an adult patient who came to see him about getting a prescription for the drug. When asked why he needed it, the patient replied, "To sell it to make money."[8]

I learned from people I interviewed how easy it was to get caught up in the drug. I spoke to a twenty-nine-year-old Knott County man who started off taking twenty-milligram OxyContin pills but soon worked his way up to a four-hundred-milligram-per-day addiction. At first, he said, the drug energized him and helped him to forget his problems. A near-deadly three-day binge, however, caused him to seek help at the only outpatient clinic in Hazard, a facility that served eight Eastern Kentucky counties. That clinic quickly reached maximum capacity with a growing wait list, making it difficult for patients to get admitted and for counselors to spend adequate time with everyone who needed help.

Law enforcement was doomed by a late start in attacking the problem. Starting with Oxyfest, I watched as they constantly tried to catch up, making a few arrests here and conducting a couple of busts there until the court system became flooded with drug cases. Perry County's top prosecutor, John Hansen, was brand new on the job when these cases started hitting the courts. In his first month in office, he got eighty-one grand jury indictments. An average month in Perry County up until that point saw only around a dozen. "That's when I realized, 'Holy crap, this is a big problem,'" Hansen recalls.[9] The volume of cases would remain high for the next several years.

But the police couldn't simply arrest their way out of the epidemic. The small rural justice and family court systems in the region couldn't handle the explosion of drug cases. The local jails became a revolving door for addicts who served their thirty days and then had a pile of pills waiting for them when they got home. Behind every user was a dealer and probably a few enablers. The court system also saw an uptick in drug-related burglaries, often committed by one relative against another, but at least on one occasion by a police officer who stole drugs and money from his department's evidence room. From January 2000 to August 2001, 7 percent of Kentucky's approximately 1,000 pharmacies were robbed or burglarized, the highest rate in the nation.[10] Even more troublingly, violent felonies connected to the drug trade spiked in some counties. "At some point, you realize there's not a damn thing you can do because it's so out of control," said Hansen,[11] who served as commonwealth's attorney from 2000 to 2006 and again from 2012 to 2018. He recalls prosecuting elderly defendants who appeared in court with their walkers and oxygen tanks after getting caught selling pills to confidential informants, sometimes members of their own families.

Chris Fugate was one of the state police troopers who served the arrest warrants, racing up hollers to haul alleged offenders off to local jails. After he got promoted to the narcotics division, Fugate's professional life became further consumed by a pursuit of "dopeheads." As someone who had always believed in compassion, it frightened him to think that he might be losing his. "I started seeing these people as problems and not as people," he says. "I was going to arrest everybody and the world was going to be saved."[12] On a round-up that netted nearly two dozen arrests, Fugate found himself in the home of a Perry County woman who had lost a son to a drug overdose. His framed photo sat next to a Bible on a dresser in her trailer. The question that the woman asked him that day is burned in his memory: "She said, 'Chris, you're a good Christian. Can you tell me if my son is going to heaven or hell?'"[13] Fugate left the holler that day questioning his calling in life.

The criminal justice system got caught flat-footed by the OxyContin scourge partly because of its own misplaced priorities. Based on what I was seeing all around me, I had a difficult time understanding why marijuana remained the centerpiece of the region's antidrug enforcement efforts. For years, the Drug Enforcement Administration had warned about the pernicious influence of marijuana on Central Appalachia. Kentucky, West Virginia, and Tennessee, three states that comprise only 4 percent of the US population, have historically produced nearly 30 percent of the nation's marijuana, which was and continues to be Kentucky's largest cash crop. The DEA proudly announced that it had "eradicated" 700,000 marijuana plants in Kentucky in 2001, the year that OxyContin and other pills were killing hundreds of people in the state.[14] In a state drug assessment the following year, the National Drug Intelligence Center and Kentucky State Police again emphasized the ongoing threat of marijuana over that of diverted pharmaceuticals, which it lumped in with club drugs and hallucinogens in a section labeled "other dangerous drugs."[15] It was easier, I suppose, to eradicate a marijuana plant than it was to figure out whether a legal drug like OxyContin is being used or sold illegally.

The OxyContin story had numerous other layers to peel back. The extraordinary human toll of the epidemic was the first. I visited with many families who told variations of the same story about the pain of watching a loved one slip into addiction and eventually get lost in the drug. I heard mothers and fathers talk about losing children and children talk about losing mothers and fathers. Though the deaths spanned socioeconomic standing, I found that the more affluent families impacted by the problem were less willing to talk about their experiences. They felt a greater sense of shame for some reason, as if addiction was something that only happened to poor families. In a region of haves and have-nots, OxyContin became the great equalizer.

The devastation of the pill epidemic can be quantified in ways that go beyond the tragic number of lives lost to overdose. Appalachian Kentucky is an area that has long prided itself on tight family bonds. Despite high rates of teen pregnancy and single-parent households, a strong network of family support has helped ensure that most children in the region get the care and nurturing that might otherwise be absent. The new emergency conditions brought on by OxyContin obliterated that paradigm. In the late 1990s and early 2000s, many teenage girls and young women with addictions got pregnant and had to turn to their parents to care for children who sometimes came into the world unhealthy. A once generally harmonious system of parent-child relationships that made it possible for young mothers to work or attend school while their parents looked after the grandbabies dramatically shifted when more grandparents started taking on primary caregiver roles amid fear for the safety of their families and the threat of the foster care system taking a young child into state custody. In many cases, young mothers signed over custody of trauma-exposed children to their parents, creating a generation of "grandfamilies" caused by drug addiction. According to a 2014 study by the University of Kentucky's Center on Trauma and Children, nearly 90 percent of "grandfamilies" in Eastern Kentucky existed because of a parent's substance abuse problem or incarceration, compared to 60 percent in the rest of the state.[16] My mother-in-law is a prime example of the phenomenon. She is raising my sister-in-law's three children due to her decades-long battle with drug abuse.

What started this tragic chain of events in motion? One of the important areas of examination is the role that physicians played in contributing to the widespread diversion and abuse of OxyContin. To give them the benefit of the doubt, many of the doctors who prescribed the drug too liberally just wanted to help patients relieve their pain with a new wonder drug. But that doesn't absolve all of these doctors of responsibility. Not everyone with a mild back problem, ear infection, or toothache needed such a potent painkiller. In prescribing this particular opioid, they were likely overtreating pain.

Dr. Mongiardo expressed the belief that OxyContin took off the way it did because too few doctors were willing to make the difficult choice to undertreat pain in some cases. Over the border in southwestern Virginia, Dr. Art Van Zee, a family practitioner, started a petition to remove OxyContin from the market. Van Zee promoted the idea that doctors should prescribe aspirin-based medications before turning to more powerful opiates like OxyContin. He also took a shot at Purdue Pharma, the manufacturer of OxyContin.

"Purdue Pharma would like everyone to believe that OxyContin is an absolute godsend and that nothing else can take its place," Van Zee said. "That's not the case."[17]

Most Eastern Kentucky doctors weren't intentionally fomenting the problem. But some were. Criminal cases against local physician Dr. Ali Sawaf and several others demonstrated just how much damage a single rogue doctor could do to a community.

Sawaf was the doctor whose arrest was announced at the kickoff of Oxyfest 2001. A week before the Lexington press conference, Harlan County sheriff's deputies arrested the urologist at his office. The case moved swiftly. Less than a year later, a federal jury convicted Sawaf of illegally prescribing OxyContin to thousands of Harlan County residents in the year 2000 alone. It emerged at trial that Sawaf routinely saw more than a hundred patients per day at his clinic. Federal prosecutors showed a law enforcement videotape of patients entering Sawaf's office and leaving with a prescription in less than a minute. Pharmacists from Harlan testified that they became so inundated with Sawaf's OxyContin prescriptions that they decided to stop filling them. Sawaf testified in his own defense that undercover police officers working the case had deceived him into writing prescriptions by lying to him about having severe ailments. In each of those cases, he made a judgment call, Sawaf said. If he had known they weren't in pain, he wouldn't have prescribed OxyContin. "There's no litmus paper to tell you about pain," he testified.[18] The jury didn't buy it. Sawaf became the first doctor in Kentucky found guilty of running a "pill mill." He was sentenced to twenty years in prison.

A medical practice in Greenup County operated by a doctor named David Procter was exposed as a training ground for a number of outlaw physicians. Procter, who is believed to have run the first large-scale pill mill in the nation just as the OxyContin epidemic was taking off, pleaded guilty in 2003 to illegally prescribing drugs, a scheme that included seeing hundreds of patients a week, prescribing over a million pain tablets, and occasionally trading pills for sex. Procter recruited other doctors to join his criminal enterprise, some of whom eventually struck out on their own and flooded other areas of nearby northeastern Kentucky and southern Ohio with Oxy-Contin and other drugs. Four of those doctors also went to prison. Another doctor convicted of running a pill mill in that area was sentenced to a quadruple life sentence for illegally prescribing painkillers that led to four overdose deaths. Procter's eleven-year prison sentence had recently ended in 2013 when the mansion that he lost when he went to prison was turned into a residential drug and alcohol treatment facility, a symbolic victory in the fight against opioid abuse and a sign of hope in an area desperately in need of places for addicts to regain sobriety.[19] The prosecutions of doctors kept coming. In 2017, a Hazard physician and his wife received prison time for running a clinic that illegally distributed millions of pills.

To truly get at the "why" of the situation, I and every other reporter working the story had to look at Purdue Pharma. How did a small, family-owned pharmaceutical company in Connecticut take a drug that generated $48 million in sales its first year on the market and turn it into a billion-dollar product just four years later? A main source of the boom in business can be traced to Appalachia and other rural areas of the country with high rates of workplace injury and disability. That is where Purdue Pharma chose to most aggressively market OxyContin to doctors, an effort that included sending a fleet of sales representatives to Kentucky to talk up Oxy-Contin to physicians and woo them with meals and gifts. The company knew the favored painkillers of these doctors, and it charged its sales reps with making a pitch for why OxyContin should be a go-to drug for people in pain.

Using these tactics, the company's owner, the Sackler family, laid the groundwork for a campaign that would make them one of the richest families in the country. But by time and again putting profits over people and avoiding the grim reality of what OxyContin was doing to communities, the Sacklers also triggered a monumental crisis.

My first interaction with a representative from Purdue Pharma came at the inaugural meeting of a state OxyContin task force that was formed a few months after Oxyfest by Governor Paul Patton, an Eastern Kentuckian who seemed genuinely concerned about the reports he was getting. The first major aim of the task force was to scrutinize the supply chain of the drug, from doctors to pharmacists to people who obtained it illegally and either used it or made a living selling it. The state police commissioner emphasized that the group wasn't just targeting OxyContin, but prescription-drug abuse as a whole. I get what he was saying, but I also believe he didn't fully grasp the long-term consequences of OxyContin's unique emergence and grip. Even when reporting stories that had nothing to do with OxyContin, I found myself getting into long conversations with interview subjects about how the drug had turned a loved one into a frightening stranger.

That first get-together of the Kentucky task force focused on how pharmacists could more effectively detect fraudulent prescriptions, a mechanism that some addicts and dealers were using to get their hands on OxyContin. This was the early days of phones with caller IDs, and apparently it was fairly common practice for people to pretend to phone in prescriptions from a doctor's office. The task force also debated whether to instruct pharmacies to check photo identification from people coming to fill prescriptions. I felt for the pharmacists. They were the last line of defense against the epidemic but had limited authority to report misgivings about the prescriptions they were dispensing. At the same time, however, I was hearing that some pharmacies had a reputation for filling suspicious prescriptions that no others would touch.

In attendance at the meeting that day was a salt-and-pepper bearded, scholarly looking man in an expensive dark suit. Dr. J.

David Haddox, Purdue Pharma's medical director, looked every bit the part of a doctor you could imagine touting the benefits of this or that medication in a television commercial. Haddox, a task force member, said that adverse publicity about OxyContin abuse in Eastern Kentucky had tarnished the reputation of the drug. But he pledged the company's support for law-enforcement efforts to crack down on illegal use of OxyContin. He also said Purdue Pharma would work with doctors to help them understand which patients would benefit from OxyContin and which simply didn't need it.

It was a nice gesture for Purdue Pharma to send its medical director out on the task force circuit, but the Sacklers were savvy enough to know that public meetings held in the areas hardest hit by Oxy-Contin abuse were not ideal forums for the company. Those meetings invariably put Haddox in the position of having to explain why OxyContin was wreaking such havoc. Purdue Pharma realized its business interests would suffer if it didn't go on the offensive, so it began sponsoring meetings of its own, featuring physicians and other speakers who extolled the virtues of OxyContin as a safe and highly effective drug for patients in pain.[20]

Purdue Pharma soon got some unlikely and high-powered help in getting that message out. Nine months after Joseph Famularo compared OxyContin to a plague at the announcement of Oxyfest 2001, he was promoting the drug as "a fine product that brings a lot of relief to suffering people" in his capacity as an unpaid consultant for Purdue Pharma. Famularo, who was replaced as US attorney in June of that year, wrote op-ed pieces praising the drug and condemning its abusers, offering a variation of the line, "Guns don't kill people. People kill people." He had befriended Haddox while both served on the Kentucky task force. Haddox floated the idea of getting Famularo a full-time job with Purdue Pharma, but Famularo was reluctant to relocate to Connecticut.[21]

The company also hired another veteran of law enforcement's OxyContin war, Jay McCloskey, who, as the top federal prosecutor in Maine, saw another of the first major waves of OxyContin abuse in the country. In his days as US attorney, McCloskey lamented how the drug was taking the lives of some of the best and brightest young people in rural Maine. A few months later, as an attorney in private practice, he had Purdue Pharma as one of his clients. The company defended its relationship with Famularo and McCloskey as part of an effort to successfully "liaise" with law enforcement.[22]

As more and more people overdosed around Central Appalachia, Purdue Pharma's message remained simple and consistent: The company had done nothing improper in marketing and promoting a drug that worked wonders for a lot of suffering people. Eventually that line would lose all credibility.

I didn't expect so soon after arriving in Eastern Kentucky to find myself in the middle of one of the most colossal public health crises of the twenty-first century. It was an incredibly consequential story that was unfolding in real time, but I found myself juggling it along with a heavy workload of other stories of importance, none more so than the Martin County sludge spill.

*

When I wrote a story about state regulators issuing a permit to the first coal-waste-burning power plant in Kentucky, it commanded a level of attention from Kentucky's US Senate delegation that was lacking when it came to the prescription drug epidemic. Only Republican Congressman Hal Rogers had treated the OxyContin crisis as a priority. The criticism he lobbed at Purdue Pharma was considered too harsh even by the editorial board of the *Courier-Journal*, which felt Rogers should be directing his anger at doctors, users, and law enforcement and not at Purdue Pharma. Rogers made it his mission in the years that followed to act as a watchdog of the opioid industry, an effort that led, among other things, to a 2019 congressional report claiming that the industry had manipulated the World Health Organization into doing its bidding.[23] Not surprisingly, Rogers has received next to nothing in donations from the pharmaceutical industry during his forty years in Congress.

I was puzzled why the GOP senators from Kentucky, Mitch McConnell and Jim Bunning, had so little to say about the spate of drug overdose deaths. Maybe it was because McConnell and Big Pharma have long been cozy, and Bunning didn't have any interest in what was happening in the godforsaken eastern part of Kentucky. In any case, neither came to his home state when it needed him most, and neither offered legislative remedies to the problem from afar. But a new coal-fired power plant was a story that the most powerful lawmakers could get behind. The first and last time I saw McConnell and Bunning together in Eastern Kentucky, they were shoveling sand at the groundbreaking ceremony for the recently approved $900 million facility in Knott County. Rogers also had a shovel in hand, as did George W. Bush's energy secretary, Spencer Abraham.

The ceremony took place on a scorching hot day on a vast parcel of strip-mined land. The dignitaries on hand touted the plant as Kentucky and the nation's future. McConnell, who had cosponsored legislation to provide tax breaks to clean-coal plants, talked about coal being "a big part of the mix" in meeting the nation's energy needs.[24] Bunning proclaimed that coal was "on the rise again after eight years of outright hostility"[25] from Bill Clinton's administration. Kentucky Mountain Power, the company that was going to operate the facility, promised that the plant would emit less than a quarter of the total emissions of existing coal-fired power plants. The two dozen or so protesters who gathered near the site weren't having any of it. I spoke to a former coal miner who came to the event to see the political bigwigs and enjoy the free barbecue being served. As he pointed to the dust-filled air at a nearby abandoned strip mine, he offered a candid assessment of the situation: "It's too late to worry about the environment. We oughta at least make some money from it."[26]

Despite all of the hoopla, no more shovels ever dug in. For four years, the project was beset by building delays and other problems. And by the time Kentucky Mountain Power announced it was ready to put more than five hundred people to work building the plant, the company's air permit had expired. The Kentucky Environmental and Public Protection Cabinet ruled that the company would have to submit a whole new permit application if it wished to move forward with construction. Kentucky Mountain Power fought that ruling for another four years before abandoning the project completely.[27]

A few days after the premature celebration of the power plant, I was flying in a fleet of helicopters whose passengers included Bush's head of the Environmental Protection Agency, former New Jersey Governor Christine Todd Whitman. Though she was the head of the EPA, her trip to Eastern Kentucky was unmistakably part two of the pro-coal tour of Bush's top energy and environmental officials. Praise for the mining industry was a major Republican talking point. Mining interests had contributed more than $250,000 to Bush's election campaign,[28] a large sum in the days before the Supreme Court's *Citizens United* decision opened the door for the unlimited spending of super PACs. In return, coal had earned itself a friend in the Oval Office. Under Clinton, the industry felt under siege as regulators and policymakers started meaningful discussions about reducing coal-based carbon dioxide emissions and other pollutants, a policy conversation related to climate change that an Al Gore administration likely would have continued. The Bush administration quashed that talk, however, and embarked on an aggressive campaign to increase coal's utility and impact.

I observed that Whitman was torn that day. As she toured the region by air, the only real vantage point for seeing the many lopped-off and mined mountaintops, she seemed on the verge of criticizing the practice. But other than lamenting that there wasn't a "better, more economical way" to mine coal, she stayed true to the party line. She expressed a belief that day that the country could achieve energy prosperity and preserve mining jobs without jeopardizing environmental safety.[29]

Back on the ground, Whitman joined a group of middle and high school students who were collecting vast amounts of garbage from illegal dump sites. I'm pretty sure that Whitman's visit to Eastern Kentucky left an impression on her, as two years after the Kentucky trip she chose to leave the EPA rather than sign a measure making it easier for coal-fired power plants to pollute the environment. Years later, Whitman would show an even greater willingness to break from the Republican Party when she accused Donald Trump of undermining the Constitution and accepted an invitation to speak at the 2020 Democratic National Convention.

But something important didn't make it onto Whitman's itinerary that day—a visit to Martin County, Kentucky, which eight months earlier had experienced one of the worst environmental disasters in the history of the American southeast, a three-hundred-million-gallon coal waste spill caused by a break in a containment dam. There was certainly something of great importance for an EPA head to see there, but I understand why she skipped it. After getting a sobering view of scarred mountains and trash-filled valleys, an up-close look at what a mining company did to destroy an Eastern Kentucky community might have led to an earlier crisis of conscience.

Up until the massive coal sludge spill, Martin County's most significant moment in the national spotlight came when President Lyndon Johnson chose the county as the location to declare a national war on poverty in 1964. Johnson's visit with locals helped popularize the image of the impoverished Appalachian. An iconic photo from the trip features LBJ sitting on the front porch of a home belonging to Tom Fletcher and his family. Fletcher, an unemployed sawmill operator, got the president's ear and became the face of American poverty, or more accurately, the white face of American poverty. The national media liked to check in on Martin County every five or ten years to see if a new buffet of federal programs had done anything to improve the county's fortunes. What they found was a county that had found a limited economic engine by belatedly tapping into its ample coal reserves. What I found was a community of residents standing knee-deep in a bog of tar-like coal waste.

Considering its omnipresence, I was surprised at how little coal I saw in coal country. But that was by design. Coal is a dirty business, sullying the land it comes from and the lungs of those who dig it. The less you see of mining in action, the better. There were plenty of coal tipples, coal trucks, and coal trains, but coal itself, except for the occasional lonely piece that found its way to the side of a road, generally remained out of sight and on the move. Sometimes I smelled coal, breathing in the fumes coming from the few remaining homes that still burned it for heat. I recognized the diesel exhaust–like odor immediately, having observed it everywhere I went during winters in the former East Berlin. I liked the smell. It filled me with warmth.

The mining industry had developed an efficient process for extracting, cleaning, and transporting the rock to power plants. One day, in October 1999, however, that system went horribly awry in Martin County. The toxic coal sludge shot out of a faulty impoundment and onto the community and into waterways as far away as the Ohio River. Luckily, no one was killed in the incident, which was similar in nature to a 1972 slurry dam breach in West Virginia that killed 125 people and left another 4,000 homeless. The West Virginia sludge spill was half the size of the one in Martin County, which was thirty times greater in volume than the 1989 Exxon Valdez oil spill. More than 27,000 residents ended up with water contaminated by arsenic, mercury, and lead, and all aquatic life in nearby Coldwater Fork and Wolf Creek was killed. After the spill, many people in the area developed red blotches on their skin from coming into contact with tainted tap water.[30]

For several years, the seventy-two-acre pond near the town of Inez held coal slurry, a tar-like goo mixture of water, rock, and coal waste particles produced after coal is washed. Coal that is washed clean of impurities burns longer and cleaner. But the resulting waste needs to be stored somewhere. In Martin County, the waste impoundment sat ominously in the hills, managed by the Martin County Coal Corporation, a subsidiary of mighty Massey Energy.

The investigation of the slurry spill got off to a promising start in the final weeks of the Clinton administration. Under the supervision of Mine Safety and Health Administration head Davitt McAteer, a team of federal impoundment experts worked to determine the causes of the Martin County disaster and to review the stability of hundreds of other similar impoundments in Appalachia.

Based on these findings, McAteer's investigative team was closing in on making recommendations for enforcement action, including possible criminal citations against Martin County Coal. That never happened. And it had everything to do with timing and politics. In January 2001, Bush entered the White House, and in quick order, he changed the face of the Department of Labor. Bush named Elaine Chao, the wife of increasingly powerful Senator Mitch McConnell, as the new head of the Labor Department. Chao replaced McAteer with a Utah coal operator named David Lauriski.

The most outspoken member of McAteer's team, a longtime mine-safety advocate named Jack Spadaro, was concerned that the new regime's investigation of other impoundments would lack thoroughness. As superintendent of the National Mine Health and Safety Academy (MSHA) in Beaver, West Virginia, Spadaro was an expert on the history of impoundment failures. He feared that another was going to happen if the mining industry and regulators didn't take what happened in Martin County seriously.

Spadaro said that Martin County Coal Corporation officials and federal regulators had concluded years earlier that the impoundment risked failure, but instead of taking steps to avoid a problem, MSHA didn't enforce its own safety recommendations and even allowed the company to increase the size of the impoundment. It also came out during a state investigation of the incident that Martin County Coal, in its original 1994 permit application, falsely stated that a seventy-foot rock barrier separated the impoundment from old underground mines beneath it. In reality, regulators discovered that the barrier was less than ten feet thick in some places.[31] Despite evidence showing otherwise, company officials maintained that the spill was caused by an "act of God," a choice of words that only inflamed passions in the deeply religious community, prompting the company to start using the phrase "act of nature." Bill Caylor, the president of the Kentucky Coal Association, defended Martin County Coal as a "good company with a good reputation" by accusing affected residents who were considering legal action of opportunism.[32] "This is a way for residents to get their property bought in an economically depressed market," Caylor said.[33]

Spadaro urged Lauriski to support his investigative team's recommendations to issue eight citations to Martin County Coal and its parent company, including one for criminal negligence. But Lauriski wasn't interested in coming down on Massey Energy, which had been—and would continue to be—a loyal benefactor to the Republican Party. Spadaro accused MSHA of whitewashing the probe. Chao supported Lauriski and criticized Spadaro for turning the impoundment probe into "a food fight."[34] There was no way Christine Todd Whitman was going to walk into the middle of this mining agency controversy.

The investigation continued in fits and bursts for more than a year, ending with a whimper in October 2002 when MSHA issued two citations to Martin County Coal, one of which was overturned on appeal. In the end, the company paid a federal fine of $55,000. Spadaro refused to sign the final report, leading to another round of sparring between MSHA and Spadaro that culminated in his retirement after thirty-five years in the field. Kentucky mining regulators were far more punitive than their federal counterparts, fining the company more than $3 million.

*

While reporting the Martin County story, I got to know Ned Pillersdorf and the greater community of Eastern Kentucky public interest attorneys. Pillersdorf would likely laugh at anyone who called him a "social justice warrior," but the term, with the meaning it had before being co-opted by the right, aptly describes him.

For decades, he and the other lawyers at the Appalachian Research and Defense Fund, or AppalReD, had provided free legal services to tens of thousands of indigent clients in Eastern Kentucky, taking aim at polluting coal companies, unsafe mining practices, illegitimate uses of power, and other nefarious targets that most attorneys in the area considered too controversial. Another of AppalReD's alumni, mine-safety advocate Tony Oppegard, had been the leader of MSHA's Martin County investigation until Bush took office.

AppalReD's founder, John Rosenberg, whose family fled Nazi Germany in 1938 and landed in segregated North Carolina, first came to Appalachia in 1970 after a stint with the Justice Department's Civil Rights Division. He came expecting to help launch a legal aid office and then go back home. But what he saw in the region moved him to stay. And his work drew other like-minded attorneys to the area. Rosenberg officially retired in 2001, but he found he couldn't sit idly by while the most vulnerable residents of the area continued to get mistreated. Nimble of body and mind, he has continued to work cases into his late eighties.

The Brooklyn-born Pillersdorf, a fanatical Mets fan who looks like a character actor from a gritty, 1970-set New York crime drama, was AppalReD's point person on the Martin County slurry spill. He represented several families in the Mullet Branch area of Martin County, one of the places most damaged by the coal sludge. Like John, Ned's name marked him as an outsider in Eastern Kentucky. He was the only Pillersdorf within hundreds of miles. His wife, Janet, was also a lawyer. She came into the world a Stumbo, a widely recognizable mountain surname shared by a former state attorney general and a gubernatorial candidate. As a girl attending high school in tiny Belfry, Kentucky, Janet scored so highly on the ACT standardized test that school officials accused her of cheating. She attended Morehead State University and the University of Kentucky College of Law and then returned home, where she met Ned, a recent hire by the public defender's office. They went into practice together and later married.

Together, Janet and Ned formed an unlikely Eastern Kentucky power couple, the brilliant and soft-spoken local girl, and the outspoken, Yankee litigator who hated nothing more than to see powerless people get screwed. They lived in Floyd County, which for a long time was the most Democratic county in Kentucky. Janet won a seat on the Kentucky Court of Appeals. Then, in 1993, she became the first woman ever elected to the Kentucky Supreme Court. She lost her seat on the high court in 2004 to a judge who publicly questioned why she insisted on using her maiden name professionally, a ploy to remind voters that she was married to an outsider. Janet lost that election, and ten years later when she ran again against that same judge, voters received robocalls informing them that Janet Stumbo's husband, Ned Pillersdorf, had contributed to the presidential campaign of "Barack Hussein Obama." She lost the rematch too.

Ned knew that Massey Energy had the resources to prolong the legal process for years, so shortly after MSHA issued its report on the Martin County spill, a group of his clients took a settlement deal in state court and received undisclosed damages from the company. It was a messy affair in more ways than one. Some of the hundreds of Martin County residents who sued the company in state or federal court complained of getting harassing phone calls from coal company sympathizers.

Nearly twenty years after the slurry spill contaminated groundwater and wells, Martin County is still struggling to provide residents with clean drinking water. As municipal water prices rise and quality remains suspect, many in the community still fill empty jugs with water that flows from mountainsides.

A decline in coal industry tax revenue has put a major dent in the coffers of every county government. In 2012, the region's coal-producing counties received $34 million from the state's Local Government Economic Assistance Fund, most of which came from a tax placed on the number of tons of coal that is mined in a given year. By 2018, that amount had dropped to $6.7 million.[35] Adding to the area's financial woes, the *Lexington Herald-Leader* reported in 2019 that a Martin County coal baron named Jim Booth owed his home county more than $2 million in past taxes.[36]

As a result, clean and affordable water is just one of the basic services that Martin County has lacked the money to offer. In 2019, Martin County Sheriff John Kirk took the drastic step of suspending all law enforcement activities in the county due to a budgetary squeeze. Kirk went on Facebook to urge residents to "lock your doors, load your guns and get a biting, barking dog."[37] Since that pronouncement, Kirk has at times served as the sheriff department's lone officer.

*

Maybe it shouldn't have come as a shock that a coal corporation and a pharmaceutical company hadn't acted as responsible corporate citizens.

At some point, Purdue Pharma realized it was futile (and bad for business) not to take any action in response to the negative news reports about OxyContin. In 2001, the company removed its 160-milligram pill from the market and provided doctors in some states with tamper-resistant prescription pads. Most notably, the drug maker pledged to work on a reformulated version of the drug that would prevent users from getting "a high."

Law enforcement groups continued to make OxyContin a priority. In 2003, Congressman Hal Rogers procured federal funding to launch a task force called Operation UNITE, which frequently announced drug arrests all over the region. The problem ran deeper than that, however. If Eastern Kentucky had built a drug treatment center for every press release sent out about a roundup of addicts, then I would have received a lot fewer of those press releases.

Most local doctors stopped prescribing OxyContin out of fear that they would come under scrutiny by law enforcement. As a result, carloads of Eastern Kentuckians traveled to walk-in pain clinics in Florida that operated as pill mills. Some of those people never made it back to Kentucky, overdosing in Florida or on the way home.[38] At a time when e-commerce was growing by leaps and bounds, shady out-of-state Internet pharmacies also helped keep the supply chain intact. According to the Government Accountability Office, the investigative arm of Congress, there were 1,400 Internet pharmacies in April 2004, up from 190 in October 2000.[39] Some of the online pharmacies employed doctors who wrote prescriptions to people without even the pretense of a doctor-patient relationship. One UPS center in Eastern Kentucky was receiving up to two hundred packages a day from a single Internet pharmacy. FedEx stopped delivering packages to parts of the region out of concern for the safety of its drivers who were carrying drug shipments. It would be years before state and federal governments cracked down on rogue Internet pharmacies.

OxyContin addicts who didn't know anyone with a valid credit card and couldn't obtain the drug online discovered other ways to get the type of high they were seeking. Methadone, more than any other drug, filled the void. Traditionally used at clinics in carefully administered doses to wean people off of heroin, methadone was also available by prescription. While many other rural parts of the country were grappling with a growing methamphetamine problem, Eastern Kentucky had methadone to reckon with. The decrease in the number of OxyContin prescriptions was more than offset by the increase in the number of methadone prescriptions being written. Kentucky law enforcement was playing a game of whack-a-mole and losing. The state lacked a system for tracking methadone overdose deaths, so I did a county-by-county survey of coroner's offices and found that more than 345 Kentuckians died from methadone-related overdoses between January 2003 and May 2004.[40] That was a conservative figure considering that only 80 of 120 coroners provided me with data. One small Eastern Kentucky county had a death toll of forty. In most of the fatal overdoses, the victims mixed methadone with another painkiller or a sedative like Xanax, creating a lethal cocktail.

To help manage the epidemic, the Kentucky justice system created drug courts in which defendants had opportunities to attend court-supervised substance abuse programs in lieu of serving jail time. But the lack of treatment facilities in Eastern Kentucky hampered these diversion programs.

Purdue Pharma is not solely to blame for the opioid epidemic. It wasn't the only company aggressively marketing pain pills. And it didn't shove OxyContin up anyone's nose or force it into their veins.

But the company should have known what would happen if communities in Eastern Kentucky and around the country became overrun with the drug. Maybe they did their research into the vulnerability of the communities there and determined it was a risk worth taking.

By the mid-2000s, the lawsuits against Purdue Pharma started coming in droves. Kentucky Attorney General Greg Stumbo filed a product liability suit against the company in 2007, the same year that Purdue Pharma reached $20 million settlements with twenty-six states and the District of Columbia for unlawfully marketing Oxy-Contin. Considering the toll the drug had taken on his state, Stumbo felt insulted by that offer, believing he had a billion-dollar case on his hands. But after several legal setbacks, Kentucky settled the case for just $24 million in 2015.[41] In 2022, state officials announced that another $483 million would flow to the state through a national settlement with several pharmaceutical companies.

We've learned a lot about Purdue Pharma's methods and practices since then.

Internal company documents obtained by the medical news website *STAT* in 2019 show how Purdue Pharma looked past or simply ignored warnings about the mass marketing of OxyContin. In 1996, for example, the company brushed off the advice of a doctor it courted in the hopes of getting his endorsement for prescribing OxyContin to a broader range of pain patients. But Swiss physician Pierre Dayer told company representatives that a patient with "low back pain" would not be a candidate for opioids in Europe, in part because of the risk of addiction with this class of drug.[42] Dayer recommended further investigation into the possible link between "the rapid onset of action in OxyContin and 'the abuse/addiction potential' of the drug."[43] Other internal company emails discuss growing concern from outside sources that OxyContin could be subject to misuse. The company encouraged a marketing plan that emphasized saying OxyContin was "effective" for pain, while avoiding use of the word "powerful."[44] An internal memo from 1999 urged sales reps to prioritize OxyContin sales, offering lucrative bonuses for doing so. "Your priority is to Sell, Sell, Sell OxyContin," the memo read.[45]

In October 2020, Purdue Pharma agreed to plead guilty to three federal criminal charges and to pay more than $8 billion in fines and penalties. The money will go to opioid treatment programs. As part of the settlement, the Sackler family agreed to cede control of the company.[46]

Looking back on the early years of the OxyContin outbreak in Eastern Kentucky, it is devastating to see how the opioid epidemic just kept spreading, in Appalachia and eventually throughout the nation, spawning the abuse of other powerful synthetic pain relievers like Fentanyl, now the biggest killer of americans aged 18 to 45, and the resurgence of heroin itself. The potential for abuse of prescription painkillers continued to grow after I left Eastern Kentucky. Between 2006 and 2014, many of the counties in the nation that averaged an annual distribution of more than 140 opioid pills per resident were in Eastern Kentucky.[47] And the Bluegrass State's rate of drug overdose deaths remains among the highest in the country. The opioid epidemic without a doubt has been one of the defining events of early twenty-first-century America, a "disease of despair" that has had widespread economic ramifications and has led to lowering of overall life expectancy. In February 2020, Federal Reserve Chair Jerome H. Powell cited opioids as a contributing factor to the nation's rate of labor force participation lagging behind other industrialized nations.[48]

At the turn of the millennium, a killer pill epidemic and an environmental disaster were two things that Eastern Kentucky could least afford. And both could have been avoided if governments and corporations hadn't shown disregard for a part of the country that had come to be viewed as expendable.

The walls caved in during my first year in Eastern Kentucky, a period of tragic human neglect that continues to scar the region. In the pursuit of profits, human beings became collateral damage. And all that remained to keep the entire roof from collapsing were increasingly thin pillars of coal.

CHAPTER 2

King Coal

The roughly 120-year history of coal mining in Eastern Kentucky can be divided into four periods. The first was the most fundamental: landowners were swindled out of their mineral rights starting around 1900 and that era created a dynamic that has come to define the region. The second was about asserting control: the proliferation of "coal camps" in the first decades of the twentieth century speaks to the coal industry's history of predatory capitalism and longstanding dominance of the region. The third was about seeking balance: the rise of the United Mine Workers of America (UMWA), whose membership peaked in the 1920s, gave miners a voice and an affiliation with an entity other than the coal company. The fourth, which is happening right now, is about identity: the rapid decline of the coal industry in the twenty-first century, worse than any downturn of the twentieth century, has forced Eastern Kentuckians to reassess their relationship to coal and prospects going forward.

The modern history of the region was shaped by outsiders coming in at the turn of the twentieth century to snatch up huge amounts of land. These business interests used "broad form deeds" to acquire the right to extract mineral deposits from underneath private property. Many of the landowners who sold these rights for next to nothing could neither read nor write and signed the deeds with an "X."[1] The document gave coal operators permission to do whatever it took to mine, leaving no obligation to repair any damage done in the process. For decades, even after strip mining started rivaling underground mining in terms of total coal production, broad form deeds remained in effect, giving companies mineral rights to both surface and underground coal reserves. As a friend of mine who was born in West Virginia and grew up in Hazard puts it, "When they stole our resources, they stole our pride, too."

Remarkably, it wasn't until the 1970s that Kentucky thought to put a severance tax on the mined coal. And it took another twenty years after that for lawmakers to realize that at least some of the proceeds from coal severance taxes should go back to the areas where coal is mined to help with economic and social development.

Eastern Kentucky has long depended on that most risky of economic models, one based heavily on the extraction of natural resources. As energy journalist David Roberts wrote in *Vox*, "Extraction industries are largely a scam through which wealthy people remove value from a region and leave behind social and environmental ruin."[2]

The people of Eastern Kentucky have had little choice but to conform to the whims of this process. The "coal camps" that sprung up during coal's early rise to supremacy offer important historical insight into the industry's ongoing grip on the region. By Kentucky historian Ron Eller's estimation, nearly two-thirds of miners and their families lived in these privately owned communities in the first years of the twentieth century.[3] Some camp residents were native to the mountains of Central Appalachia. Others came from Southern and Eastern Europe in search of jobs. At one point, so many Italian miners poured into the region that the Italian government opened a consular office in West Virginia. Miners from thirty-eight different countries lived in a US Steel–owned coal camp in Lynch, Kentucky, at one time the largest coal camp anywhere.[4] During this era, the region also got its first taste of integration from Southern Blacks who came to work in the mines. Some of the descendants of these miners remain in the area today, giving Eastern Kentucky small pockets of significant diversity.

The out-of-state companies that ran these mostly unincorporated towns exerted control over their workers by borrowing the concept of the nineteenth-century company town and adding an extra dose of indentured servitude. There were no elected officials or independent law enforcement agencies in coal camps. Most everyone lived in a boxy, wood-framed house with wood siding. Companies paid workers in "scrip" that could only be used to buy goods at company stores, which were frequently sold at marked-up prices. Most children went to company-run schools, though some coal camp kids left their home base to attend one of the several settlement schools that educators established in Eastern Kentucky in the early twentieth century. The sick got treated by company doctors.

For coal camp residents who followed all of the rules set forth by the company, it was a regimented but pleasant enough existence. As long as miners did their work and didn't stir up trouble, they were provided for. It was forbidden to be both a member of a camp church congregation and a union. The texts in the English classes taught to foreign-born workers warned of the threat that unions posed to industrial capitalism. The West Virginia coal wars of the 1920s and the Harlan County War of the 1930s resulted from coal companies trying to violently prevent camp "agitators" from labor organizing.

By the mid-1950s, coal camps were well on their way to extinction, but they remain a central part of Eastern Kentucky's history and identity. They transformed societies. James Still's celebrated novel *River of Earth*, which shared the Southern Author's Award with Thomas Wolfe's *You Can't Go Home Again* in 1940, tells the story of a struggling Eastern Kentucky family choosing between maintaining independence by staying in their home or moving to a nearby coal mining camp to take advantage of the job opportunities there. I credit Still's works with helping me to get a handle on mid-twentieth-century life in the Kentucky mountains. The cold, hungry days of the Baldridge family's winter are palpable. When Still died in April 2001 at the age of ninety-four, I attended his memorial service at the Hindman Settlement School. As one of the speakers at the service noted, "Thomas Wolfe said you can't go home again. James Still said you can never leave home."[5]

In the mid-1920s, the coal mining industry employed more than 800,000 workers nationwide, around 65,000 of them in Kentucky. Coal mine employment in Kentucky peaked at 75,000 in 1948.[6] But due to decreased demand and increased mechanization of the mining process, nearly 400,000 mining jobs were lost nationally between 1948 and 1968, an industry trend that resulted in Kentucky's mining workforce being trimmed by two-thirds.[7]

With mining came death, but there was a dramatic drop in coal mine fatalities beginning in the early 1950s, mostly due to a watchful union fighting for improved safety conditions and fewer miners working underground.[8] The perception of coal mining as a deadly trade was starting to change. "Coal mining in Kentucky is safer year after year, thanks to the efforts of management, labor, the government and a number of organizations which promote mine safety," *The Messenger* of Madisonville, a town in the heart of Western Kentucky coal country, wrote in a 1963 editorial.[9]

The coal industry still needed an image boost, however, because the next wave of coal extraction brought the ugliness of mining to the surface. The industry was no longer only extracting coal from miles beneath the earth. It was using strip mining, also known as mountaintop removal mining, to blast the earth's surface to pieces. In Western Kentucky, an area at low elevation, the practice left fewer visible scars. In Eastern Kentucky, however, it was impossible to overlook strip mining's reengineering of the earth's landscape.

*

I started covering Eastern Kentucky at a time when bituminous coal, at the ripe age of 2 million, was experiencing a sort of late-life crisis. Since the first seam of coal in the region was tapped at the turn of the twentieth century, the coal industry had played a dominant role in meeting local employment and national energy needs. By the year 2000, however, the industry was locked in a fight for survival against critics, changing norms, and reality itself.

The dip in demand for coal in the mid-twentieth century was partly brought on by increased production and consumption of other energy sources, including renewables, natural gas, and petroleum gas. Natural gas in particular posed a threat as it steadily encroached on coal's primacy through the increased use of hydraulic fracturing, or fracking. But thanks largely to steady coal production in Appalachia, the mining industry warded off the challenge and experienced a resurgence over the next several decades, riding waves of boom and bust to remain a force even at its lowest point. In 2000, coal still provided more than half of the nation's electricity.

Other energy sources may have been cleaner or less expensive, but the coal industry had a mystique that other industries couldn't match. Coal mining's images of helmeted men carrying carbide lamps, returning from their daily underground shift with soot-blackened faces, perfectly captured the can-do spirit that the country has always liked to present to itself and to the outside world. Coal mining was the proverbial honest day's work for an honest day's pay that is so deeply ingrained in American mythos. Yet it wasn't your average blue-collar job. At the same time that we exalted coal miners for their industriousness in working to help quench the nation's growing thirst for electricity, we pitied them for lacking safer, more conventional places to earn a paycheck. The famed canary went into a coal mine, not into a steel mill or a chemical plant, and definitely not into an office lined with cubicles.

Coal miners are a devoted lot. In a documentary series called *Our Appalachia*, produced in the 1980s by the Division of Media Services at Morehead State University, several miners who worked for the Martin County Coal Corporation, which was twenty years away from the infamy of the massive slurry spill, touted the virtues of their vocation. One gave the following testimonial:

> My dad was a coal miner. When he was a coal miner, it wasn't really a great glamorous job, but through the efforts of a lot of organizations, they've made coal mining safe now. Inside is no different than working in a garage. You've got a roof over you, and they've got it supported. It's just a safe job now. It's a little dirty, but a man who don't want to get dirty, he don't want to work too much.[10]

The *Courier-Journal* had long served as an unofficial watchdog of the coal industry, a role that media outlets in Eastern Kentucky were reluctant to take on for a variety of reasons. I admired Hazard-based WYMT's commitment to providing a uniquely Eastern Kentucky perspective on the news, but the CBS affiliate had a coal-friendly advertising base to please, which killed its appetite for critical coverage of the mining industry. Similarly, with one notable exception, *The Mountain Eagle* of Whitesburg, the many local papers in the region opted to focus on ribbon cuttings, high school sports, and youth beauty pageants. A local reporter who stepped out of line and decided to investigate a coal company's misconduct could expect an angry phone call to their editor from a company representative. If that wasn't enough to get the reporter reassigned to a story about the new bakery that just opened in town, then someone from the coal company might take direct action by digging into the journalist's past. I saw it happen to a reporter I know. He hung in a lot longer than most journalists would have, but after a couple of stories critical of the coal company's safety record, he backed off.

Coal companies knew better than to try to intimidate the *Courier-Journal*. The paper's George Polk Award–winning 1998 series, *Dust, Deception and Death*, was just one of its successful efforts to shine a spotlight on the industry's long history of cutting corners when it came to worker safety and environmental protection. The articles got the attention of policymakers and forced coal operators to finally address why so many coal miners were dying from black lung disease. That didn't mean that everyone in a position of power had a positive opinion of the paper's coverage. One pro-coal state legislator named Jim Gooch told the paper in 2001 that its stories about coal "don't have any credibility with this legislator."[11]

Under the leadership of truly great editors like the legendary John Carroll, the *Lexington Herald-Leader* had established itself as a worthy competitor to the *Courier-Journal* in its coverage of college athletics, state government, and Eastern Kentucky. The *Herald-Leader* had two veterans stationed in my area, Lee Mueller to the north in Pikeville and Bill Estep to the south in Somerset. Both natives of the region, Lee and Bill benefited from impressive Rolodexes. They were two of the reporters on a 1994 series about local politics in Kentucky called *Little Kingdoms*, which remains one of the best pieces of newspaper journalism about the eastern part of the state. I wasn't going to be able to beat the competition every time, but based on the *Courier-Journal*'s proud history of covering coal mining, my editors expected me to own that part of the beat.

The coal industry and its chief critics—including those at the *Courier-Journal*—both realized that the first years of the twenty-first century were a critical time for coal mining in the United States. With the election of George W. Bush, the industry added a coal-friendly presidential administration to its allies in Congress and statehouses throughout Appalachia. The coal industry contributed $30 million to political campaigns from 1997 to 2002 and spent more than three times that amount on lobbying.[12] On the other side of the cavern stood the United Mine Workers union and an increasingly vocal group of environmental and mine-safety activists trying to prevent coal companies from running roughshod over people and the planet. The two sides clashed frequently over consequential subjects, but unlike in the violent coal wars of decades past, this battle played out much more civilly, with rules and regulations taking the place of guns and knives.

The coal industry believed that tight government supervision had helped companies install safeguards and promote environmentally conscious operations. It pointed to a flurry of governmental activity in the 1960s and 1970s as evidence that it was as strictly regulated as any industry. In 1969, Congress passed the Federal Coal Mine Health and Safety Act, a law that required federal inspections of all coal mines, gave mine inspectors authority to shut down dangerous mines, and set limits on miners' exposure to coal dust in the atmosphere of mines. Over the next decade, those and other provisions of the law were tightened, leading up to the creation of the Labor Department's Mine Safety and Health Administration in 1977. That same year, the passage of the Surface Mining Control and Reclamation Act increased enforcement of environmental laws at active and abandoned surface mines.

On my beat, mining industry officials were feeling emboldened to speak out against what they perceived as an onslaught of burdensome regulations. With Bush making coal a centerpiece of his national energy policy and former coal operator Paul Patton sitting in the Kentucky governor's mansion for a second term, the industry saw an opportunity to expand its activities and to ward off new mandates. But the industry's public relations problems hung over the early years of the new millennium. The disastrous Martin County slurry spill in 2000 had raised troubling questions about coal mining's environmental footprint. That same year, thirteen Kentucky miners were killed in work-related accidents, the most in the state in nearly a decade and the most in the nation for the third consecutive year. These events revealed that, in fact, some mining regulations in Kentucky were lagging behind other states.

The *Dust, Deception and Death* series hadn't been kind to Patton. It showed that many of the air-quality tests performed in the coal mines that he operated in the 1970s yielded impossibly low levels of dust, a sign that the tests were fraudulent. After the stories were published, Patton denied having any "conscious knowledge" of testing improprieties at his mines.[13] Patton had already alienated some of the state's most vulnerable miners by criticizing the leniency of the state's black-lung compensation program. His comments led to a legislative overhaul of the system that made it much harder for miners with the disease to collect benefits. At the end of 2000, Patton took another hit from the paper, this time in a series of stories by former Eastern Kentucky correspondent Ralph Dunlop about the state mining board's failure to help enforce safety laws that might have prevented deaths and injuries. Again, Patton went on the record saying he was unaware of any problems.

Despite growing evidence of a culture of corner-cutting, the Kentucky Coal Association stuck to its talking points. "Coal is not the 'pick and shovel' industry that is too often portrayed," Kentucky Coal Association President Bill Caylor wrote in a 2001 opinion piece in the *Courier-Journal.* "Today's coal industry is a high-tech industry that stresses safe working conditions for its miners. Safety is serious business."[14]

In order to avoid saying anything too inflammatory, media-shy coal executives usually left the talking to Caylor, but I was able to build rapport with a few company officials who felt comfortable speaking their minds on the record. One of them was Paul Matney, the director of human resources at the TECO Coal Corporation, a subsidiary of Tampa-based TECO Energy that generated more than $300 million in revenue in the early 2000s.[15] The company's influence was impossible to miss in Eastern Kentucky. In addition to sponsoring programming and running ads on the local TV station, an imposing TECO coal-processing tipple provided an unofficial welcome to Hazard for anyone entering town traveling west on the Hal Rogers Parkway, which had dropped Daniel Boone from its name to honor the coal-friendly congressman.

Matney's grandfather had been a United Mine Workers organizer in the early days of the union. "The day he got the job was the day someone died inside a Virginia mine," Matney told me. "The mine operator told the other miners to throw the body on a coal car and to take it out when the shift ended. That's the way it was back then."[16]

A Pike County native, Matney recounted how, as a younger man, he had passed up a scholarship to attend Harvard in favor of going to the University of Kentucky, where he double majored in mathematics and physics and then received a master's degree in statistics. After graduation, he again resisted the siren's call of the Northeastern United States to remain at home, where he found a fulfilling career in coal. When I first spoke to him in 2001, he acknowledged that the industry was having a difficult time recruiting young Eastern Kentuckians. "We're losing people, and we're losing miners," he told me. But he remained hopeful that coal could overcome its growing reputation as a dying industry if the politicians in charge would just cut it some slack.

*

I don't know if Patton experienced a crisis of conscience or just grew tired of the bad press, but shortly after Ralph Dunlop's follow up pieces to *Dust, Deception and Death* ran, the governor took dramatic action by recommending a complete overhaul of Kentucky's mine-safety system. As I familiarized myself with the events that led to Patton's proposal, I realized I was looking at something more than a dry, process-heavy story about a tweaking of government bureaucracy. The board shake-up cut to the core of the longstanding tension between the coal industry and the groups that felt the industry lacked adequate oversight. Patton abolished the former mining board and at his prodding the state legislature approved the creation of two new governmental bodies, a board to administer the safety program and a commission to deal with enforcement. I was still early in my journalism career and hadn't yet acquired the cynicism that caused me to view boards, commissions, and blue-ribbon panels as a performance to convince the public that a problem is being taken seriously. To his credit, Patton laid to rest any mistrust of his intentions by putting the already established mine safety advocate Tony Oppegard in charge of prosecuting cases before the new commission.

Oppegard scared the hell out of the coal industry, and with good reason. For most of the previous eighteen years, Oppegard had been the only lawyer in Kentucky to specialize in cases involving coal miners who lost their jobs because they complained about safety conditions. He had aggressively led the US Mine Safety and Health Administration investigation into the Martin County slurry disaster, setting the stage for the issuance of major citations, until the Bush administration replaced him. As the new general counsel for the Kentucky Department of Mines and Minerals, Oppegard would be in a position to prosecute violations of safety regulations that he was going to help write. When coal operators found out that Oppegard was a candidate for the job, they demanded to talk to the governor. They left the meeting thinking they had a promise from Patton not to hire Oppegard.

But Patton identified Oppegard as the most qualified person for the job. The mine workers union praised Oppegard as a tireless fighter for workplace safety. The Kentucky Coal Association said it feared that he would bring a "hidden agenda" to the job.[17] I spoke to a Harlan County coal operator who said the mere mention of Oppegard's name made him uncomfortable. Patton acknowledged that some coal companies had reason to feel uneasy. "Anybody that doesn't want any change in Kentucky mine safety procedures might not want Oppegard," the governor said.[18]

Oppegard, who grew up in a coal mining region of Southwestern Pennsylvania, arrived in Kentucky in 1980 to work for the crusading Appalachian Research and Defense Fund (AppalReD). The following year, a coal-dust explosion at an Eastern Kentucky underground mine killed eight men. To that point, AppalReD hadn't worked on cases related to mine safety. But John Rosenberg, the organization's founder, gave Oppegard the green light to investigate the Topmost mining disaster in Knott County. Oppegard represented the victims' families, who urged the federal government to convene a public hearing to examine why the blast occurred. They wanted to know how inadequate ventilation systems and an improperly high amount of coal dust discovered in the mine after the incident had escaped the notice of inspectors.

Oppegard and the families met with then-MSHA head Ford B. Ford, presenting him with a petition containing 11,000 signatures of people demanding a hearing on the Topmost incident. But Ford wasn't swayed. After the meeting, Oppegard told the *Courier-Journal*, "I got the impression that Ford has a total lack of understanding of coal mining in Eastern Kentucky."[19] Oppegard later wrote that he found Ford, an appointee of President Ronald Reagan, "evasive, disingenuous and far more concerned with his and MSHA's public image than with learning why a massive breakdown of safe mining practices had occurred at the Topmost mine."[20]

The day after the Topmost disaster, thirteen miners were killed in a methane explosion at an underground mine in Tennessee. About a month later, seven more Kentucky miners were killed in another coal-dust explosion in Floyd County. Oppegard had found a calling.

His work on the Topmost case was a valuable and painful learning experience. The deaths could have been prevented if the mine had been equipped with an inexpensive and readily available filter that removes electrical charges from coal dust. As it stood, the eight miners were less than an hour into their eight-hour afternoon shift, crawling on hands and knees through a thirty-one-inch coal seam, when the mine exploded. All eight victims died from carbon monoxide poisoning that resulted from smoke inhalation. Oppegard grew close to the deceased miners' families, taking their children to ball games and attending their weddings as they grew into adulthood. The tragedy that took their fathers' lives nagged at him. If coal operators and officials running mining agencies didn't understand or care about basic matters of safety, then he would have to work extra hard to make sure more lives weren't needlessly lost. He resisted the idea that coal mining was a dangerous job in which deaths were inevitable. As a private attorney, he took a hands-on approach to his job, venturing down into coal mines on a regular basis and taking up the cases of miners who blew the whistle on unsafe working conditions. Oppegard understood that most people weren't mining wonks like him, and he took the time to patiently explain jargon and concepts like "retreat mining," "clay dummies," and "shooting from the solid."

Kentucky mine operators got a brief reprieve from Oppegard when he left to go to work for the federal government in 1998. But after three years with MSHA, he was back in the Bluegrass State, this time with orders from the governor of Kentucky to help rein in outlaw mine operators. In his new office in the state capital of Frankfort, Oppegard kept a framed poster with a quote from renowned labor activist Mother Jones, who helped organize coal miner strikes in the early twentieth century: "Pray for the dead and fight like hell for the living."

Oppegard quickly got to work, drafting new and tougher state rules to protect miner safety. Among the new regulations was a three-strikes-and-you're-out measure for repeated problems at the same mine. And for the first time, the state could assess fines for violations, a reform that had immediate impact. Over the next three years, Oppegard filed complaints against 117 alleged mine-safety violators.[21] In one of those cases, a mining instructor admitted to selling training certificates at an Eastern Kentucky flea market instead of providing actual mine training. In another case, a coal company was fined more than half a million dollars for a fatal explosion. Oppegard's work didn't confine him to a desk. While investigating the case of a miner who was seriously injured in a roof collapse after his foreman ordered him to use a piece of bolting equipment that he hadn't been trained on, Oppegard squeezed into the mine's nineteen-inch seam of coal for a few hours to get a firsthand look at the working conditions of the mine. Thanks to Oppegard's efforts and presence, Kentucky coal operators started to take state inspections seriously for the first time.

*

With Oppegard coming at them from one side, the early 2000s Kentucky coal industry found itself on the defensive from other sides as well.

Every now and then a celebrity environmentalist touched down in Eastern Kentucky to lament the ecological toll of coal mining. Following a helicopter tour of the area in 2002, Robert F. Kennedy, Jr., whose daughter Rory made a 1999 documentary set in eastern Kentucky, lashed out at strip mining operations for polluting the Kentucky River, a waterway that runs from the mountains to the Ohio River. Before he became a prominent anti-vaccination advocate, Kennedy devoted much of his time to speaking out against corporate polluters that he believed were treating Kentucky and other states "like a business in liquidation."[22]

"They're allowed to create slurry ponds and chop off the top of entire mountain ranges," Kennedy said on that trip, speaking before a group of educators and activists who assembled for the launch of an initiative called Kentucky Riverkeeper. "The landscape has been dismantled by this industry . . . We're not protecting the environment for the sake of the fishes and the birds. We're doing it because nature enriches us."[23] Backstreet Boy Kevin Richardson, a native Kentuckian who attended the event, nodded approvingly as Kennedy spoke.

It was a reach to place all of the blame for the pollution of the river on the coal industry. Other infrastructural problems like the illegal dumping of trash, faulty septic tanks, and raw sewage running directly from homes into streams have long contributed to the problem. But Kennedy's presence in the area served its intended purpose of sending a message to the industry and the public that the grassroots movement against coal was gaining strength. Even Hollywood was getting in on the act, casting actor Steven Seagal in a movie filmed partly in Hazard about a brawling environmental cagent who puts the hurt on polluting mine owners.

The articles that I or our environmental reporter wrote about high pollutant levels in rivers and streams or about tainted drinking water and dead aquatic life didn't have the immediacy of another aspect of strip mining that was literally hitting people where they lived.

In pursuit of a story on this new symptom of strip mining, I went to interview a man who returned home one day to find his double-wide trailer, or what remained of it, with a boulder in its living room. The company that operated the strip mine a few hundred feet above his house had set off too powerful of a blast, sending the massive piece of rock hurtling through the air and down on the man's roof. It was becoming an all too common problem in the area. Coal companies, looking to blow as much coal as possible out of the earth, were detonating explosives well in excess of legal limits, causing these dangerous "fly-rock" incidents. I figured the man with the boulder in his living room would be hopping mad. Anyone inside the house at the time of the incident likely would have been killed. But he didn't want to talk with a reporter, and he firmly but politely asked me to get back in my car and leave him alone. Maybe he had other things on his mind, like getting rid of his uninvited spherical house guest, and just wasn't in the mood to talk. Or maybe, more likely, I thought, he didn't want to risk saying anything that would alienate the mining company that employed dozens of people in his community, maybe even a cousin or brother.

I spoke to a former strip mine blasting supervisor who quit his $37,000-a-year job because he said his company had pressured him to set off blasts in excess of the depth limit allowed by the company's permit. With attorney Ned Pillersdorf's help, he sued the company and settled out of court for $142,500.[24] Following three fly-rock incidents at the site, the company determined that it couldn't mine there anymore, at least not legally, so it closed shop. A fly-rock incident or a mudslide caused by a strip-mining company pushing earth and rock from mountaintops onto hillsides was just part of life in coal country for some. "Falling rock" signs are ubiquitous in the region, and ignored at one's own peril.

Other people whose homes were on the receiving end of boulders from the heavens didn't hesitate to air their grievances. In 2002, I talked to a man named Jerry Pinson who was out grocery shopping when an errant eleven-foot boulder from a strip mine blast crashed down on his Pike County mobile home. Several of Pinson's neighbors were forced to evacuate their homes as other boulders dangled perilously from the hillside. The top fine in Kentucky at the time for a fly-rock violation was just $5,000. It brought cold comfort to Pinson that surface mining officials in Frankfort were discussing ways to more strictly regulate blasting practices and to increase penalties for fly-rock incidents. He had habituated himself to the boom of detonating explosives from the hill above his home and had long since learned where to place his dishes and pictures so they rattled but didn't fall. "My house is tore up, and I don't know what to do," Pinson told me. As we spoke, he managed to locate a few articles of clothing from the rubble before joining his neighbors at a nearby motel.[25]

Thankfully, no one was killed by fly rock during my time in Eastern Kentucky. But in 2004, a three-year-old boy in Virginia was crushed to death by a half-ton boulder that was dislodged by a bulldozer operator at a strip-mine operation. The rock fell 650 feet before crashing through his family's house. The company received the maximum fine of $15,000 for the fatal incident. County prosecutors opted not to bring criminal charges in the case. The boy's family reached a confidential settlement in its civil lawsuit against the coal company whose actions caused his death.[26]

As long as fly-rock incidents took place in remote hollows and only victimized mobile-home residents, coal companies could afford to downplay their frequency and seriousness as a public health hazard. Then, in 2005, a flying boulder chose the wrong target: a Walmart Supercenter in Hazard. Like in many rural American communities, Walmart had come to dominate Central Appalachia's retail landscape. That banjo-playing kid from the movie *Deliverance*? He works at a Walmart in Clayton, Georgia, not far from where the movie was filmed. In addition to being a top employer, it is a main hangout, especially in the early days of any given month, when many Eastern Kentuckians have a government check to spend. There are people who spend an entire day at the local Walmart, catching up with friends and acquaintances they run into as they make their way through the store. When my mother-in-law says she's going to Walmart, her kids and grandkids know not to expect her home for several hours. The Hazard Walmart's sales numbers for Nabisco and Coca-Cola products were so impressive one year that the corporate office in Bentonville, Arkansas, awarded the town with a softball game between store employees and an all-star team of Hall of Fame baseball players including Ryne Sandberg, Ozzie Smith, and Brooks Robinson. I attended the game, which took place at a high school softball field not far from the park known as Pillville.

A greeter at the Hazard Walmart claimed that she was injured when the vibration from the fallen boulder caused her to fall against an ice machine. Walmart accused the woman of exaggerating her injuries, but an administrative law judge awarded her temporary disability benefits for physical and psychological injuries.[27] Kentucky regulators issued citations to the company that operated the strip mine, and over the next decade, state and federal agencies became more vigilant about regulating the use of explosives at strip mines. Once again, this time in an unexpected way, Walmart reasserted its central role in the lives of people of the region.

*

A century of enjoying the coal booms and enduring or fleeing the coal busts helped shape Central Appalachia's self-image and gave the coal industry a powerful symbolic and economic hold throughout the area. But groups like Kentuckians for the Commonwealth and the Kentucky Resources Council had been increasingly successful in fighting for environmental reform since the 1980s.

I attended any number of events at which critics assailed mountaintop mining. One of the more memorable gatherings featured several local clergymen, one of whom lamented the "scarred and marred mountains" around him and called mountaintop removal "a waste of God's creation."[28] When I called Bill Caylor of the Coal Association for comment, he told me he resented the religious bent of the protest. "I disagree when people try to justify their actions with quotes from the Bible," he said. Without missing a beat, he then cited what he viewed as a pro-mountaintop removal passage in the holy book about "every valley shall be filled in, every mountain and hill shall be made low."[29]

The coal industry fought back with a simple message: less coal mining would be devastating for a place like Eastern Kentucky that loved and depended on coal as much as coal loved and depended on it, even if those statements were becoming less true with each passing year. To maintain the hearts and minds of the region, Big Coal launched an initiative in 2002 called "Friends of Coal." The volunteer organization was the brainchild of the West Virginia Coal Association, which felt aggrieved by talk of increased enforcement of limits on the weights of coal trucks in that state. I knew the issue well. In Eastern Kentucky, I had seen firsthand and written about "choking clouds of gray dust that spew from convoys of heavy coal trucks" that roared down highways and two-lane roads with equal gusto. West Virginia coal operators had grown frustrated with negative media portrayals of their industry. They wanted to help shape the narrative about coal. "We have a lot of friends out there," a

Beckley, West Virginia, coal operator named Warren Hylton said during one of the group's brainstorming sessions. "If we ask for their help, they'll help us."[30] Friends of Coal and affiliated groups soon sprouted up in Kentucky and Virginia. None charged membership fees. The only criterion for joining the program was an abiding love of coal.

The campaign sought to build upon existing pro-coal sentiment in Eastern Kentucky. From the day I arrived there, I was reminded by stickers on cars and in store windows that "Coal Keeps the Lights On!" Eventually the slogan earned its own state license plate. Central Appalachian coal associations hoped to turn that popular sentiment into bedrock principle by suggesting that people needed to make a zero-sum choice between being friends of coal or enemies of coal. The industry had some advantages in that quest. A rank-and-file miner in the early 2000s earned more than thirty dollars an hour. A miner who advanced to the job of foreman could make even more than that. Few jobs in the area paid as well. So were you a real Eastern Kentuckian whose family had toiled in the mines for generations, or were you one of those tree-huggers and do-gooders who hated both Appalachian heritage and jobs that paid decent wages? The choice was yours.

Bill Bissett worked for the public relations firm that helped build the Friends of Coal movement. As he puts it, "How many jobs are there in rural America that pay people $70,000 a year to do something they love?"[31] Bissett, who went on to serve as the president of the Kentucky Coal Association from 2010 to 2016, felt the industry could maintain its influence through savvier public relations. "The coal industry has always been run by lawyers, engineers, and accountants who are horrible at public relations," he says. "They even filter out the good news that is happening."[32]

The coal industry had timed its public relations blitz perfectly. By the early 2000s, membership in the United Mine Workers had declined steeply, partly because the UMWA didn't fight the rise of strip mining, which coal companies performed with a much smaller workforce. There were only a couple of thousand union coal miners left in Kentucky in 2000. The downward trend continued all the way up until the last union mine in Kentucky shut down in 2015.[33]

The diminution of union involvement in the workplace created space for coal companies to portray themselves as the protectors of the working man. Autocratic coal camps were a thing of the past, but the industry discovered a new way to tap into the coal-camp mentality of loyalty and codependency. Other trends of the time helped bolster the industry's cause. The opioid crisis ravaging Eastern Kentucky heightened the region's desire to see Big Coal succeed, because a downturn in mining could only serve to plunge a struggling society into deeper despair. Coal mines were hardly free from the prescription pill epidemic that was affecting society at large, prompting Kentucky to become the first state to require drug and alcohol tests for miners. The September 11, 2001, terrorist attacks shook Eastern Kentuckians' sense of comfort and security even further. In times of turmoil, people there yearned for something familiar to rally around. And as was historically the case, coal presented itself as the best option.

The Friends of Coal movement turned technical debates over how coal trucks polluted and endangered public roads into a full-fledged cultural war with far-reaching political ramifications. "It started with sponsoring football games and car shows, very apolitical stuff," says Dee Davis, the president of the Eastern Kentucky–based Center for Rural Strategies. "Over time it brought people together behind coal, Democrats and Republicans, and created a cultural zeitgeist."[34]

Critics derided the movement as a faux-grassroots attempt to win or buy allegiance by making a pro-coal message as ubiquitous as possible. If a coal company already sponsored a Little League baseball team, for example, the team agreed to wear a "Friends of Coal" patch on their jerseys.

Bissett recoils at the suggestion that the movement lacked spontaneity. "It wasn't an Astroturf campaign," he says. "That support was always there. It was just never under a single banner." Bissett argues that the campaign also fostered a sense of pride within the industry, especially among miners who "felt like everyone hated them" for just doing their job.[35]

"Friends of Coal made rank-and-file miners think like CEOs," Bissett says.[36]

*

As the region's dominant cultural and economic force, it's no wonder coal mining has always had a tremendous impact on the electoral politics of Appalachian Kentucky. Influential mine union leader John L. Lewis, who died in 1969, is the main reason why most people in the region remain registered Democrats despite having views and voting habits that are much more closely aligned with today's Republican Party. Lewis, a domineering figure who served as president of the United Mine Workers of America from 1920 to 1960, organized periodic strikes, fought for the collective bargaining rights of miners, and advocated for federal mine safety legislation. Known for his fiery rhetoric and tough-guy personality, Lewis was a supporter of Republican President Herbert Hoover but shifted his allegiances in 1932 when the Democrats won control of Congress and the White House. Lewis and the Democrats forged a productive partnership throughout the 1930s. Franklin Roosevelt's pro-union New Deal policies helped the UMWA secure high wages and benefits for its members. It hardly mattered when Lewis broke from FDR in 1940. Over the course of eight of the toughest years in the nation's history, the Democratic Party had established itself as the party of the laborer and the trade union, creating a symbiotic relationship between the UMWA and the Democrats that led to widespread support for the party throughout the mining regions of Appalachia. Democrats supported the union's ideals and engendered a feeling of solidarity among miners. Republicans did not. And party affiliation and loyalty got passed down through the years, almost like an inheritance.

And so it remained for many decades. It used to be a common

sight in Eastern Kentucky homes to see framed photos of Jesus, John F. Kennedy, and John L. Lewis hanging alongside family portraits. But the slow and steady decline in UMWA membership caused allegiances to shift, and the Democratic Party started losing support of the constituency that Lewis helped bring into the fold. The sometimes-hostile relationship between miner and coal company abated as the two sides came together to embrace the GOP-supported goal of keeping the coal industry strong.

"Companies preached to miners that unions were evil and only wanted to take their money for dues," mine-safety expert Tony Oppegard says. "They told the miners that unions like to go on strike, and if that happened, the company might have to pull out of the area and take its jobs with it. That kind of talk turned a lot of employees into company men."[37]

Big Coal not only kept the lights on. It also paid to put Christmas presents under trees and food on tables. Factor in the social conservatism of Eastern Kentucky and you ended up with a lot of registered Democrats who increasingly started voting Republican in state and federal races. Floyd County, for example, had more than 25,000 registered Democrats and fewer than 5,000 registered Republicans at the beginning of 2017, yet county residents supported Donald Trump by a three-to-one margin against Hillary Clinton.[38] The county's support for Mitt Romney in 2012 was only slightly less robust. Republican organizers in some counties have tried to bring attention to the disconnect between what the Democratic Party used to represent to people of the region and what it represents now. As visitors to Harlan County's annual Poke Sallet Festival listen to bluegrass music and gorge on fried foods, they can also stop by a booth run by county Republicans trying to woo away Democrats. Those efforts have been successful. Around 2,000 of Harlan County's 20,000 registered voters have switched their registration from Democrat to Republican since 2017.[39]

Neighboring Perry and Leslie counties also illustrate the strong generational influence of party politics in the region. In Perry County, registered Democrats outnumber registered Republicans by more than two-to-one. Drive a few miles down the Hal Rogers Parkway, however, and you'll come to one of the most Republican counties in the entire nation, where nine out of every ten registered voters are Republican.[40] Why is that? Primarily because in Leslie and other Eastern Kentucky counties that have little or no history with the UMWA, Republicans have always far outnumbered Democrats.

It was none other than Richard Nixon who helped Leslie County cement its Republican bona fides. After resigning the presidency in disgrace in 1974, Nixon holed up at his beachside estate in Southern California for four years, refusing all invitations to appear at events. Then, in 1978, Leslie County Judge/Executive Allen Muncy called to see if Nixon might be interested in coming to the county seat of Hyden for the dedication of a recreation center named in his honor. Much to Muncy and everyone else's surprise, Nixon said yes, making Leslie County the location of Nixon's first public appearance since leaving office. Many prominent state Republicans stayed away from the event, but the positive reception that Nixon received from the people of this tiny dot on the map prompted him to end his period of self-seclusion. As *The New York Times* wrote on the occasion of the visit, "In southeastern Kentucky, the Appalachian Mountains close over Leslie County like a fist. Isolated and independent, the county has repudiated the railroads, the United Mine Workers and almost all Democrats since the Civil War."[41]

When, with the passage of time, the UMWA sunk into irrelevance in Eastern Kentucky, the region had to recalibrate its political leanings. Friends of Coal was there to help by courting both lawmakers and the voting public. For coal to overcome the double blow of increased competition from cleaner forms of energy and the threat of stricter regulation, it was going to have to wield as much political influence as possible. One of the campaign's leaders, Massey Energy CEO Don Blankenship, learned firsthand the benefits of having allies in government when the aggressive investigation into the malfeasance that led to the 2000 sludge disaster at Massey's Martin county impoundment was put on ice as a Republican administration took office mid-investigation. Furthermore, in the new George W. Bush administration, former Massey executives ended up in positions of leadership at federal mine safety agencies.

*

Since I was writing a lot about what went on inside of coal mines, I felt compelled to see one for myself. But you can't just show up at a mine and say, "Take me underground, please." You need to be invited. There were hardly any union mines to visit because there were hardly any union mines left in Eastern Kentucky at the time. And no coal operator in his right mind was going to let a reporter, especially one from the dreaded *Courier-Journal*, inside a working mine. That meant I had to settle for the Kentucky Coal Association mine tour, by no means a worthless experience, but not exactly a true-to-life one either. Bill Caylor of the Coal Association, a couple of industry people, and a reporter from the local television station also joined the field trip that day. The outing started with an elevator ride down to the mine entrance and then a trip on a personnel carrier called a "mantrip" through a mined-out seam of coal. The mantrip came to a stop a couple of miles down the line, where we exited into a walkable tunnel. The mine was well lit and ventilated. Its roof was high. The weight of the mountain above caused a crackle-and-pop sound that would have been a lot more ominous if I had been crawling through a seam instead of walking aside a cadre of coal industry representatives. The tour gave me a point of reference when it came to the mining experience. But when talking to miners who described working in dark, cramped, and dirty conditions, I still had to rely on my imagination.

The one time I actually saw the inner workings of an active mine, the circumstances were much different. It came after twenty-five-year-old Harlan County miner Edwin Pennington was killed when a mine roof collapsed and crushed him. The tragedy had a macabre twist: Pennington was filming his crew at work right up until the moment he was buried under tons of rock and dirt. He had had a close call at work the day before and smuggled a video camera inside the mine so that he could show his girlfriend the dangers of his job. His girlfriend had joked with him the day before that he better not scratch the video camera, which had been a Christmas present. The footage survived, and Pennington's family shared a copy of the videotape with me. The miners were performing what is called "retreat mining," which involves chipping away at massive pillars of coal to induce a roof fall as miners retreat toward the entrance of a played-out mine. Pennington wasn't positioned far enough away when the roof caved in. The last moments of his life are haunting. The miners engage in gallows humor about life insurance policies and the condition of the mine roof. His camera remains trained on the roof until the recording abruptly ends.[42]

Caylor called the incident "a fluke,"[43] but investigators determined that a foreman at the Bell County Coal Corporation mine knew about large cracks in the roof but didn't give miners proper warning.

Pro-coal forces were correct that overall working conditions in mines had vastly improved since the lawless first decades of the twentieth century when thousands of people were killed on the job annually. By the mid-1980s, the number of coal mining deaths nationally dropped below a hundred a year, and by 2000, that figure was fewer than fifty.[44] But those statistics don't account for the miners who died slow deaths after contracting coal workers' pneumoconiosis, or black lung, a disease caused by prolonged exposure to silica and asbestos dust.

I covered mining at a time when the federal government was making it increasingly difficult for afflicted former miners to receive black-lung benefits. The federal Black Lung Benefits Act was established in 1969 to help miners who suffered from the condition. In the first years of the program, around three-quarters of miners filed successful claims. But the coal industry lobbied successfully to tighten compensation rules and to delay the disbursement of benefits. On the state level, where benefits also had been slashed, Patton, the former coal operator, was gearing up for the next phase of his unlikely crusade for miners and mine safety.

During his first term as governor, Patton railed against the state black-lung program, declaring it "totally out of control"[45] for awarding benefits to miners he didn't believe were actually disabled. He cited his own black-lung diagnosis, which came as the result of an X-ray, to back up his assertion that reform was needed. He supported a 1996 law that required miners to show proof of disability through a lung-function test in order to collect benefits. The system for deciding who got compensation was complicated by the high rate of smoking among miners. Kentucky, a leading producer of burley tobacco, was known for cheap cigarettes and the highest overall smoking rate in the nation.

Over the next six years, the state program accepted less than 5 percent of new cases, compared to an approval rate of around 80 percent under the old law, prompting Patton to take the bold step of admitting that he had made an enormous mistake by virtually eliminating compensation for black lung. "I don't know how to say it any more plain—I was wrong. I have wronged the coal miners in Kentucky," Patton said at a news conference in 2002. "I want the opportunity to correct that wrong."[46]

Miners like Leonard Shepherd exemplified the flawed nature of the state and federal systems for awarding black lung benefits. Shepherd, who I interviewed in 2001, had worked about twenty years above ground as a coal crusher when MSHA began offering free chest X-rays to screen for black lung. His X-ray came back abnormal and a follow-up pulmonary test showing swelling of the lungs confirmed that he had black lung. His doctor ordered him to quit his $30,000-a-year job. When I met him, Shepherd was forty-three years old, sleeping with an oxygen mask and struggling to walk short distances without gasping for breath. Despite his diagnosis and condition, his federal black lung application was rejected, leaving him, his wife, and their teenage son to survive on monthly $262 welfare checks.⁴⁷ The change in state law that Patton was pushing for stood to help miners like Shepherd, who died in 2013.

The time I spent talking to Eastern Kentucky miners with the disease further opened my eyes to the hold that coal mining had on the local culture. The men I interviewed were mostly in their forties. Some wore breathing devices. All were slowly suffocating. None expressed any regrets about the line of work that had landed them on death's door. On the contrary, every single one of them longed to still be doing the job that had come to define them. It reminded me of the former NFL football players who suffer from degenerative brain disease but who speak warmly and nostalgically about suiting up on Sundays.

In 2001, I met Russell Kidd, a forty-one-year-old black-lung victim in Floyd County who for twenty years crawled into a thirty-inch seam to dig coal. Kidd, a husband and father of two high-school-aged children, echoed the opinion of the Martin County miner from the 1980s. "It's the dirtiest job you'll do in your life," Kidd said. "But I'd work tomorrow if I could."⁴⁸ After his initial black-lung diagnosis in the early 1990s, Kidd received $20,000 for retraining but chose to continue going underground, something the law allowed at the time. His health gradually deteriorated. The final time I spoke to Kidd, he talked about friends of his who died from black lung. "We need to change the law to help the coal miner who worked his whole life," he told me. He died a few years after our last interview.

In my personal life, I saw the ravages of black lung up close and over an extended period of time. I was dating my future wife, a Harlan native, whose father had worked as an underground miner for close to twenty years. When I met him, he was hooked up to an oxygen tank, teaching one of his granddaughters the alphabet and watching Disney movies, sports, and *Who Wants to Be a Millionaire* on television. He, too, desperately wished he could return to the mines. I watched him take his last breaths in a Lexington hospital. It was gut-wrenching. For days afterward, friends and neighbors sent buckets of fried chicken and covered casserole dishes over to the house in Harlan, where we sat and mourned his passing. The personalized metal tag that he used to check in and out of the mine before and after every shift hangs on a hook in the kitchen of our home in his memory.

*

Patton made good on his promise to work with the state legislature to reform black lung compensation law. Despite his early missteps, he left office with a positive legacy on mine safety, having added teeth to state enforcement efforts and undone the problematic black lung legislation that he had earlier supported. The new law allowed any miner with X-ray evidence of black lung to qualify for retraining benefits. It made older miners with the disease eligible for cash payments.

Coal operators felt betrayed by Patton. "The coal industry helped elect him the first time, but in his second term he turned his back on us a little bit," Matney says.[49]

We'll never know if Patton would have brought his newly discovered commitment to mine safety to the US Senate. Considered the likely Democratic challenger to incumbent Senator Jim Bunning in 2004, Patton opted against running for the seat after his second term as governor was marred by a sex scandal. Patton's successor as governor, Ernie Fletcher, the first Republican to be elected Kentucky governor in thirty-two years, quickly dismantled some of Patton's achievements. He killed the jobs- and economy-focused Kentucky Appalachian Commission. And as part of a broader executive branch shake-up to eliminate "redundancies" in government, Fletcher did away with the Kentucky Department of Mines and Minerals and the state Department for Surface Mining Reclamation and Enforcement, leaving the door open for the federal government to once again play a chief role in mine-safety and environmental regulation. This was problematic, because under George W. Bush, MSHA cut the number of safety officers and issued fewer and smaller fines to safety violators. The Bush administration also took a hands-off approach to coal's environmental impacts by touting so-called "clean coal technology" while also promoting a fossil fuel–friendly energy plan that placed no cap on the emission of carbon dioxide by coal-burning power utilities.

Somewhat surprisingly, Fletcher waited over a year to fire Oppegard from his mine-safety post. Fletcher provided no reason for his decision, but the Kentucky Coal Association later admitted lobbying the governor to dismiss Oppegard. Fletcher was indicted near the end of his lone term for taking state employees' political loyalties into account when hiring, firing, or reassigning them.

Fletcher was a proponent of smaller government, and on mining he probably would have gotten away with ceding back regulatory authority to MSHA and the federal Office of Surface Mining. But a couple of weeks before I left the *Courier-Journal* in 2006, an underground miner in Eastern Kentucky was crushed to death when a slab of rock twenty feet long, ten feet wide, and four-and-a-half feet thick crashed down on him. The incident happened less than two weeks after twelve miners were killed in an explosion at Sago Mine in West Virginia. The Sago disaster sparked renewed interest in mine safety and brought pressure on Fletcher to acknowledge that an extra layer of mining regulation didn't qualify as redundant. A new package of legislation gave state regulators the authority to fine companies that violate safety laws and increased the $30,000 starting salary of mine inspectors.[50]

In covering the day-to-day machinations of coal mining for more than five years, I observed the constant push and pull between the coal industry and the advocates and government agencies that monitored its activities. Only after leaving Eastern Kentucky and taking a step back did I realize the region's central paradox: coal was fading away as an energy source of the future but managing to remain as culturally and politically relevant as ever.

Fading or flawed empires rely on propaganda to keep themselves propped up. And as much as Big Coal would have loved to see John McCain defeat Barack Obama in the 2008 presidential election, Obama's victory had a silver lining. It gave the industry the perfect villain to blame for what it called "The War on Coal," as the Obama administration put in place new measures designed to reduce the health and environmental impacts of mountaintop removal and conventional strip mining.

"When companies had to lay off miners, they'd say, 'That damn Obama and those regulations,' even if the layoffs had nothing to do with Obama and regulations," said Paul Browning III, a Harlan County magistrate whose jurisdiction includes the old coal camp towns of Benham, which is home to a solar powered coal museum, and Lynch. "That's what miners and their families were told again and again. It had a big impact."[51]

That helps explain the region's overwhelming support for Donald Trump in 2016. Trump promised a resurgence in the coal industry. Hillary Clinton, meanwhile, handed Trump and Friends of Coal a gift by commenting on the campaign trail that her renewable energy plan was "going to put a lot of coal miners and coal companies out of business."[52] It didn't matter that Clinton went on to praise the work ethic of miners and to talk about helping them transition to other lines of work. The sound bite hurt Clinton not just in coal communities but among a large swath of working-class voters across the country. The politics of it aside, her comment showed a lack of respect and understanding for a fundamental part of regional culture and identity.

Anti-Obama and Clinton sentiment also explains how billionaire coal operator Jim Justice, the wealthiest person in West Virginia, won that state's governorship in 2016 despite his companies' long history of mine-safety violations and unpaid fines. Like Trump, Justice owned a luxurious resort, the Greenbrier, which one journalist wrote "looks like it was airlifted out of a Wes Anderson movie and dropped into the Allegheny Mountains."[53] To the concern of many in the coal industry, Justice ran as a Democrat, beating the suitably named Republican candidate Bill Cole. A few months after taking office, Justice switched parties and pledged his unwavering support to Trump.

Big Coal came out in force behind Trump in 2016. Trump's most generous coal supporter was Hazard-born coal operator Joe Craft, who, along with his wife, Kelly, kicked in $2 million to Trump's campaign and inaugural committee.[54] Trump then appointed Kelly Craft as US ambassador to Canada. After twenty months in that post, a period during which her travel records showed that she spent a considerable amount of time in Kentucky, she was promoted to replace Nikki Haley as ambassador to the United Nations.[55] Following his election, Trump rolled back some coal regulations, including one that strongly encouraged mining companies to reforest strip-mined lands as part of the reclamation process. Trump also appointed the former CEO of a coal company with a record of repeated safety violations to head the federal Mine Safety and Health Administration. In 2017, the Republican-controlled Congress, with Mitch McConnell as its Senate leader, repealed a rule that banned coal companies from using waterways as a dumping ground for potentially toxic debris.[56] Trump's pro-mining views went beyond coal. His goal of reviving the nation's nuclear energy sector included a plan to extract uranium from the Grand Canyon.[57]

But despite Trump's best efforts to end "the war on American energy" and attacks on "beautiful, clean coal," the coal industry hasn't experienced anything close to a resurgence. In 2019, before the coronavirus pandemic further hurt the coal industry, US demand for coal fell to a forty-two-year low,[58] once again forcing coal mining regions of Appalachia to contemplate their economic future and the toll that mining took on their land and people.

Eastern Kentucky's mountains are scarred, its waterways tainted, because of rampant strip mining. The bodies of its former miners are also scarred. But over the past twenty-five years, fewer than 6 percent of federal black lung claims have been approved, a shockingly low figure considering that one in every five people in Central Appalachia who had worked at least twenty-five years as a miner had some form of black lung, according to a 2018 report by the National Institute for Occupational Safety and Health.[59] And the cheating on dust tests has continued. In 2019, eight employees of a bankrupt Western Kentucky coal company were indicted on conspiracy charges for falsifying monitoring samples at two mines.[60]

Coal mining employment in the United States declined 42 percent between 2011 and 2018 due to decreased demand.[61] Appalachian coal-mining employment, which accounted for more than 60,000 jobs in 2011, fell to around 30,000 in 2018.[62] In 2019, six coal companies, including mining giant Murray Energy Corporation, filed for bankruptcy, prompting Congress to authorize $10 billion in taxpayer money to save the industry's quickly evaporating pension fund.[63] It was the first time the federal government intervened to bail out a fund for private sector workers. McConnell, who had long blocked such a bill from coming to a vote, said he was motivated to take action after Murray Energy declared bankruptcy.[64]

Though Kentucky only trails West Virginia in its number of coal mining jobs, the Bluegrass State has two-thirds fewer coal jobs than it did ten years ago. Coal production in Kentucky has also precipitously dropped. In 2019, there was more coal mined in Illinois than in Kentucky—a sentence that deserves to be written in all-caps. [65] More coal is now produced in Western Kentucky than in Eastern Kentucky, where coal production is split about evenly between surface and underground mines.

Coal production is falling nationally, but not as dramatically as one might expect, due in large part to an abundance of coal mining in the Powder River Basin of Wyoming, which accounted for more than one-third of coal production in the country in 2019.[66] A significant amount of Western-mined coal ends up in China, a nation that relies heavily on coal as an energy source. Nearly 150 coal-fired power units were idled during Trump's first term, a series of shutdowns that diminished the nation's coal-generated capacity by 15 percent.[67]

Even pro-coal politicians like Trump's former energy secretary Rick Perry have written the industry's obituary, putting the blame on Obama for killing the industry.[68]

Bissett, who left the Kentucky Coal Association in 2016 for a top post at the chamber of commerce in Huntington, West Virginia, says Trump isn't to blame for not delivering on his promises to coal. "There are leaders in the industry who think he didn't do enough,"

Bissett says, "but he put people in power who knew the industry or were part of the industry. He did everything he could, but he couldn't call up all the major utilities and say, 'You're going to start using more coal.'"[69] From what we know about his mob-inflected business tactics, that sounds exactly like something Trump would do. Maybe he did make the call and the utilities simply told him no.

Bissett isn't a fan of the phrase "War on Coal." He prefers the more tongue-in-cheek rallying cry, "Legalize Coal." And despite ample signs that the industry is in steep decline, he thinks coal isn't dead quite yet, at least not everywhere. "People in the energy industry say if you don't like the current state of the industry, just give it ten years, and it will change," he says. "Maybe someone will figure out how to burn coal without affecting the climate."[70]

Paul Matney retired from the coal business in 2014 after TECO Energy sold off its coal division for next to nothing. He is nostalgic about the forty-two years he spent in the industry. "I guess I'm living the American dream," he muses. "The coal industry was wonderful to me." But he is also realistic about coal's future. "If you do away with the market for a product, then you basically do away with the product," he says. "And you can't just turn on the switch of a coal-fired power plant once its been mothballed. It costs hundreds of millions of dollars to put them back online . . . It's part of the 'cancel culture' movement. Environmentalists tried to cancel the culture of coal mining, and they were successful."[71] I took note of Matney's use of the phrase "cancel culture," a Trump-era nod to the perceived evils of political (and ecological) correctness. In polarized times, Trump's supporters believed the "radical Democrats" and "fake news media" joined forces to cancel the man himself. The culture wars continue to run as deep as an old underground coal mine.

*

A recent incident in southeastern Kentucky perfectly encapsulates mining's past, present, and future. On July 1, 2019, the Blackjewel coal company, at one time the country's sixth largest coal producer, declared bankruptcy and shut down all of its operations, including a non-union mine in Harlan County. The move came without warning and put around six hundred local coal miners out of work with no severance pay or continued health benefits. Even worse, the final paychecks that Blackjewel had issued a few days earlier bounced, leaving some miners and their families stranded on summer vacation in Myrtle Beach and other popular summer spots without funds to get home.

Later that July, when Blackjewel attempted to remove a trainload of coal worth around $1 million from the mine's property, a handful of miners showed up and stood on the tracks to block the departure. The protest soon grew to dozens of miners, who were joined by labor and civic leaders. Then-presidential candidate Bernie Sanders sent pizzas to the protesters. The candidates in a heated Kentucky gubernatorial race used the situation to stump for votes. The national media flocked to Harlan County to witness the first large-scale labor protest there in several decades. Every story about the blockade alluded to the area's coal strikes of decades past, sometimes violent events that earned the place the nickname "Bloody Harlan." This blockade of the train tracks remained peaceful and arrest-free with miners holding signs reading NO PAY WE STAY. No lawyers in Harlan County wanted to get involved in the labor dispute, so county judge/executive Dan Mosley called in Ned Pillersdorf, who was based a couple of hours away in Prestonsburg, to represent the miners.

Blackjewel miners Chris Lewis and his son, Dalton, helped organize the protest. The shared experience helped further tighten their family bonds. "You know there's a lot of pride that comes with coal mining, and I'm proud of Dalton," his father said that summer. [72]

Jerod Blevins, a twenty-nine-year-old Blackjewel miner joined the protest on the first night. Every day for several weeks, Blevins stayed on the train tracks until around one o'clock in the morning, returning home for a few hours of sleep before trekking across a treacherous mountain road to rejoin the Lewises and the other aggrieved miners. "It's just an awful, awful thing to happen," Blevins said at the time. "Myself and the others, we all have kids. And that's one of the best ways around this area to provide for your family, is the coal mines."[73]

The number of protesters dwindled as the miners started finding jobs elsewhere, mostly out of state. The Lewises left to take mining jobs in Alabama. Blevins found other mining work in Virginia. In September, the protest ended, but the notoriety it generated helped force Blackjewel's hand. In October, the Blackjewel miners finally received the money that was owed them.

I view the Blackjewel protest as a tipping point, and possibly even a coda to the century-plus history of Harlan County coal mining. And I am startled to hear how candidly some local officials assess the future of coal compared to fifteen or twenty years ago.

"Coal has taken more than it's ever given, whether it's miners' health, the landscape, clean water, roads," said magistrate Paul Browning III. "All it's really given is a wage. Every time we realize we need to do something differently, King Coal comes back with a mini-boom and we get complacent."[74]

Loyalty to coal still defines the area. SUPPORT COAL PRODUCTION. IT IS OUR ECONOMY, implores a gas station sign along Kentucky Highway 119 in Harlan County. But the reality is that most southeastern Kentucky counties can no longer depend on coal, creating an economic situation filled with both potential opportunity and peril. Because, without coal, how does the region celebrate its uniqueness? How does it ward off the generalized poverty that has already seeped in? How does it avoid getting left further behind?

CHAPTER 3

Life Beyond the Mines

President Bill Clinton spent the scorching July 4 weekend of the final year of his presidency vowing that the country would not leave Eastern Kentucky behind. Sipping on the region's reluctant trademark soft drink, Mountain Dew, to stay hydrated, Clinton toured the region that had strongly supported him during his two runs for president, and after taking in what he saw, he stepped up to a podium on a jam-packed main street in Hazard and explained how his New Markets Initiative was going to inspire the private sector to breathe life into struggling economies all the way from Appalachian Kentucky to Watts, California. Flanked by local officials like Perry County judge/executive Denny Ray Noble and dignitaries including the Reverend Jesse Jackson, South Carolina Congressman James Clyburn, and Housing and Urban Development Secretary Andrew Cuomo, Clinton reflected on the nation's history: "I'll bet you some of you here are actually the descendants of those people Governor Patton talked about, the Revolutionary War heroes who helped to settle this state. But, you know, whether our parents and their parents came here on the Mayflower or slave ships, whether they landed on Ellis Island in the 1890s or came to Los Angeles Airport in the 1990s, around the 4th of July we're supposed to celebrate what we have in common as Americans, to reaffirm that what unites us is more important than what divides us. Well, if we believe that, we have a shared stake in one another's success."

Then, Clinton zeroed in on why he was there: "If we, with the most prosperous economy in our lifetimes, cannot make a commitment to take every person along with us into the twenty-first century, we will have failed to meet a moral obligation and we will also have failed to make the most of America's promise."[1] In Eastern Kentucky, that meant making a post-coal future an economic reality.

To give his words more weight, Clinton came with the goods in hand, announcing that a company called Sykes Enterprises would soon be opening information technology call centers in Eastern Kentucky, at industrial parks located near the regional hubs of Hazard and Pikeville. Company president John Sykes stood beside Clinton to affirm his commitment to developing a stable workforce in the region. His call centers were going to employ hundreds.

And Sykes did create jobs . . . for a few years. Local Eastern Kentucky governments had put together multi-million-dollar tax incentive packages to lure the company to the area, but when those benefits ran out, Sykes realized it would be more cost effective to move many of its operations overseas.[2] Over the years, Sykes call centers have come and gone and come again, to and from towns in Central Appalachia and other rural parts of the country. In 2019, another round of massive layoffs took place at a Sykes location at the already largely empty four-hundred-acre Coalfields Industrial Park outside of Hazard. But later that year, Sykes partnered with Intuit Inc., the maker of TurboTax and other products, and started operations back up again, promising a newly renovated facility and hundreds of jobs by 2021. By and large, the history of call centers in the area has been marked by this type of instability. Like many of the industrial parks scattered around the region, the one in Hazard has struggled to come anywhere close to full occupancy. Rather than helping to diversify and move beyond a coal-based economy for southeastern Kentucky, Sykes stands out as an example of the failed promises that have plagued the region for decades. As Bill Gorman, the longtime mayor of Hazard who was standing behind President Clinton that July 4 weekend, said a couple of years after our snowy dinner together, Sykes had picked Eastern Kentucky's pocket.

Almost every topic I wrote about in Eastern Kentucky connected back to economic marginalization in some way. The opioid stories focused on an impoverished population that was vulnerable to drug abuse. The coal stories shed light on what happens to workers and the environment when an area's economy is dominated by one fickle industry. The resulting outbreak of political violence—which will be the subject of the next chapter—centered on control of an illicit black market that can only exist when the traditional economy has floundered for a very long time.

Once or twice a year, usually motivated by the release of new socioeconomic data or a damning report, I had to write what I came to refer to as "a straight poverty story," a statistics-heavy piece that directly addressed poverty and its elusive antidote—economic growth and development. I found these stories challenging, but not because they were difficult to execute. They followed a simple formula, ranking them among the easiest stories to write. The problem was evident. The numbers quantified the problem. And with a little legwork, it was easy enough to find people who put a face to the problem. What I found frustrating was trying to make these stories something more than just what people had been reading about Eastern Kentucky for decades. There was a lot to understand about generational poverty there, and even stories that clocked in at 2,500 words ended up feeling overly facile.

It is my aim here to assemble the pieces in a way that gives not only a three-dimensional view of the region's long-standing economic woes but also a possible road map of its economic future.

In my early days at the *Courier-Journal*, around the same time that I was covering Governor Paul Patton's state OxyContin task force, Patton, a former Eastern Kentucky coal operator, was outlining a strategy for promoting economic opportunities in the region. "We have to break down the stereotype that there is a lack of education and sophistication in Eastern Kentucky," Patton told me. "It's the Li'l Abner syndrome," he said, referring to the hillbilly family featured in a once-popular comic strip.[3] Patton spoke of visiting Chicago, Detroit, and New York City to drum up business interest in the area. Two years later, Patton and others were still talking about Li'l Abner, this time at a session of the East Kentucky Leadership Conference called "Li'l Abner Doesn't Live Here." It struck me as meaningful that the region's political and business leaders were so fixated on a comic strip that had ceased publication nearly twenty-five years earlier. When Patton described the region as having "pockets of poverty like in any metropolitan area,"[4] it didn't give me pause as much as it would later when I started contemplating the similarities and differences between rural and urban poverty. Some commentators, mostly conservative ones, have no qualms about using the loaded term "white ghetto" to describe struggling parts of Appalachia. When a later job would take me to some of the most depressed urban areas of the country, I saw the flaws in this comparison. While I think there is ample overlap in the challenges facing generationally poor urban and rural communities, and both have been stigmatized by a certain otherness, the historical background and potential solutions to those challenges diverge significantly. The most notable difference is that the white rural poor do not face the added hurdle of overcoming institutional racism.

The concept of Central Appalachia's otherness in the eyes of the rest of the country swings both ways. I don't think some of the people I met there knew what to make of me, with my wavy hair, thickish eyebrows, and olive complexion. But it wasn't my appearance that elicited comments. It was how I spoke. One of my most indelible memories of Eastern Kentucky is how often people matter-of-factly told me, "You talk proper." Though they never uttered the words in a derogatory manner, I was taken aback the first few times I heard them. Proper? How so? I started to feel self-conscious. Even when I lived in Germany and handled most of my daily business in German, I hadn't really thought much about how I talked. Nor, after I reached a certain level of fluency in the language, did many people comment on the way I spoke. But now that I was back in my home country, I found myself getting called out every other time I opened my mouth.

The "you talk proper" comment would come at odd points during a conversation, sometimes when I was in the middle of a sentence. It was as if the person I was talking to could no longer suppress the urge to comment on whatever properness they detected in my speech. I wasn't using fancy words or anything like that. I was just talking. After a while, I came to understand that they were simply observing, "Yer not from aroun' here, are ya?" I guess there's a reason that line has made it into so many movies. But I could live with it, because after all, it was true that I wasn't from around there.

My colleague Roger Alford, a born and bred Eastern Kentuckian who covered the region for the Associated Press, was always good about passing along cultural tips that might make life easier for me. He once told me that if a state trooper ever stopped me for speeding, a regular occurrence because of the miles I logged, that I should apologize to the officer and explain that I had been blasting a Jerry Reed song on the tape deck and got so caught up in the spirit that my foot came down a bit too heavy on the gas pedal. Reed, the singer of the country divorce anthem "She Got the Goldmine (I Got the Shaft)," had cult status among Kentucky troopers for his many hits and his starring role in the Burt Reynolds highway caper *Smokey and the Bandit*. Roger phrased it beautifully, including just the right amount of emotion to where I could see him getting off with just a warning about slowing down. I wasn't so sure it would work for me, however. I could picture being halfway into my explanation when the trooper would interrupt me to say I talked proper.

Roger had an interesting take on why people couldn't hold their tongues when it came to my apparently discernible Northern accent and pronunciation. He told me about the subset of Eastern Kentuckians who, during the coal industry's down times, had ventured north to Ohio, Indiana, or Michigan for work, only to return home talking in a completely different way. No more "might could." No more "afeared." It was a kind of formal and upwardly mobile code-switching, and according to Roger, it irritated the hell out of friends and family who felt the person was trying to disown home. I didn't blame them for feeling that way. I remember how I felt when friends from college who studied a semester abroad in London returned home sounding like heirs to the British throne one moment and Cockney taxi drivers the next. Dialect acquisition isn't so fluid.

Not all Eastern Kentuckians speak alike. Some have migrated from other places. Others just don't develop what is considered a typical regional speech pattern. Some have impressive vocabularies. Others don't. I once gave a talk to the Hazard Rotary Club and was asked by a woman during the question-and-answer session for my thoughts on the "hegemonic relationships" of the region. Obviously there are brainy people in Eastern Kentucky, as there are everywhere. But the regional dialect there is definitely entrenched, a result of relatively little in-migration over the generations. It is considered "one of the most ancient forms of living English spoken in the world."[5] The dialect manifests itself in vocabulary, grammar, and pronunciation. Sometimes it is difficult, for example, to determine whether someone in town is looking for a pin or a pen. If someone there is sleepy, they are "tarred." In her 2010 PhD thesis in linguistics at Stanford University, Rebecca Dayle Greene, a native of the area, wrote, "I was motivated to study language in rural Eastern Kentucky in part because I grew up in that region and language is by far the most salient aspect of my regional identity. When I left my small hometown to go to college at the University of Kentucky, only an hour and a half away from my home, people commented on or made fun of my rural Eastern Kentucky accent multiple times each day. My social identity shifted very rapidly from 'the good student' to 'the girl with a hillbilly accent.'"[6]

I thought a lot about dialect during my first months in Hazard. After all, this was the moment at which Sykes Enterprises was hiring minimum-wage workers for its new technical-assistance call centers in Eastern Kentucky. Sykes encouraged employees to use standard elocution and grammar, but call center managers still got complaints from far-flung customers about the difficulty in understanding the heavy mountain accents on the other end of the phone. From what I could glean, the turnover rate at these call centers was enormous.

To most of its speakers, the Eastern Kentucky accent is far more a source of pride than a source of shame. But that hasn't prevented some people from working to shed it, the idea being that self-consciousness will diminish and job prospects will improve if they learn to speak more conventionally. I was intrigued by the subject of how Eastern Kentuckians partly view themselves through the lens of language and ended up writing a story about it. A middle school speech and debate teacher in Hazard told me that she coached her students to speak in a nonregional accent because she was afraid (not "afeared") that competition judges would penalize them for their accents. I met a twenty-six-year-old pharmaceutical salesman who recalled the teasing he received on a trip to Ohio because of his "hillbilly" accent. Through the use of audiotapes, he built his vocabulary, practiced his elocution, and learned to speak without his native drawl, achievements, he said, that helped bring him "to parity" with his physician audience, or at least made him talk like a TV news anchor from Anywhere, USA.[7] The pharmaceutical salesman altered the way he spoke on his own, while others in the region sought outside help, hiring "accent modification" professionals to help with the task. I spoke to a linguistics professor who did a study showing that employers were less inclined to hire candidates with heavy accents to perform duties involving a lot of contact with the public. A strong New Jersey accent was deemed least desirable in the study.

In reporting that story, I interviewed Tyler Medaris, one of the middle school students on the speech and debate team. He told me that he could turn his accent on and off like a light switch—on when he was in Eastern Kentucky and off when he traveled. He had recently won a statewide speech competition in the broadcasting category. A few years later, he became only the second southeastern Kentucky high school senior in nearly fifty years to take home top honors in broadcasting from the Kentucky High School Speech League (motto: "Mind over chatter").

I was curious to know what Medaris was up to in adulthood. Had this linguistic chameleon flown above the nets of language and culture? And if so, how did he view the place in which he was born and raised? Maybe, I thought, he had stuck around Hazard and put his broadcasting skills to use as the anchor of the WYMT evening news. Or, more likely, he had sought a life for himself somewhere in the vast Central Appalachian diaspora. It turned out that after some colorful detours he had landed back in the Bluegrass State, where he was operating a landscape design business in Lexington. Though it took place twenty years ago, he remembered the first conversation we had in his school library.

The son of a prominent Hazard attorney, Medaris told me that his childhood "was pretty damn privileged" and included summers at a SeaWorld camp in San Antonio, where he developed a passion for marine science.[8] He was standing with the throng on Main Street when Clinton came to Hazard. He has two vivid memories of that day: his best friend's sister passing out because of the heat, and the president of the United States waving to him. He was co-president of his senior class, and in addition to speech and debate, performed in musical theater productions.

After graduating from Hazard High School in 2005, he left Eastern Kentucky to attend the University of Miami. His randomly assigned freshman roommate was from Staten Island. To help break the ice at first-year orientation, he and his dormmates played the game "Two Truths and a Lie." Medaris shared a story about his house getting raided by drug enforcement officers in Hazard. It was a lie. The truth was that police making an OxyContin bust had mistakenly busted down the door of his eighty-seven-year-old grandmother's home. Mayor Gorman and his wife sent flowers and a new door.

In Coral Gables, Medaris hosted annual Kentucky Derby parties that featured a strict dress code and lots of bourbon. His undergraduate studies took him to Austria, China, and South Africa. And most significantly from a personal standpoint, college is where he came out as gay.

He left Miami with a bachelor of arts degree in marine affairs and thoughts of following his father's lead by pursuing a career in law. He got within one semester of finishing law school at the University of Kentucky before dropping out. "I realized I didn't want to do this after all," he says.

When we spoke in the spring of 2020, Medaris had recently attended a funeral in Hazard. It was the first time he had been to his hometown in two years. "My parents have a condo in Lexington that's two blocks from me, and most of my friends aren't in Hazard anymore," he explained. He doesn't expect he'll ever live in Eastern Kentucky again. I asked Medaris what he thinks of the region now that he has the benefit of time and space. I expected that he might try to distance himself from the region.

During one of our conversations, Medaris turned on the mountain dialect to make a point about something. It didn't come out sounding quite right. I figured he had simply lost that part of his identity—and everything that goes with it. But once we came around to talking about the future of Eastern Kentucky, rather than dismissing the subject as not his problem anymore, he spoke proudly of his heritage and expressed deep concern for the region. He made it clear that he is no friend of coal.

"When people signed away their mineral rights, they lost everything they had and that created a second-class citizenry," he says. "The coal industry has been bald-faced lying to people forever. Every outsider who has come in has screwed the place over right, left, and center."

Medaris, who was helping to organize Black Lives Matter demonstrations in Lexington when we reconnected, argues that Eastern Kentucky needs to take advantage economically of natural resources that "you don't need to dig to get," referring to the natural beauty of mountains and waterways.[9]

Since the early 2000s, this idea has gained begrudging acceptance. Back then, for the first time, health-care sector employment surpassed that of the mining industry, a trend that has only grown in the past two decades. The medical center in Pikeville is now among the largest job creators in the entire state. But only the groundbreaking of proposed coal-fired power plants proved able to bring the political elite out in force. Congressman Hal Rogers, a powerful member of the House Appropriations Committee, saw an opportunity after the 9/11 terrorist attacks to bring homeland security jobs to the part of Eastern Kentucky that I came to think of more as south central Kentucky based on its terrain and relatively prosperous communities.

In 2004, Rogers secured funding for the National Institute for Hometown Security, a facility housed at the Center for Rural Development in his adopted hometown of Somerset. Rogers's efforts to create a high-tech footprint in Eastern Kentucky prompted the coining of two tongue-in-cheek nicknames: the "Taj Ma-Hal" for the rural development building and "Silicon Holler" for Rogers's home district, an ode to the many rugged Appalachian valleys that dot the region and a reference to the tech jobs he hoped to bring to the hollows of Eastern Kentucky. Rogers himself also gained a nickname: The Prince of Pork.[10]

Job creation in Eastern Kentucky was a challenging storyline. Rogers and Patton wanted the public and the media to believe that great things were happening in the region. I wasn't willing to buy into it without getting a broader perspective. Others took the bait, and in my opinion, committed a journalistic error. Just as it has always been important to resist going too far to the extreme when discussing the area's poverty, it was equally problematic in the early 2000s to overplay signs of progress.

On April Fool's Day 2001, *The New York Times* published a news article about the annual Hillbilly Days festival in Pikeville. Maybe it was recompense for decades of portraying Eastern Kentucky in a negative light, because the little piece of fluff that ran on page A14 of the nation's paper of record that day looked like something ghostwritten by the Southeast Kentucky Chamber of Commerce. The article was ostensibly about an area's self-deprecating embrace of the stubborn hillbilly stereotype. It recounted how some of the nearly 100,000 people who attended the hillbilly festival that year came dressed for the occasion, wearing overalls, carrying moonshine jugs, and displaying other trappings of hillbilly life. But then, author Francis X. Clines oddly slips into "Mission Accomplished" hyperbole about the health of the economy of the area. "Four-lane highways broke through years ago from the larger world, and the telecommunications and health care industries are booming the way mining once did," Clines writes.[11] He allows Governor Paul Patton to serve up a quote that Patton never would have dared give to a newspaper more attuned to daily life in Eastern Kentucky. "The old days of Lyndon Johnson's foray into eastern Kentucky to highlight domestic poverty are gone," Patton said. "What we offer now is intellectual service to people around the world."[12]

In the governor's native Pikeville, a town home to several coal barons and more than a few members of the region's oligarchy, talk of progress was more than just bait for reporters. Still, the article provided no numbers to back up the boast about the telecommunications and health-care industries, not to mention how on Patton's watch the private prison industry had aggressively moved into Kentucky. There was no mention of the prescription pill epidemic ripping through the region. In fact, the *Times* didn't get around to running an in-depth story about OxyContin in Kentucky until eight months later, when it reported that the head of the DEA blamed aggressive promotion of the painkiller by its maker for contributing to widespread abuse of the drug. I like fun stories, but not when they provide a superficial take on what is happening somewhere. Those stories are as much of a disservice to an area as the ones that only focus on the negative.

Pikeville today continues to make strides. A recently opened microbrewery in thriving downtown Pikeville, serving a wide array of IPAs, is a sign of the times in which moonshining and bootlegging have largely been relegated to the dustbin of history, although a good mason jar of moonshine is still pretty easy to come by. A few blocks from the brewery is one of the top-rated high schools in the state, as well as a private university and school of osteopathic medicine that aspires to go public. For years, there has been debate over whether to use coal severance tax money to turn into southeastern Kentucky's only state university. Among the backers of the idea is Patton, who has served the university as president and chancellor. Relatively speaking, Pikeville is doing well. But most of Eastern Kentucky is not.

*

When I tell people that I lived in Appalachian Kentucky one of the most common first responses I get is, "Oh, it's so beautiful there." This "beauty" is key to understanding Eastern Kentucky's future challenges and opportunities. Yes, there is undeniable beauty in Eastern Kentucky, like the area around Buckhorn Lake in Perry County or the view from the top of Pine Mountain between Letcher and Harlan Counties. On a day trip, you can see soaring mountains, rambling streams, an old-growth forest, and struggling but charming main streets. There is an extraordinary calm and quiet to much of the area. But the fact is, Eastern Kentucky has been its own worst enemy when it comes to preserving and cashing in on its topography for a purpose other than coal mining.

Strip mining poses an obvious threat to the purity and beauty of the landscape. But it's not the only blemish on the land in Eastern Kentucky. The region also has a trash problem, and it's been piling up for years. Think of the littering incident that got the narrator of Arlo Guthrie's classic song "Alice's Restaurant" thrown in jail, drain it of its humor, multiply it by thousands of such acts, and you'll have a pretty good sense of the illegal dumping dilemma in Eastern Kentucky, where many residents, rather than signing up for mandatory garbage pick-up services that they often can't afford, resort to throwing trash on the side of a road or down creek and river banks. Every year, hundreds of people in the region are fined for not registering for waste pickup and dozens more are charged with illegal dumping, a Class D felony, but the practice continues.

The PRIDE program, a regional clean-up initiative that Congressman Rogers helped fund, never fully took off, leaving each county in the area to devise a personalized strategy for dealing with its trash. One local politician during my time in Eastern Kentucky took an aggressive approach to combating the problem of bottles and cans that littered his county. Frustrated that the Kentucky legislature time and again voted down "bottle bills," Letcher County judge/executive Carroll Smith proposed one of his own that would have placed a five-cent deposit on most beverage containers and fast-food cups sold in Letcher County. Operating in a county that was home to the feisty *Mountain Eagle* newspaper and the arts collective Appalshop, Smith, a former coal miner, was a maverick who didn't shy away from unconventional politics. He shunned the support of the coal industry and had earlier been unsuccessful in trying to pass a timber ordinance to monitor the logging industry. Many of the causes Smith advocated would have been political suicide for any other elected official in the region.

In support of his container initiative, Smith cited a state study showing that beverage containers accounted for a majority of all the litter in Kentucky ditches. From personal observation, that seemed about right, though it was easy to overlook the bottles and cans that lay among bigger-ticket items like old refrigerators, televisions, and car tires. The Letcher County Fiscal Court rejected Smith's measure, citing concerns over the practicality of enforcement and general dislike of the idea overall.[13] Despite the outcome, I had to applaud Smith's effort and creativity.

Down in the ditches, you had trash. Up in the hills, autumnal Appalachia was on fire. The sight and smell of blazing forests came to be a perennial reminder of the arrival of Eastern Kentucky's annual arson season, which runs roughly from Halloween until Christmas. I had no idea about the tradition until I received an email from one of my editors in the fall of 2001 that read, "It's just about time for Eastern Kentuckians to torch their trees. And as dozens of accelerant-wielding pyrotechnics take to the forests from Pikeville to Paintsville, let's keep an eye on the arson problem and try to be as proactive as possible."[14]

Many Eastern Kentucky counties are 80 percent forested, making the timber and logging industries a significant contributor to the state's economy. But the region has always had a culture of arson. Well over half of all the forest fires in any given year are intentionally set, a far higher percentage than any other place in Central Appalachia. Compounding the problem, Kentucky has also lacked the resources to aggressively fight the blazes, forcing the state to rely on underpaid and volunteer firefighters, the National Guard, and even prison inmates to do the job, often after the fires are already burning out of control. My first Kentucky arson season happened to be the most severe in many years. Nearly 200,000 acres of forest burned that year, resulting in millions of dollars of lost timber revenue.[15] I spent Thanksgiving 2001 shadowing firefighters earning six dollars per hour to trek deep into the burning forests of Breathitt County. Many of the crew members had spent every Thanksgiving in recent memory fighting fires. Along with fireproof blankets, goggles, and other firefighting equipment, someone on the crew always brought along a portable grill to cook deer meat. As I tailed the ground team, National Guard helicopters carrying massive bags of water flew overhead. And this was all because someone decided to start a little fire that turned into something much bigger.

The total number of acres burned in the state started to dip in the early 2010s but shot up again dramatically in 2016, according to the Kentucky Division of Forestry.[16] Arson is still very much a rite of autumn in the hills of Eastern Kentucky.

Why do the arsonists do it? As I microwaved Thanksgiving dinner back at my apartment that evening, I pondered this question. Then, while out jogging the following day, I noticed a luminescent glow on an adjacent hillside. It suddenly clicked. The main reason seemed to be that the fires provided entertainment value. Set a fire on one ridgeline and then maneuver an all-terrain vehicle to the opposite ridgeline and admire the light show. The firefighters I embedded with saw a recreational arsonist speed off on a four-wheeler, but they were pinned in by flames and couldn't follow him. Some arsonists surely have a more practical purpose in mind: the blazes clear spots for marijuana cultivation in the spring. A year before I arrived in Eastern Kentucky, federal authorities "eradicated" 184,000 marijuana plants from the Daniel Boone National Forest, far and away the highest total of any national forest.[17]

*

Its difficult-to-access location will always present challenges, but there is growing recognition that a clean, hospitable, and technologically advanced Eastern Kentucky will be a more desirable place for people to visit and companies to locate themselves. "I always tell people to be cautious with our transition narrative," Shane Barton—an economic development specialist in Eastern Kentucky—said. "There are some folks who are too focused on one industry. We can't think of tourism as the silver bullet. We have to look at the big picture."[18]

For two decades, local economic development officials have worked the tourism angle, with some mildly successful results. But word has spread slowly. Take for example a recent *USA Today* article about tourist attractions in "Eastern Kentucky." The four towns featured on the list, Corbin, Maysville, Lexington, and Winchester are all located along the I-75 or I-64 corridors. With the exception of Corbin, the birthplace of Harland Sanders and the location of the first Kentucky Fried Chicken, none of those places fell in my coverage area or in what I would consider Eastern Kentucky.[19]

The "Winchester Wall" is not a tourist attraction. It is a geographical divide that separates Eastern Kentucky from more flourishing areas of Central Kentucky. It is where Interstate 64 ends and the less high-speed Bert T. Combs Mountain Parkway begins. For years, state officials have planned an expansion of the Mountain Parkway in the hopes of making Eastern Kentucky less cut off from the rest of the state.

To assess the recent history of the area's tourism initiatives, I revisited a story I wrote in 2005 about the reintroduction of elk to the region. Elk hadn't roamed Eastern Kentucky since the mid-1800s, but the Mid- and Southwestern United States apparently had elk to spare. So with the help of wildlife biologists, mountaintop removal mining, and plenty of out-of-state elk, the animals became a focal point of the area's tourism drive. "Elk Crossing" signs started sprouting up in the sixteen Eastern Kentucky counties where the animals were placed. Soon, Kentucky's elk population became the largest in the eastern United States. I never personally set eyes on anyone who came to Eastern Kentucky specifically to see elk, but tourism leaders assured me that private planes full of wildlife watchers were regularly flying into a small airport in the region situated on strip-mined land for the purpose of communing with the large mammals.[20]

Once the elk population grew to the point where local residents complained that the animals had become a nuisance, it was only a matter of time before watching elk became shooting elk. The state started issuing a limited number of hunting licenses to elk hunters. That news filtered down to Donald Trump, Jr., who, in 2018, came to Eastern Kentucky with his son for an elk-hunting trip followed by a meal at one of my old stomping grounds in Hazard.[21] The *Courier-Journal* published a brief piece about Trump, Jr.,'s visit. The headline: "Donald Trump Jr. Makes a Stop at Applebee's in Eastern Kentucky." As is often the case nowadays on newspaper websites, I had to navigate around a full-screen advertisement and answer a few survey questions to get to the rest of the article. But I really wanted to know more about Trump, Jr.,'s visit. The opening sentence of the story read, "There's no place like the neighborhood for Donald Trump Jr.," a lead that positioned the first son as a true man of the people and helped to promote an advertiser or potential advertiser.[22] Genius. The story went on to note that Trump, Jr., and his son worked up an appetite for all-you-can-eat riblets that day by learning about falconry and then bagging some elk.

I remember well when that Applebee's opened. It marked a significant cultural moment for Hazard and the surrounding area. Even a regional hub like Hazard had struggled to provide locals and visitors with a dining experience that existed almost everywhere else. With the launching of the Applebee's, Hazard could boast having a national chain restaurant that served alcohol. To that point, fast-food and diner-style establishments dominated the region's culinary landscape. The best of the bunch was France's Diner, where a woman named Frances served home-cooked comfort food, not cassoulet or crepes as the misplaced apostrophe in the restaurant's name suggested. The diner was located across the street from what was arguably Hazard's biggest attraction, the Mother Goose House, a circa-1940 home with an enormous shingled roof forming the shape of a goose, yellow bill and all. The stone dwelling beneath is "the nest," with egg-shaped windows.

But if you craved more than ham and eggs and novelty architecture, you had limited options. The closest sit-down chain restaurants with alcohol licenses were sixty miles away. You really had to have a craving for Chili's or TGI Fridays to make that trip. There was an excellent Mexican restaurant in Hazard, brilliantly named El Azul Grande (The Big Blue) to appeal to University of Kentucky fans who understood rudimentary Spanish. Located in the only "wet" county in the vicinity, Hazard was well positioned to become the first town to take its restaurant offerings to a level that almost every other place in the United States had already been for decades. It just needed a business owner with the guts to take the chance. The Hazard Applebee's arrived at the inauspicious moment when the OxyContin epidemic was wrecking everything in its path, making it challenging for business owners to find a drug-free workforce. But the plan came to fruition when an Applebee's opened on the north side of Hazard. No longer did Hazard-area residents have to venture to the dark, smoky, heavily 1970s-influenced Cliff Hagans Rib Eye for a glass of beer and slab of meat. Applebee's, with its bright interior spaces and walls chock full of University of Kentucky sports memorabilia, quickly became a hot spot, and as the only margarita-serving establishment within a hundred miles of most of its patrons, it drew customers from hours away. For weeks, there were lines outside the door until well into the evening.

The scene reminded me of the images of Soviets with their faces pressed up against the windows of a McDonald's that opened a few months after the fall of the Berlin Wall. I was told by locals that a similar scene had played out when a McDonald's opened in the Eastern Kentucky town of Paintsville in the 1980s. After a few weeks, the Applebee's hysteria settled down, and I was able to find a seat at the bar most nights. Located just down the road from my apartment, I often stopped in after returning to Hazard from an out-of-town assignment. I also met sources there. With an increasing number of Eastern Kentucky towns and counties voting to "go wet" over the years, the Hazard Applebee's has become less of a novelty, but, in my mind it remains a central part of the region's recent history.

If you build it in Hazard, they will come, and the steady increase in nationwide chains opening in the region is one sign of its slow transition toward a more traditional consumer economy. When an Italian fast-food restaurant called Fazoli's opened in Hazard in 2018, it shattered company records, both in terms of sales and number of people served in its first week.[23] For an area not known for having a population with a lot of disposable income, I found these figures stunning. But it's worth noting that Fazoli's first week in business coincided with the first week of a new month, meaning many residents had just received their government assistance checks. A bite at Fazoli's can be followed by a short trip across Route 80 to the Walmart Supercenter, boulder-free since 2005.

*

Some Eastern Kentucky tourism officials have gazed longingly over the border into northeast Tennessee and wondered if they too could become a mecca for visitors. The two areas have similar topographies. Southeastern Kentucky has the Cumberland Gap National Historical Park. Northeast Tennessee (and northwest North Carolina) have the Great Smoky Mountains National Park. But there is a key difference between the two areas, one that helps explain why the half-million-acre Great Smoky Mountains National Park is the most visited national park in the country, drawing more than ten times as many people per year as its Kentucky counterpart.[24] Next to the park is the town of Pigeon Forge, home to the wildly popular Dollywood theme park, which pulls in another three million visitors a year. Down the road from Pigeon Forge is Gatlinburg, a mountain town that has Tennessee's only ski resort. Pigeon Forge caters to families. Gatlinburg appeals to couples. It is a winning formula that draws plenty of visitors to an area that has sacrificed authenticity for Disneyfication.

Eastern Kentucky still has hopes of replicating the success of this part of Tennessee. Tucked away off of Kentucky Highway 119 near the Harlan County line in Bell County is the future site of Boone's Ridge, a 12,000-acre nature and wildlife reserve located on a reclaimed mine site. The privately owned park in Miracle, Kentucky was originally conceived as a modest attraction where visitors could hike trails in an area teeming with elk, black bears, and bobcats. But over the past decade, the vision has grown by leaps and bounds. The Appalachian Wildlife Center, as it was originally named, got rebranded as Boone's Ridge, a quasi–theme park that is expected to have a visitor's center, three museums, a theater, a zoo, an artisan hall, and several gift shops and eateries.

Boone's Ridge is a $50 million home-run attempt that its CEO, David Ledford, says will create almost 3,000 new jobs and draw almost a million visitors a year, generating nearly $175 million for the local economy.[25] The company's website has featured a count-down clock ticking down the days, hours, minutes, and seconds until its projected May 2022 opening. Congressman Hal Rogers and former Kentucky governor Matt Bevin have helped steer federal and state funding to the project. In 2016, it was the recipient of a $12.5 million grant from the US Office of Surface Mining and Reclamation Enforcement.[26] The Appalachian Regional Commission is also backing the venture.

It feels like this swing for the fences is coming with two strikes in the count. The land where the park is going up has a tortured history. For years, it belonged to Asher Land and Mineral, which made it the site of Kentucky's first mountaintop removal operation. Once the coal got mined and the land reclaimed, local economic development officials saw an opportunity to develop the area as an industrial park. In 2001, the Pine Mountain Regional Industrial Development Authority bought the land for $850,000, using coal severance tax funds, a pot of money the state receives each year based on the value of the total amount of mined coal. To provide access to the site, the state paid for a bridge across the Cumberland River. Years passed, but no businesses moved in. The bridge came to be known locally as the "Bridge to Nowhere."[27] Until Ledford's Appalachian Wildlife Foundation leased the land from the development authority in 2016, it was being used as an ATV park.

Ledford is a wildlife biologist by trade, but he also possesses the skills of a born salesman. He sees Boone's Ridge as a one-of-a-kind attraction. "There's really nothing like this in the entire country," he has said.[28] He compares the potential appeal of the nature reserve to the Ark Encounter, a popular biblically themed attraction in Northern Kentucky that features an enormous replica of Noah's Ark and a decidedly creationist message. As of late 2020, no road signs along Route 119 promoted the area as the future site of the reserve, but Ledford said Boone's Ridge plans to spend $35 million on marketing and advertising in its first three years of operation. "If you build it and people know about it, you can get them to come," he said.[29]

Boone's Ridge isn't Applebee's, however.

Many of the development officials I spoke to while covering Eastern Kentucky struck me as political animals who showed more interest in photo ops and helping buddies with pet projects than seriously contemplating what the region needed to do to build lasting economic momentum. When I attended public meetings or watched the "Issues & Answers" segment of the local television news, I heard from old, entrenched interests that were reluctant to outline a plan for the future that would alienate King Coal and the coal severance tax money it generated. I don't recall ever hearing anybody under the age of fifty speaking in either of these forums.

As a result of a steep decline in coal production, there just isn't that much in the coal severance pot anymore. And what is there hasn't always been used to benefit Eastern Kentucky. In 2013, for example, $2.5 million from the fund went toward renovating the University of Kentucky's basketball arena in Lexington.[30]

In a move that came at least twenty years too late, Kentucky Senator Mitch McConnell took note of the area's revenue crunch when, in 2019, he and Rogers simultaneously introduced a bill in the Senate and House that would direct money from the federal Abandoned Mine Lands fund to economically distressed communities that have depended heavily on mining. The funds would go toward repurposing abandoned coal mines, cleaning up the waterways they polluted, and investing in projects like Boone's Ridge.

*

Twenty years after my first conversations with local leaders about life after coal, the region has finally tapped some smart and innovative thinkers to confront the enormous challenges of the future.

Shane Barton is a proud ninth-generation Appalachian with an encyclopedic knowledge of the people and places of Central Appalachia. One of his first memories is of his uncle being killed in a rock fall at a Virginia coal mine in 1984. Unlike his counterparts from earlier this century, Barton doesn't feel a need to pay lip service to coal. In fact, he brushes aside the rhetoric of Friends of Coal and speaks about the industry in the past tense.

"The narrative around coal has changed," said Barton, who works for the Community and Economic Development Initiative of Kentucky. "It used to be if you were critiquing the coal industry or mountaintop removal or cancer or particulates from dust, you were in fact desecrating the value of the coal mining family. Now we have the 'coal expiration date,' as we refer to it, and we're trying to move on."[31]

Born and raised in the mountains of Southwestern Virginia, he attended Virginia Commonwealth University in Richmond and eventually returned home with a Nigerian wife, a master's degree in urban and regional planning, and a desire to see the region he loved get out of the economic doldrums. His specialty is downtown revitalization, an assignment that became that much more daunting with the toll that the 2020 shutdown took on small businesses. Soon after a recently opened independent bookstore on Main Street in Hazard recovered from the North Fork of the Kentucky River overrunning its banks and flooding the store, the pandemic forced it to close again. Similar scenes played out across the region.

Besides location, the other main obstacle facing Eastern Kentucky,

Barton told me, is commitment to the cause. Other Appalachian towns have spent years building tourism industries, using inherent historical advantages, a high level of regional coordination, and a healthy marketing budget to create thriving visitor economies—the deleterious effects of the COVID-19 shutdown notwithstanding.

Can Eastern Kentucky find its marketable niche? I think about this question every time I'm there. I believe the answer is yes, but two things need to happen first. The region has to come together and make beautification efforts a priority. If people are going to choose to spend time and money in a place, they need a reason to come and a reason to stay. They need a few nice amenities and a host community that will make them feel welcome. This might sound hokey or like the subject of a lecture delivered on the first day of an Introduction to Hospitality and Tourism class, but I think it could be a key to a more promising future for Eastern Kentucky, both in terms of drawing visitors and courting businesses and creating a higher quality of life for locals. It alarms me to hear Ledford say that future visitors to Boone's Ridge "are not going to spend three or four days here. . . . It's not the end destination. It's a stop on the way to someplace."[32]

Whenever I drove over Stone Mountain from Harlan County into Lee County, Virginia, I observed what looked like a discernible cleanliness gap between the adjacent counties. I thought it might just be my imagination. It wasn't. Barton told me that Southwestern Virginia is cleaner for a reason. "It has taken littered roads and illegal dumps very seriously," Barton said. "That part of Virginia has one of the largest 'Keep America Beautiful' programs in the country, and Lee County was one of the first adopters. It shifted the culture."[33] Whether the topic is litter or just about anything else, Barton said, Eastern Kentucky has traditionally lacked a regional approach to confronting challenges.

From what he observed growing up in Southwestern Virginia and later as an economic development official, Barton sees a template that could work for Eastern Kentucky. I have visited the area he is talking about and see what he means. Abingdon, the seat of

Washington County, is a town of about 8,000 located in the Blue Ridge Mountains, making it comparable in size to the larger towns in Eastern Kentucky. Abingdon's location right off of well-traveled Interstate 81 gives it a geographic edge that Hazard, Pikeville, and Harlan don't enjoy. But it is the rural areas around Abingdon that are helping to drive a burgeoning tourism industry. The thirty-five-mile Virginia Creeper Trail follows an old railroad path up into the mountains. The trail's ominous-sounding name derives from the sight of old steam locomotives creeping their way up steep mountain inclines. In the 1970s, the US Forest Service repurposed the land as a hiking and biking trail. Many residents of the town of Damascus were not pleased about the area opening up to the nature crowd. "The people whose property it ran through hated the Creeper Trail and everything it stood for," Barton said.[34] He remembers a farmer burning down a trestle because he didn't want the trail near his property.

With time, the people of Damascus came around to the idea that the Creeper Trail could benefit the community. But it took years of work and regional cooperation to get that message out and to create an outdoor experience that would draw in outsiders. Abingdon has museums, playhouses, and farm-to-table restaurants. Damascus, with a population of less than 800, is one of a handful of American towns that has earned the title "Trail Town, USA" from the American Hiking Society. Along the town's main street are several bed and breakfasts and bike and kayak rental shops. Up in the mountains in tiny communities like Konnarock and Whitetop are a host of rental cabins. That's how a once-struggling area of Central Appalachia grew its economy.

There are signs of progress in Eastern Kentucky. The North Fork of the Kentucky River is cleaner than it was twenty years ago. Trash is scattered along its banks, but not as much as once was. Sewage still leaks into the water in certain places, but fish-and-wildlife officials have made fixing that problem a priority. There are fishing and boating opportunities that didn't exist twenty years ago. Perry County Park, which used to be known as Pillville during the peak of the OxyContin epidemic, is now a popular departure point for boaters and paddlers. The park has a welcome center and a hashtag: #PerryProud.

*

There is one economic resource Eastern Kentucky simply does not have enough of: people sticking around to build their jobs and careers. According to US Census estimates, every county in the region lost population between 2010 and 2018.[35] Thanks to an influx of auto manufacturing jobs in central Kentucky, the Appalachian Kentucky diaspora now has an outpost closer to home. The town of Bowling Green, home to the National Corvette Museum, has had a plant that makes that iconic car since the early 1980s. But in the early aughts, Ford, Toyota, and other manufacturers started setting up camp all over the state. By the mid 2010s, Toyota's largest plant outside of Japan was in Georgetown, Kentucky. No longer do young Eastern Kentuckians in search of manufacturing work *have* to migrate to Ohio, Indiana, and Michigan, making it easier to keep intact their ties to home, but many have found broader opportunities and happiness in the big cities of Kentucky and other states.

Barton detests the term "brain drain," which he says discredits people, highly educated and otherwise, who choose to stay in the area. He looks at outmigration from Eastern Kentucky as part of the natural human impulse to want to experience new places and things. The key, he believes, is to work toward making migration a two-way street. "We have to be willing to be open to newcomers if they do show up," Barton says. "We are asking people to come, but are we ready for company?"[36]

For Eastern Kentucky to realize a promise of prosperity that Bill Clinton didn't deliver on that sweltering day in Hazard, it needs a well-coordinated plan geared toward improving physical and technological infrastructure, obtaining private and public funding, and transcending old, broken ideas. There will always be an alphabet soup of organizations that try to bring the region's leaders together.

I saw several such groups come and go during my years there. The latest initiative, called SOAR (Shaping Our Appalachian Region), is using a plan called the "Blueprint for the Future of Appalachia" to transform Eastern Kentucky.[37] SOAR has touted the region's decline in opioid overdose deaths and marginal successes in workforce and industrial development as proof that the blueprint is working. Some of SOAR's ideas are intriguing, like trying to make Eastern Kentucky's cleared land a hub for "drone ports" at which unmanned aerial vehicles are tested and studied. But SOAR's leading initiative to "wire" Eastern Kentucky with affordable, high-speed broadband service faltered at a time when students stuck at home because of COVID-19 most needed reliable Internet service to participate in distance learning.[38]

In a 2019 column in the *Lexington Herald-Leader*, Jared Arnett, SOAR's then-executive director, channeled the 2001 *New York Times* article about the hillbilly festival by proclaiming victory over economic hardship in the region. Arnett wrote, "We are not what is wrong [in Kentucky]. We are a shining example of what is right. I want to be abundantly clear: The debate is over. . . . We are creating a future in Appalachia."[39]

I admire Arnett's confidence and optimism, but from my perspective, the future of Eastern Kentucky is still very much open to debate. The region seems to have taken a major first step by relegating the glories of coal to the past. Now the work really begins. Beyond a professional class of teachers, lawyers, and medical professionals and pockets of great wealth are masses of struggling people. Fifteen of the one hundred US counties with the highest percentage of food stamp recipients are in Eastern Kentucky.[40] In some Eastern Kentucky counties, one in every four people receives Social Security disability payments.[41] The high school graduation rate in Eastern Kentucky, though higher than in past decades, is still the lowest of anywhere in Appalachia.[42] The teen pregnancy rate in Appalachian Kentucky is nearly 70 percent higher than the national average.[43] Due in large part to the opioid epidemic, some Eastern Kentucky counties have seen the biggest drop in life expectancy of anywhere in the nation.[44] The region has one of the highest cancer rates in the country.[45]

I purposely haven't dwelled on those numbers or others like them. They are well documented. But it is important to remember that they represent the fact that poverty has consequences, both direct and indirect. Another of those consequences is chaotic local government, which, like the serpent eating its own tail, then turns around to become another impediment to economic progress. And in an Eastern Kentucky in danger of falling further behind, local corruption, vote buying, and even cold-blooded murder of political opponents had become shockingly normalized.

CHAPTER 4

Killing Season

Almost from day one, I had gotten an eye-opening glimpse into Eastern Kentucky's most pressing challenges. I expected that coal, prescription drugs, and economic development would remain the centerpieces of my coverage. But as German writer Thomas Mann noted in his celebrated 1924 novel *The Magic Mountain*, "Everything is politics,"[1] and when election season rolled around in the mountains of Eastern Kentucky, the area became consumed by a level of political violence and dysfunction that still haunts me. The terrible acts of that year started in a place with a storied history of hostility.

Harlan County re-entered the public consciousness in the year of the American bicentennial with the release of filmmaker Barbara Kopple's acclaimed documentary *Harlan County, USA* about a violent 1973 coal miners' strike sparked by company opposition to unionization of a mine. The film, which won an Academy Award for Best Documentary Feature, chronicles day-to-day life in the county during the strike, which lasted over a year and led to the murder of a striking miner by a mine foreman. The events depicted in the film reinforced the county's hardscrabble reputation as "Bloody Harlan," a nickname that dates back to a Great Depression–era labor dispute that featured shootings, bombings, and widespread civil unrest that had to be quelled by the Kentucky National Guard. Kopple's film captures a simmering tension that never really went away in Harlan County, a rough-and-tumble place that even other Eastern Kentuckians tend to politely distance themselves from.

Despite what movies like *Deliverance* would have us believe about Appalachia, Eastern Kentucky isn't a place of stranger-on-stranger violence (though the 1967 murder of Canadian documentary filmmaker Hugh O'Connor, who stepped onto the wrong man's property, serves as a tragic exception). I walked into some tense situations in Eastern Kentucky, but I never felt in danger, even when the Lexington-based photographer I frequently worked with raised the stakes by taking pictures. The family feuds that marred the area for generations are a vestige of a bygone era. And the months-long, non-violent protest in Harlan County led by Blackjewel's laid-off coal miners in 2019 suggests the area's fabled coal wars are also history. But there remains an unmistakable air of violence in some parts of Eastern Kentucky, where the pursuit of power and control over local fiefdoms has led to corrupt rule and, occasionally, bloodshed.

Five years after Kopple accepted her Oscar, Harlan County doubled down on its reputation by voting in Vietnam veteran and former coal miner Paul Browning, Jr., as sheriff. Browning won the election in a landslide despite having a misdemeanor conviction on his record for pointing a gun at a former county sheriff. But he possessed the type of persuasive skills that convinced voters he could make the county safer by expanding the purview of his department. To that point, the sheriff's office was mainly responsible for collecting property taxes, an activity that provided the office with funding to operate. The vast majority of law enforcement activity in the county was left to the Kentucky State Police post in Harlan. Browning intended to change that.

Browning's tenure as Harlan County sheriff was brief and tumultuous. Shortly after taking office in 1982, someone shot him in the arm on his way to work, an act he blamed on a network of drug dealers that he planned on busting. Browning used that incident to win an additional $44,000 in funding for his office, a request that was opposed by some members of the Harlan County Fiscal Court who said they didn't like that a man who had threatened the former sheriff was now the county's top law enforcement officer. Browning didn't appreciate the criticism one bit. A few weeks later, he was arrested again, this time by the Kentucky State Police, for conspiring to kill two people, a fiscal court member who voted against his funding request and the chairman of the county school board who joined the debate by calling Browning "a flaky SOB."[2] The police took credit for foiling the plot in the nick of time.

The theatrics in Harlan garnered the attention of the national media. *The Boston Globe* wrote, "The Browning case is seen by some here as a setback in Harlan County's efforts to attain a degree of respectability in the eyes of the rest of the state and country."[3] Browning's trial on the murder conspiracy charges revealed even more salacious details. State police offered up an audiotape of Browning trying to recruit a local bootlegger to commit the murders. Browning was also caught on tape delivering cash and a gun to undercover officers posing as hitmen. In denying the allegations against him, Browning suggested that his dealings with the moonshiner and the undercover cops were part of his own elaborate sting investigation aimed at finding out who shot him and why. In a jailhouse letter published by the *Harlan Daily Enterprise*, Browning wrote that nefarious interests were trying to bring him down because of his efforts to fight cocaine trafficking and bootlegging.[4]

Because most people in Harlan had a strong opinion about Browning, but also out of safety concerns, his trial took place 130 miles away in Danville, Kentucky. Browning's defense unraveled when several of his own deputies testified that he told them about his desire to kill his political opponents. Another deputy testified that he was the one who shot Browning in the arm and that he had done so at Browning's behest, as part of a plan to help the sheriff win the sympathy of county residents and the fiscal court.

Browning was found guilty and received a ten-year prison sentence. Though confined to a jail cell, he legally remained sheriff while he appealed his conviction. A group called "Save Our Sheriff" collected 1,700 signatures on a petition asking Kentucky's governor to re-examine the case. The same group raised $10,000 for Browning's legal fees.[5] After the trial, the commonwealth's attorney who prosecuted the case said Browning was "one of the most charming, charismatic, intelligent people I've ever met. He's Jim Jones and Charlie Manson in an All-American boy package."[6] The governor ultimately stripped Browning of his badge.

Browning won parole after three years and moved to Ohio to plot his return. In 1995, another Kentucky governor restored Browning's civil rights, allowing him to vote in elections, and if he ever got the itch, to make another run for public office.

In 2002, twenty years after his conviction for conspiracy to commit murder, Browning decided to try to win back the sheriff's job. "I was doing a good job when I was sheriff, and they can't take that from me," Browning said in announcing his candidacy. "They can slander me, but the people who know me around this county, they can't take that from me, and it's those people who will put me back in office."[7]

Browning's mission to unseat two-term incumbent Steve Duff had an added level of drama. As a state police officer in the 1980s, Duff had slapped handcuffs on Browning and taken him to jail. And as was his tendency, Browning held a grudge. An affinity for a good old-fashioned feud and the high stakes of a devastating prescription pill epidemic combined to make the sheriff's race the talk of Harlan County. Browning promised to be tough on OxyContin dealers. More than just destroying lives, the drug was corrupting Harlan County to its core, Browning said, alluding to reports that women were prostituting themselves to earn money to buy Oxy-Contin. Browning vowed to clean up the drug problem and bring the worst dealers to justice. He promised to drain the swamp.

Browning campaign signs sprouted up all over the county, in its two main towns, Harlan and Cumberland, and up remote hollows in communities like Evarts, Loyall, and Wallins Creek. His unlikely political comeback was gaining traction and alarming his opponents.

"For the first few weeks, they laughed and laughed at him, thinking he had no chance," Browning's son, Paul Browning III, now a Harlan County magistrate, says. "The next few weeks, they were like, 'Is he really going to win this thing? What in the hell are people thinking?' He was upsetting the apple cart in a big way."[8]

Browning fashioned himself as an Eastern Kentucky version of Buford Pusser, the uncompromising Tennessee lawman whose battles against bad guys and corruption formed the basis for the 1974 movie *Walking Tall*. Browning had a commanding presence and a fifth-degree black belt to go along with it. He hoped Harlan County voters would focus on his positive attributes rather than dwell on his checkered past.

With two months to go before the Democratic primary, it appeared Browning was poised to pull an upset. Then he didn't come home one Friday evening. His wife and son couldn't reach him by phone, but that wasn't cause for alarm considering the area's spotty cell phone reception. On most nights, they would have just assumed he was out politicking. But this night was special. Browning's beloved Kentucky Wildcats were squaring off on CBS against the University of Maryland in an NCAA basketball Sweet Sixteen tournament game. Browning never missed a game, not even a meaningless regular-season matchup, and he always watched the games in the comfort of his home. His absence during Kentucky's most important game of the season struck his family as more than odd. They watched the game, hoping he would walk through the door before the final buzzer.

It was a rough night. Kentucky lost the game by ten points. And when the game ended, Browning still hadn't appeared. His son waited until the next morning to report him missing, and later that day, state police found his Toyota pickup truck in a neighboring county with a badly burned body inside. Four days later, the remains were identified as Browning's.

The people willing to speak to me about the Browning murder fell into two camps, just as they had twenty years earlier. His detractors believed that Browning was a charlatan and sociopath who was asking for trouble. His supporters viewed him as a populist reformer who had the courage to run for office again despite knowing he might not make it to election day alive. Whether they loved or loathed him, no one expressed surprise at his death.

The echoes of the 1980s feud only got louder. Before police identified any suspects or a possible motive in the killing, they released a videotape that Sheriff Duff said he received about a month before

Browning's body was found. The tape showed Browning taking $2,500 in cash from a man that the sheriff's department identified as a cocaine dealer. On the videotape, Browning could be heard saying, "This is all I needed to put me in that office. This is the best money you've spent in your life."[9] Browning was also recorded threatening to kill or imprison a number of people in Harlan County whom he held responsible for derailing his life and political career. His targets included Sheriff Duff and Ron Johnson, the prosecutor at his murder conspiracy trial who had likened him to notorious cult leaders. At the time of Browning's murder, Johnson served as the county's top criminal judge. Browning told the man whose cash he was filmed taking that Johnson sat on the top of his list of targets. In a familiar defense, Browning's son said that his father had once again been conducting a sting operation that required him to gain the confidence of the drug dealer. "He hoped to break something open before [primary day]," the younger Browning said. "He didn't want to beat Steve Duff. He wanted to humiliate Steve Duff."[10]

As state police investigated "a lot of motives from a lot of people" in the case, attention focused on Browning's sworn enemies. Judge Johnson was a particularly compelling subject of conjecture for locals and investigation for reporters. He was even something of a minor celebrity, as his dramatic and colorful criminal court proceedings aired each afternoon on local cable television. It didn't surprise me that a convicted defendant would have animus toward the prosecutor who sent him away to prison, but it struck me as unusual that the victorious prosecutor had clung to his hostility for so long. But I learned through my reporting that Browning wasn't just another defendant in Johnson's eyes. He had taken tremendous personal satisfaction in building a case against Browning, and it ate him up inside to think the man could once again be sheriff.

I learned from Johnson himself and Browning's son just how much the men's antipathy for each other had festered over the years. When Browning came back to live in Harlan County in 1998, he moved into a house right next door to Johnson and his family. The homes were on an isolated country road with nothing but forest surrounding them. Once the men became neighbors, they started engaging in psychological warfare. Browning often stood outside and stared for extended periods of time at his neighbor's property. Not to be outdone, Johnson regularly went into his backyard and fired guns into the air.

Watching Johnson's court proceedings on television was a purely voyeuristic exercise, and for the early 2000s, somewhat ahead of its time. People could tune in and see which of their friends, ex-spouses, and neighbors were being hauled in front of the judge to answer to criminal charges. Occasionally viewers would be treated to a defendant's courtroom outburst, but generally speaking, the star of the show was Johnson, who liked to deliver sermons from the bench that didn't always relate to the cases before him. During one afternoon's programming, Johnson interrupted the sentencing of a drug dealer to share some pointed thoughts on why he didn't want his longtime adversary, Browning, regaining control of the sheriff's office.

"I had to deal three or four years with that devil. He doesn't give up," Johnson told the courtroom and viewing public. "Sometimes I think we have to pray for Michael the Archangel to come down and do his business."[11]

Who was the Archangel Michael and what was his business? Well, according to the New Testament, he was the leader of God's army who went to battle against the forces of evil and vanquished Satan during a war in heaven. On most days, Johnson's words might have been brushed off as the type of personal slander that the two men routinely engaged in. But coming when they did, on the very afternoon that Browning was last seen, the words took on greater significance.

Browning was dead, yet critics like Johnson seemed to revel in kicking him one last time. They could no longer investigate him or beat him at the ballot box, so the next best thing was to finish him off in the court of public opinion. About a month after the murder, I interviewed Johnson in his chambers about the controversy. He admitted leaking the incriminating tape of Browning and the drug dealer to the public. And he flatly denied having anything to do with his murder . . . not that he seemed to mind that it happened. "The guy was just evil," Johnson told me.[12]

The Browning family had buried their patriarch quietly and were now left searching for answers. On my visit to the house, his wife, Jayne, sat somberly in the living room, while his thirty-four-year-old son, Paul Browning III, told me he was contemplating entering the sheriff's race as a way to honor his father and avenge his death. As we talked, a toddler bounced around the living room. When young Paul Browning IV heard us talking about his grandfather, he took a pause from his activities and proudly informed me, "My papaw's running for sheriff!" Amid all of the feuding and mudslinging, it was easy to forget the ugliness of violence and the impact that it has on families.

I wanted to stay in Harlan County to follow this story. And I mostly did, making the ninety-minute daily commute from Hazard to Harlan to keep tabs on developments in the investigation. But other things were happening on my beat, including the discovery of 300-million-year-old footprints on a slab of sandstone in Perry County, 135,000 gallons of coal waste shooting from a burst pipeline into local waterways, and Senator Mitch McConnell comparing Palestinian leader Yasser Arafat to dictators Saddam Hussein and Muammar Gaddafi during a speech in Eastern Kentucky.

During those eventful weeks in Harlan covering the Browning murder, I also broke away to write a story about the death from natural causes of Robert E. Cornett, the top elected official in Breathitt County, which readers of *Hillbilly Elegy* may remember as J. D. Vance's ancestral home. Cornett, in addition to being county judge/executive, was also a beloved country doctor who continued to make house calls to the farthest reaches of the rural county up until his death. His wife told me he hadn't taken a day off in nearly thirty years. The turmoil in Harlan provided a window into a certain side of Eastern Kentucky, but hearing Cornett's constituents share their memories of him reminded me that the region had its saints as well as its sinners.

*

I soon returned to the sinners, because the killing season wasn't over. This time, the scene was Pulaski County, less remote and impoverished than Harlan and located seventy-five miles due south of Lexington. My previous trips there to the county seat of Somerset were to cover events at the Center for Rural Development, or the "Taj Ma-Hal," as it was known in honor of Congressman Hal Rogers's efforts to build it and to attract economic opportunities to the area. Despite enjoying a higher level of prosperity than counties to its east, Pulaski County had been no less affected by the scourge of OxyContin and other drugs in the early 2000s.

It fell on forty-eight-year-old Sheriff Sam Catron, who was seeking a fifth term in office in 2002, to help bring the pill problem under control. In 2000, two years after a coin toss broke an election tie between him and a challenger, Catron had supervised the largest drug roundup in the county's history, a series of raids that primarily turned up methamphetamine, cocaine, and marijuana. Catron took a hands-on approach to the job, flying helicopters around his county—the third largest by area in the state—in search of marijuana plots and personally patrolling the roads on the graveyard shift, looking for any kind of illicit activity. He was a bachelor, and those who knew him said he had no real hobbies. His job as a lawman consumed him. When not at the sheriff's office or out on the roads, he spent time at his childhood home, which he shared with his eighty-six-year-old mother, who had been widowed for more than four decades. Many years earlier, her late husband, Lewis Catron, a local police chief, had been shot on his front porch by a bootlegger. He died from his wounds seven years later. His son told friends that he would never consider getting married as long as he was in law enforcement because he didn't want a woman to experience what his mother went through.

Catron knew that the pill epidemic sweeping the region presented a new set of challenges for his office. During a twilight campaign speech at a fish fry at the Shopville-Stab Volunteer Fire Department, the soft-spoken Catron introduced himself—as if anybody at the event didn't already know who he was—and told the gathered constituents that he would appreciate their vote. And that was all he said about the sheriff's race. He spent most of his time on the stage auctioning off cakes to raise funds for the fire department. Catron bought two of the cakes himself and left the gathering to put them in his police cruiser, which was parked across the street. As a bluegrass band prepared to play another set, a loud bang pierced the evening air. The startled crowd looked over to see Catron sprawled on the ground, the victim of a single deadly shotgun blast to the head.

In an awful twist, Catron's murder came almost forty-five years to the day after his father's death. And there was another eerie coincidence. On the same day as the fish fry, Catron appeared in a taped segment of the television show *America's Most Wanted*, talking about his department's efforts to apprehend a white supremacist militia member who was on the run.

Unlike Browning's death in Harlan County, which took place on a remote rural road with no apparent witnesses, Catron's murder unfolded in the full view of about 350 people, some of whom instinctively looked up to a ridgeline above the fire station and saw a man dressed in camouflage running toward a motorcycle, a rifle strapped over his shoulder. A sheriff's deputy and firefighter jumped into their vehicles, cut over to Highway 80, and gave chase. The pursuit lasted a few miles before the gunman lost control of his motorcycle on a wet road and crashed. Danny Shelley, an unemployed thirty-year-old local man with a history of minor crimes, was taken into custody and charged with capital murder.

The motorcycle that Shelley fled on provided the first clue that he didn't act alone. It was registered to Jeff Morris, a former sheriff's deputy and one of four candidates challenging his old boss in the Republican primary. Morris had quit working for Catron the previous summer over a dispute about vacation time and allegations that he had lifted a wallet from the department's evidence room. Nobody gave him much of a chance in the race. The other candidates vying for the post included the man who had tied Catron in the previous election and a well-respected Somerset city police officer with long-time ties to the area. Morris wasn't originally from Pulaski County, which was considered a huge disadvantage when running for sheriff. Morris was at the fish fry when the shooting happened. I interviewed Shelley's brother, who told me that Shelley and Morris were close friends. Others in the community said that Shelley had played an active role in Morris's campaign, serving as Morris's witness when he filed papers to run for sheriff. Catron's chief deputy, who was sworn in as sheriff after the murder, said he had no knowledge of any animosity between Catron and Morris.

As the community prepared to bury its beloved sheriff, investigators learned a lot more about Morris's movements and activities on the day of the murder. Within forty-eight hours, they had unraveled the murder plot, charging Morris and a third man named Kenneth White, a drug dealer whom Catron had arrested for cocaine possession a year earlier. White, it turned out, was bankrolling Morris's run for sheriff.[13]

The three suspects spent the hours before the murder together, campaigning around the county and visiting a Walmart to buy a battery for Morris's 1985 Yamaha Virago motorcycle, the one that Shelley used to flee the scene. Shelley, detectives learned, was an OxyContin addict who got his drugs from White. The last call that Shelley made on his cell phone prior to pulling the trigger was to White. In police interrogation rooms, the suspects helped flesh out the details of the conspiracy. Shelley told detectives that Morris planned to hire him as a deputy after he won the election. In a jail-house interview with me, Morris denied involvement in the murder and pointed the finger at Shelley and White.

The division in public opinion that I observed in Harlan County after the Browning murder was absent after the Pulaski County incident. Everyone, other than drug dealers, adored Catron. Anger and sadness filled the community. Out to dinner one night, a fellow reporter from the area scolded me for breaking the gloom and laughing at something another of our dining companions had said. It's true, the restaurant and everywhere else in the county was awfully quiet during those days, as if everyone was participating in an extended moment of silence for Catron.

Around two thousand mourners, including law enforcement personnel from around the state and country, packed the Center for Rural Development for his funeral. Dozens more people stood outside the building listening to the service over loudspeakers. "I've never witnessed such widespread and universal grief," Congressman Rogers said in his eulogy. "Everyone feels as if they've lost not just a family member, but a close family member."[14]

*

The previous few weeks had been dizzying, but the political drama still wasn't over.

A few days before the Kentucky primary, I got called down to Clay County to cover yet another election-related threat of violence connected to a drug ring. Clay County couldn't match Harlan County in terms of its place in popular lore, but it had its own history of belligerence. It was the site of the nearly hundred-year-long Baker-Howard feud, a violent conflict triggered by what we today would consider a small-claims court matter. In 1899, journalists from around the country journeyed to Clay County to cover a particularly violent chapter in the feud. Despite being under military protection, Tom Baker, the leader of his family's clan, was murdered outside of the Clay County courthouse just moments after receiving a change of venue in his trial for the murder of the county sheriff's brother. A journalist from *The St. Louis Republic* newspaper wrote from the scene, "In the grim mountains of Kentucky, where for nearly two centuries the peace of the Blue Ridge has been undisturbed except for the mountaineer, there lives a race of people separate and distinct from all the world."[15] The reporter wrote that the only blight on this part of Appalachia were the Appalachians themselves, continuing, "For this man, simple and plain as he may be, and poor, as men go, has but one creed—to slay."[16]

The residents of Harlan County, inured to political shenanigans, seemed to view the death of Paul Browning as an occupational hazard facing any sheriff's candidate, especially one with as shadowy a past as Browning. The quick arrests in the murder of Sam Catron allowed the people of Pulaski County to focus on mourning a fallen hero, and while there certainly was anger directed at the trio believed to be responsible for his death, I never sensed that more violence was in the offing. In Clay County, however, a sense of menace hung over the area, and drugs, violence, and politics had become intertwined. The first major OxyContin bust in Kentucky took place there in 2000, when police arrested ten people who operated a multi-million-dollar drug ring that supplied tens of thousands of customers with illegal drugs.

The deeply entrenched factions in the county didn't like the idea of a group of journalists from Louisville, Lexington, and beyond descending on the county to monitor the run-up to the election. I don't know what out-of-town reporters arriving in Clay County in the late nineteenth century thought they were getting into, but reflecting on my own experience, I felt the same way I did when I went to Serbia in September 2000 to cover the controversial election that resulted in the overthrow of President Slobodan Milosevic. In both the airy squares of Belgrade and in the claustrophobic Clay County seat of Manchester, I felt under observation.

A man named Jennings White, no relation to the Kenneth White implicated in the Pulaski incident, stood at the center of Clay's 2002 election turmoil. His ancestors knew a thing or two about county feuds. Way back when, the Whites got mixed up in the Baker-Howard conflict owing to the fact that the sheriff and his murdered brother were both Whites. It surprised no one when the sheriff himself was arrested for the murder of Tom Baker.

As clerk of the county since 1994, Jennings White was responsible for running elections and tallying votes. His job, as well as his family ties to the local mayor, state representative, and circuit court clerk, made him one of the most powerful figures in Clay County. In 2002, White was seeking a third term as clerk. It had already been a consequential year for men in this position. About twenty-five miles up the road in McKee, Jackson County clerk Jerry Dean was running for reelection while awaiting trial on charges that he murdered a former employee who filed a $30 million sexual harassment suit against him. The woman was shot to death in her garage a few days before she was set to testify in the lawsuit. Dean was acquitted in 2004 of the murder charges.[17] My most vivid memory of Dean's pre-trial hearings is of the snipers positioned on the roof of the county courthouse each morning to protect Dean and testifying witnesses from vigilante justice. Dean narrowly lost his bid for reelection in 2002 and never held public office again. In 2020, at the age of seventy-six, Dean was arrested on burglary charges, seven years after he was arrested on drug charges.

White's lone competitor in the Republican primary was a hardware store owner named Freddy Thompson. About two weeks before the election, an assailant allegedly fired thirty shots at White's minivan. Right before that incident, someone took aim at a private investigator who was helping Thompson dig up dirt on White. And that same night, Thompson's home came under attack. No one was injured in any of the incidents.[18] Not long after the flurry of gunfire, I interviewed White inside a van that was flanked by two other vehicles in a fast-food parking lot. He was all jitters but tried to downplay the shootings and the attention that the election was receiving because of them. "It's Clay County," he told me. "Things just happen here."[19] Things like having one of the tires of my car slashed while I was out doing interviews in Manchester.

Over the following days, the county sheriff, a White ally, twice suspended absentee voting at the county clerk's office because of large and disruptive crowds. In a related development, Thompson's supporters went to court to protest that they were being prevented from working as election monitors on primary day. The events of that week prompted the Kentucky attorney general's office to dispatch representatives to Clay County to do some monitoring of their own. Other dark-suited law enforcement agents who wouldn't identify themselves to me were also roaming around the county. At issue was whether some Clay County residents were receiving drugs in exchange for pledging their vote to certain candidates. All around Eastern Kentucky, OxyContin pills had replaced a fifth of whiskey as the currency of choice in such vote-buying schemes. In order to ensure that they were getting a proper return on their investment, a representative of the buyers, whenever possible, would accompany the sellers into the voting booth, often under the pretext that the person casting a vote was illiterate or otherwise needed assistance pulling levers.

That year, in one of the most high-profile vote-buying cases in recent Eastern Kentucky history, federal prosecutors alleged that coal mine operator Ross Harris funneled $41,000 in illegal cash to a friend in Pike County running for a judgeship. The plot involved Harris bankrolling the campaign through a series of "straw contributions" supposedly from others. That money was divvied out fifty dollars at a time, purportedly for the legal practice of vote hauling, but instead went to people willing to sell their votes. To help facilitate the process, the people behind the scheme mailed vote sellers sample ballots showing them what box to check. Harris's friend lost the race by several thousand votes, raising questions about the effectiveness of the vote-buying efforts. Harris was convicted in 2004 and sentenced to eighteen months of home incarceration.[20] He died of cancer before completing his sentence.

*

Fortunately, election day came and went without any additional acts of violence in any Eastern Kentucky counties.

In Pulaski County, with Jeff Morris and Sam Catron's names both still on the ballot, the candidate endorsed by Catron's family handily won the Republican primary and the general election six months later. In Harlan County, where no one had yet been charged with Paul Browning's death, Sheriff Steve Duff held onto his office by a wide margin. Browning's son mounted a write-in campaign in November's general election and received about 16 percent of the vote. In Clay County, Thompson soundly defeated White in the primary and went on to become the new county clerk.[21]

The rest of the stories played out in the criminal justice system.

Danny Shelley and Jeff Morris pleaded guilty to their involvement in the murder of Sheriff Catron. By doing so, they avoided a possible death penalty. As part of their respective deals, they agreed to testify against White, who was convicted at a 2003 trial.[22] In 2018, White died in prison.

The Browning murder in Harlan County wasn't as easily solved. The investigation played out for eight years, culminating in the arrests and convictions of four men, including Roger Hall, a longtime Harlan County narcotics detective who was Sheriff Duff's right-hand man. Duff himself was cleared of any involvement in the crime after police concluded that Hall masterminded the crime on his own. Concerned that Browning would win the sheriff's race and fire him, Hall enlisted the help of Dewayne Harris, the drug dealer who was seen on the videotape giving cash to Browning. Harris, who was paying Hall for protection, got his cousin and another man to help carry out the hit on Browning, police said. The defendants received prison sentences ranging from twenty years to life in prison for the gunman Raymond Harris.[23]

Sixteen years after his father's murder, Browning III won a seat on the Harlan County Fiscal Court by sixteen votes. Duff is no longer sheriff, and many of the people in public service are new. Browning spends his days working on behalf of the communities he serves, but every now and again he reflects on his father's life and death. He believes Hall's acceptance of a plea deal and refusal to testify at the trials of his codefendants prevented the full truth about the plot from coming out. Browning is left, he said, with a "half-painted picture" of what happened to his father.[24]

Browning III left the county for a number of years but felt pulled back.

"I think every single person who lives in Harlan County, and I could probably expand that to include every single person who has ever lived in Harlan County, has a love-hate relationship with this place," Browning said. "I believe that to my core, because I certainly feel that way."[25]

The fallout from the 2002 election in Clay County was more sweeping.

The law enforcement agents who wouldn't identify themselves turned out to be from the FBI. Their investigation led to a combination of drug, vote-buying, and corruption convictions for more than a dozen Clay County officials, including Jennings White, Freddy Thompson, a former state criminal court judge, and a former county school superintendent. White pleaded guilty to his involvement in a lucrative drug ring being run by a pawnshop owner who doubled as a county election commissioner. Thompson was convicted of vote buying and manipulating vote totals in elections after becoming county clerk.[26] Thompson's attorney admitted that his client bought votes in the contentious 2002 race, but only because the well-connected White had perfected the practice. "There was no way that incumbent Jennings White, an accomplished vote-buyer from an entrenched family, could be defeated unless votes were bought on behalf of Freddy Thompson," attorney Russell Baldani wrote in a court motion. In Eastern Kentucky, some politicians really do try to manipulate elections, creating a misguided belief among some in the region that even presidential elections can be stolen.[27]

*

The Harlan, Pulaski, and Clay intrigues all happened in a single year. That is more than just a coincidence. But beyond being provocative, what do the violent incidents of 2002 tell us about Eastern Kentucky then and now?

The bloody family feuds of the late nineteenth and early twentieth centuries suggest that there is something exceptional about the area's history of violence. My wife's deep dive into "her people" in Harlan County offers an astonishing genealogical glimpse into the mayhem and bloodshed of years past. As Malcolm Gladwell writes of Eastern Kentucky's unique brand of entrenched violence in his 2008 book, *Outliers: The Story of Success*, "When one family fights with another, it's a feud. When lots of families fight with one another in identical little towns up and down the same mountain range, it's a *pattern*."[28] Gladwell, who singles out Harlan in the chapter, attributes the prevalence of feuding in the region to the Scots-Irish immigrants who settled the area coming from "one of the world's most ferocious cultures of honor . . . placing loyalty to blood above all else."[29] He believes parts of Appalachia simply have violence in their DNA.

In *Outliers*, Gladwell promotes the "10,000-hour rule," his idea that it takes that amount of time to become an expert on any given subject. As someone who spent nearly 50,000 hours in Eastern Kentucky, I feel qualified to challenge Gladwell's theory about violence in Appalachia. His analysis ignores the structural conditions that engender violence. In struggling Eastern Kentucky—with its unstable economy and longstanding reliance on an extractive industry, and its bare-knuckles reputation for generating revenue and demanding loyalty—violence has always been used to achieve and hold onto power. With the passage of time, conflict in the name of family bonds gave way to violence rooted in avarice and desperation.

There is no getting around the fact that the region has long been beset by government corruption, a cancer on the body politic that seems only to metastasize during the heat of election season. "Corruption is not a mountain stereotype or a comic form of local color. It's real, and it impedes investment," a 2013 *Lexington Herald-Leader* editorial noted. "Public corruption has abetted a drug abuse epidemic and denied youngsters a decent education."[30] As evidence of the problem, the editorial cited the 237 public-corruption convictions in the Eastern District of Kentucky between 2002 and 2011, the 17th most in the nation during this time period. Most of the federal court districts above Kentucky on the list are located in heavily populated urban areas or encompass entire states.

In Eastern Kentucky, garden-variety corruption is only part of the story. After all, measured against places like Illinois, where, in recent history, nonindicted governors barely outnumber indicted governors, the area doesn't look particularly troubled. But healthy and functioning economies can withstand a bit of graft and greed at the top. Areas with developing economies simply cannot. There's a lot more riding on the corrupt acts of Eastern Kentucky officials, from both the standpoints of personal gain and public loss. The addition of a catastrophic prescription pill epidemic to an already unstable political climate created especially dangerous conditions. Fortunately, Eastern Kentucky hasn't seen anything close to the level of political violence it experienced in 2002. But that doesn't mean the region is clear and free of the dangerous intersection of corruption and violence. In the absence of traditional economic engines found elsewhere, the illegal drug trade continues to fill a void in the mountains. That makes for volatile local politics.

No one, it seems, has been immune to the Clay County corruption bug, not even favorite son Richie Farmer, a star on Clay County's state championship–winning 1988 high school team and a key member of the University of Kentucky men's basketball squads of the early 1990s. His senior class was nicknamed the "The Unforgettables" and had their jersey numbers retired and hung from the rafters of Rupp Arena. After his college career ended, Farmer transitioned into state politics, bringing to the table a level of name recognition and popularity that few Kentuckians possessed. Farmer won two terms as state agriculture commissioner. A basketball-playing ag commissioner named Farmer was a match made in heaven. Until it wasn't. In 2013, a year after leaving office, Farmer was indicted by a federal grand jury on charges that included using hundreds of thousands of dollars in state funds for personal use. He pleaded guilty and received a twenty-seven-month prison sentence.[31] But proving that basketball is still king, a judge allowed Famer to delay reporting to prison for a week so that Farmer could watch his son play for his high school alma mater in the state basketball tournament. After completing his prison term, Farmer returned to where it all started, Clay County, and declared bankruptcy.

Farmer returned home just in time for another local political

scandal, this time involving the county's top elected official, Judge/
Executive Joe Asher, who was indicted along with a county road
foreman on bribery and corruption charges. According to prosecutors, the men made thousands of dollars by using county materials
to install tile and a concrete wall on private properties. Asher, who
had served as judge/executive for six years, resigned his post and
avoided jail time by taking a plea deal.[32] Though not exactly the
crime of the century, the controversy surrounding Asher's actions
crippled Clay County government for an entire year.

Clay County is still wary of outsiders asking questions, and justi-
fiably so. Dating back to the Baker-Howard feud, no one has said or
written anything flattering about the place. For decades, the county's poverty rate has hovered around 40 percent, and fewer than 10
percent of adults there have college degrees, making Clay County
a popular setting for poverty stories. I know because I wrote them
myself. The thing about it is that I kind of like Clay County, or at
least the idea of Clay County. Getting to the county seat of Manchester is relatively easy. It's only about twenty miles from Interstate
75 along a mostly four-lane road. Once outside of Manchester, you
drive along some of the prettiest back roads in the region, a landscape that shifts between swinging bridges, historic barns, and lush
forest. It is "Daniel Boone Country," potentially a marketer's dream.
The president of the Kentucky state Senate is from Clay County.
Eastern Kentucky University now has a campus in Manchester. But
it is also a place where crooked politicians have ruled the day for so
long that it has impeded the possibility of any meaningful progress.
And the public officials there are guarded because they know the
county has earned its poor reputation time and again.

Clay County judge/executive Johnny Johnson, who has been in
office since 2016, recently told me that the county now understands the importance of honest government and meaningful
economic development efforts. He says Clay County is about five
hundred well-paid jobs away from becoming the place he would
like to see it be.

"Them boys that done run the county back then done a good job, but come election time, they wanted their man in, whatever it took," Johnson said. "Now everything is much better. Everybody tries to do the right thing. It's nothing like back in the day. We don't see that foolishness no more . . . Our problem is that we need jobs in our county, something to boost us up."[33]

*

Even in its darkest hours, Harlan County has always felt more penetrable. The people there might not always want to talk to a journalist, but at least they'll tell you in a raised voice where they're coming from. The current Harlan County judge/executive and I go way back. I first met Dan Mosley when he was an eighteen-year-old community college student. Back then, when he wasn't in school or working at a local tobacco store, he spent his time at government meetings and community events, keeping tabs on everything of significance that was happening in the county. Mosley liked to wear suits and hold court over a few beers with reporters from the local paper, the *Harlan Daily Enterprise*. I attended some of these off-the-record sessions and came away impressed with Mosley's firm handshake and understanding of public policy.

As a politician-in-training but not yet an elected office holder, he didn't have to worry about a provocative quote ending up in the newspaper. I could tell the kid had a promising political future, so it came as little surprise to learn that in 2014, the thirty-two-year-old Mosley won Harlan County's top elected position, becoming the youngest serving judge/executive in all of Kentucky. By comparison, Senator Mitch McConnell was thirty-five when he launched his political career by winning election to the judge/executive post in Louisville in 1977. Mosley's immediate predecessor, Joe Grieshop, had clashed for years with the county sheriff, who wound up arresting him for the unauthorized use of a public building. "Politics is one thing, theft is another," the sheriff said at the time. "I don't play favorites and I don't go out of my way to pick on people. Ain't nobody above the law."[34] The case against

Grieshop didn't go any further, but the sheriff ended up getting convicted on felony theft charges.

Mosley has arguably one of the most challenging jobs in the state. Harlan County's population, which peaked at 75,000 during coal's boom years, has been dropping ever since. He has seen the exodus from Harlan up close. "People get laid off and just take off and leave their houses behind," he told me. "They'll come in and give me the keys and tell me to show the house to anyone who's interested."[35] Mosley says the opioid epidemic compounded the area's problems, creating unsafe communities and a "lost generation"[36] of people who got hooked on the drugs.

Mosley is a believer in the idea that Eastern Kentucky can benefit economically from more transparency and fewer little kingdoms. He doesn't run from Harlan's feisty reputation and counts himself among the biggest fans of the critically acclaimed television drama *Justified*, which was set and partially filmed in Harlan. In *Justified*, a stetson-wearing deputy US Marshal named Raylan Givens navigates the seedy underbelly of rural crime and justice. Mosley says the show got the spirit and roughness of his home county just right. *Justified* featured a version of the oft-covered song "You'll Never Leave Harlan Alive," an atmospheric gem about late sunrises and a historical primer about the legacy of stolen mineral rights rolled into one amazing tune.

Justified packed so much aberrant behavior into its run that a writer for MTV News compiled a list of the show's thirty-seven greatest villains on the eve of the premiere of its sixth season. Boyd Crowder was Givens's biggest nemesis, but the writer pointed out that Boyd was "just one of many villains in the hive of scum and villainy better known as Harlan County, Kentucky."[37]

I don't know if the writer of the article was taking a shot at the actual Harlan or the one depicted in the show or both. It doesn't really matter. A throwaway line in a listicle that disparages real or fictional Harlan Countians isn't going to inflame passions, while a similar sentiment expressed by a politician will be remembered and resented for years and years.

Paul Browning III could never bring himself to watch the show because of certain plotlines that seemed inspired by his father's murder. The violence and corruption in Harlan County is an extension of a "bully mentality" that has been around for generations, Browning says: "It started when the first people moved into the area. It went from the biggest guy in the holler to the coal company bully to the sheriff and politician bully. Because of that, people around here understood Donald Trump on a whole different level than most people do. People here by and large speak their piece, even when they know what the consequences will be."[38]

CHAPTER 5

God and Country

As I traversed Eastern Kentucky at the beginning of the twenty-first century, I had no way of knowing that those years would have such a profound psychological and political impact on the region. Beyond the effect of pills, coal, and corruption on society and politics, I saw something else equally era-shaping when the post-9/11 "War on Terror" collided with the somehow more vague, Fox News-propagated "War on Christmas." Both have to do with the role of God in society, and religious zeal helps explain a lot of things, including how people define American culture and values and how they vote in national elections. Eastern Kentucky took a lead role in those religious battles of the early 2000s.

When I showed up in March 2001 for a rally in front of the federal courthouse in London, Kentucky, I anticipated seeing a lively demonstration against a judge's previous order that three Eastern Kentucky county governments—Harlan, Pulaski, and McCreary—remove displays containing the Ten Commandments from schools and other public spaces. And I got what I expected. "Our Christian heritage is under attack," the Reverend Herschel Walker, head of the Ten Commandments Advancement Fund, told the assembled crowd. "There's an evil force—a group trying to rewrite our history."[1] Another speaker, Jimmie Greene, the top elected official in McCreary County, laid out the issue as he saw it: "America was based on Christianity. I respect other religions, but historically they had nothing to do with the founding of America."[2]

The issue had a long and contentious history in Kentucky. A landmark 1980 US Supreme Court ruling struck down a Kentucky law that required every public school classroom in the state to post a copy of the Mosaic code. But in 2000, the Kentucky General Assembly passed a resolution that encouraged local governments and schools to post the Ten Commandments, a move viewed as a ringing endorsement of the displays at the Pulaski and McCreary county courthouses and at Harlan County schools. The state legislature also passed legislation ordering the creation of a monument inscribed with the Ten Commandments on the Capitol grounds.[3] That law was later struck down by the courts.

A couple dozen of the 150 people who attended the London rally squeezed into a courtroom for a three-hour contempt hearing that could have resulted in Greene and other county officials going to jail for refusing to take down copies of the biblical text. US District Judge Jennifer Coffman declined to take that step, partly because the counties had tried to assuage the American Civil Liberties Union, which was representing the plaintiffs in the case, by posting copies of the Bill of Rights, the Declaration of Independence, and the Magna Carta alongside the Ten Commandments. The ACLU still wasn't having it, and Coffman gave the parties some time to agree on a mutually acceptable display. If they couldn't do so, litigation would continue. The case was right in the ACLU's wheelhouse, and I wondered whether the defendants had an appetite for an extended court battle with such an experienced foe. But the county governments made it clear in court that day that the Ten Commandments would remain up. They just needed to find the right window dressing to make the display pass constitutional muster.

A few weeks after the federal court hearing, a public high school in Harlan County took the bold step of converting a teachers' lounge into a prayer chapel featuring an altar, pews with crosses, and a framed inscription of a biblical passage. A local couple who came up with the idea for the chapel said God had inspired them to have the room renovated. The proposal received unanimous support from a site-based council responsible for making decisions about the use of school space. Needless to say, the ACLU was alarmed by what it perceived as Harlan County doubling down on unlawful religious displays. After the organization threatened additional legal action if the teachers didn't get their lounge back, school officials slapped a lock on the door of the chapel while they assessed their options. The *Courier-Journal* editorial page weighed in on the controversy, writing, "We'd urge a compromise. Keep a meditation room but remove the Christian imagery, so students of all faiths will consider it a place to come when they want to think or pray, as they already have the right to do anywhere in the building."[4] The school didn't heed the advice. A week later, the room reopened with only a slight makeover. Gone was the framed Bible verse, but everything else, including the crosses, remained in place. Johnnie L. Turner, a state representative and the attorney for the school board, said he believed the school had taken the necessary steps to bring the room in compliance with the establishment clause. "The 't's,' which could be called crosses, are a grayish area," he admitted. "It depends on how you look at them."[5]

That comment summed up the gulf in worldviews between the plaintiff and the defendants. The ACLU was a professional outfit that knew better than to introduce emotion into this or any other legal dispute. But I got the feeling that behind the organization's measured statements was a desire to remind the hayseeds that they still needed to follow the Constitution. And I know that the Eastern Kentucky counties wanted to do whatever they could to stick it to the godless ACLU, just one of the forces they believed was waging an all-out assault on Christianity. That narrative would gain further traction after the 9/11 terrorist attacks.

The drama deepened when the counties recruited the help of a Florida-based legal group with a growing reputation for taking on cases of interest to the evangelical Christian community. A year before getting involved in the Ten Commandments case, Liberty Counsel threatened to sue a Florida public library for staging an event that included readings of Harry Potter books and distribution of Hogwarts certificates to children. The group's founder, Mathew Staver, argued that the library was promoting the religion of witchcraft in violation of the separation of church and state.[6] The Kentucky case had more meat on the bone, and Staver appeared thrilled to be a part of it. He started coming to every hearing and associated rally to stir up the faithful with warnings about government infringement on religious freedom. In the years to follow, Staver's group would return to the Bluegrass State for more litigation, including a case in which it represented an Eastern Kentucky county clerk named Kim Davis who, on religious grounds, refused to issue marriage permits to same-sex couples in 2015, in defiance of a Supreme Court ruling that legalized gay marriage in all 50 states. The case garnered international attention and helped earn Liberty Counsel a place on the Southern Poverty Law Center's list of hate groups. "Liberty Counsel is an organization advocating for anti-LGBT discrimination under the guise of religious liberty," the law center wrote.[7]

In June 2001, to the dismay of Staver and his clients, Judge Coffman ruled that the displays in the Harlan County schools and McCreary and Pulaski county courthouses still violated previous US Supreme Court decisions banning Ten Commandments displays that have specific religious intent. She ordered them to come down "IMMEDIATELY," as she wrote in her ruling.[8] The defendants reacted as if a witch had used a Confundus Charm to cast a spell on the judge. "I am shocked that we have to take down history from the walls of the schools," Turner lamented after hearing the ruling.[9] But McCreary County judge/executive Greene promised that his crew would fight on.

Harlan County had to decide whether it could afford to continue fighting both the Ten Commandments and the school chapel battles. The ACLU hadn't yet filed suit seeking another injunction against the school district, but in the wake of Coffman's ruling, it seemed only a matter of time before the civil libertarians came for the chapel. They avoided having to take that step, however, when Cumberland High School voluntarily closed the chapel and converted the space into a restroom. A few years later, the high school itself closed, the result of a school consolidation trend that hit the region. A Pike County high school's recent attempt to create "prayer lockers"—a sort of prayer request box in the form of a high school locker—in its hallways brought to mind the prayer chapel controversy of twenty years ago.[10] Every so often, a new attempt to smuggle church into school is likely to take place.

Liberty Counsel and the counties devised a game plan. Elsewhere in Kentucky, in Mercer County, the ACLU was struggling to get a Ten Commandments display removed from the courthouse. The case was being litigated in a different federal judicial district and pitted the ACLU against the ACLJ, the American Center for Law and Justice, a legal group established by the Reverend Pat Robertson to advocate for evangelical causes. The ACLJ's chief counsel was Jay Alan Sekulow, who went on to become President Donald Trump's personal lawyer and part of Trump's legal team at his 2020 Senate impeachment trial.

The Mercer County display also featured the Bill of Rights, the Declaration of Independence, and the Magna Carta, the difference being that these documents were included from the get-go and not added later. Staver advised his clients to stand firm behind the Mercer County strategy. Too late, came the response from the ACLU, which argued that the counties had already shown intent to endorse religion. In order to meet a secular educational standard, the ACLU contended the displays would need to include a wide range of texts related to the foundation of systems of law. The counties, for example, could consider emulating a marble frieze in the US Supreme Court building that features Moses holding the Ten Commandments alongside Hammurabi, Muhammad, and other "great lawgivers of history."

That seemed unlikely. The Eastern Kentucky counties had begrudgingly agreed to hang American and British historical documents. There was no way Muhammad was going to grace the walls of any of their schools or government buildings.

Harlan, McCreary, and Pulaski Counties took the next step together by appealing Judge Coffman's district court ruling to the Sixth US Circuit Court. To support their case, Staver pointed to a federal court ruling upholding the constitutionality of Ohio's state motto, "With God All Things Are Possible," a biblical phrase that the court determined acknowledged religion but did not endorse it. The appeals court upheld the lower court's ruling.

The fight ended there for Harlan County, which voluntarily removed the religious displays to save further legal expenses. But McCreary and Pulaski Counties continued with the litigation . . . for another ten years. They lost every appeal, including in front of the US Supreme Court, which declined to review the case in 2011 after ruling against the counties in a five-to-four decision six years earlier. The Ten Commandments came down, and Pulaski and McCreary counties were ordered to pay the ACLU's legal fees, a sum of more than $450,000.[11] The ACLU, which had refrained from commenting on the cases outside of a courtroom, declared victory. "It is unfortunate that despite having lost before every court to consider this case, county officials nonetheless prolonged this litigation for more than a decade thereby increasing the financial burden on taxpayers," ACLU of Kentucky attorney William Sharp said in a statement. "This case reaffirms that government officials may not use public office to promote a religious agenda, and failure to abide by that basic constitutional limitation on governmental authority can be costly."[12]

And the display in Mercer County, Kentucky? It withstood every court challenge by the ACLU and remained up.

*

As they do today, the culture wars of the early 2000s kept civil libertarians plenty busy in Eastern Kentucky. The ACLU got the call when public school officials in a northeastern Kentucky county came under attack in 2002 for allowing a gay-rights group to meet on high school grounds. The Boyd County school district took the position that it was constitutionally required to give the Gay-Straight Alliance the same access to school facilities as other nonacademic clubs. Many community members strongly disagreed with that assessment. Out of protest, hundreds of Boyd County High School students skipped school on an agreed-upon day.

The county school board tried to defuse the controversy by taking a drastic measure. It sought to ban *all* nonacademic clubs from meeting at the high school, including the Bible Club and Fellowship of Christian Athletes. A school-based council composed of teachers and parents blocked that idea, leading the school board to go even further by banning all academic and nonacademic clubs from *every school in the district* from meeting after school. The ACLU compared that move to an era in American history when communities closed down public swimming pools rather than allowing minorities to swim there.

Clergy members in the area weighed in with a counterproposal: ban the Gay-Straight Alliance from school grounds and start teaching a course that teaches tolerance but also that homosexuality is wrong.

After several fraught months, the ACLU reached a settlement with the district that allowed the Gay-Straight Alliance to meet at the school after hours. In exchange, the ACLU agreed to drop its lawsuit against the county.[13] As part of the agreement, all students and teachers had to undergo sensitivity training. By this time, however, the thirty students in the club had all graduated and the teacher who led it had left the district. The club never reorganized.

The divide between religious and secular America was widening before my eyes. And fights over the public posting of the Ten Commandments and over gay rights served as undercards to what had long been the main event in this conflict: the issue of abortion. In January 2000, ACLJ counsel Sekulow looked ahead to a series of upcoming US Supreme Court cases with an archconservative cultural warrior's glee: "This is shaping up as quite a term, the most interesting in many years. It has everything from abortion protests to gay and lesbian issues, church-state disputes, school prayer, and maybe partial-birth abortion, too."[14] Sekulow had enough savvy to know that these issues fired up the faithful and helped create a loyal base of voters for the Republican Party.

With the election of George W. Bush later that year, abortion opponents got the born-again, pro-life Christian president they dreamed of. And Bush took up their cause. In 2003, he signed into law a federal ban on late-term abortions, a piece of legislation that Bill Clinton had twice vetoed. An equally provocative and symbolically powerful abortion-related development of Bush's first term came when Norma McCorvey, the plaintiff in the landmark *Roe v. Wade* case, spoke out publicly against abortion and renounced her role in helping to make it legal.

It was getting more difficult by the day to separate religion from the politics of religion, and all of the posturing and grandstanding disgusted me. Then the Reverend Billy Graham entered my extremely secular life.

In June 2001, Graham came to Kentucky for what turned out to be one of the final stadium crusades of his career, a four-day extravaganza that took place on the first days of summer at Papa John's Cardinal Stadium, home to the University of Louisville's football program. This represented a major spiritual opportunity for church congregations throughout Eastern Kentucky, including several in the former Letcher County coal camp town of Fleming-Neon, where the churches got together and rented two school buses to travel to the revival. I got their permission to tag along. In a pre-interview, the pastors who organized the trip told me that they felt compelled to see Graham partly because of the ongoing Ten Commandments controversy in Eastern Kentucky. The time had come, they said, for all Christians to stand together and promote their values. A 42,000-seat stadium playing host to the most influential preacher of the twentieth century seemed like an ideal place to show that united front.

In preparation for the crusade, I had some homework to do. An evening of reading up on Graham's life and career confirmed some of my preconceived notions about him but challenged others. Graham integrated his revivals in the 1950s. Martin Luther King, Jr., and Jimmy Carter counted him as a friend. And George W. Bush credited him for helping him to quit drinking in the 1980s. Though Graham helped spawn the televangelism craze that took off in the 1970s, he maintained the gravitas that earned him recognition as

"America's pastor," "the Protestant Pope," and one of the most admired people on earth.

Graham certainly had his flaws. Out of anti-Communist conviction, he advocated an escalation of American involvement in Vietnam. He was caught on a "Richard Nixon tape" expressing anti-Semitic views about supposed Jewish control of the American media. And he had retrograde views on feminism and homosexuality. But because I had always lumped him together with hucksters like Jerry Falwell and Pat Robertson, I found myself on the eve of the trip grading him on a serious curve. For one thing, I liked that he had largely shunned partisan politics. A lifelong Democrat, he served as a spiritual advisor to US presidents of both parties. And despite repeated overtures, he never fully aligned himself with Falwell, Robertson, and others on the "religious right," who had weaponized religion for personal and political gain. Graham was vehemently pro-life but recognized that abortion was a complex and polarizing issue that allowed for differing opinions. He acknowledged that there were cases where abortion is "the lesser of two evils."[15] He had an enormous pulpit and, for the most part, he used it to preach unity and share his desire to make the world a more hospitable place for believers and nonbelievers alike.

As I crisscrossed the counties, Eastern Kentucky's ubiquitous churches, along with its tiny rural post offices, became my guideposts. On remote mountain roads with little signage, the houses of worship, and their place-specific naming conventions, helped orient me. Not always, though. For example, the tiny Floyd County community of Buck Branch is located three miles north of Pilgrim, but the Buck Branch United Baptist Church is located five miles southwest of Pilgrim. Go figure.

The Second Great Awakening of the early nineteenth century solidified Central Appalachia's Baptist and Methodist leanings. Having heard the same stories as everyone else about snake-handling and feet-washing, "mountain Christian" rites that took hold in Appalachia in the early part of the twentieth century, I could only speculate about what went on inside these buildings. I finally got an up-close look on New Year's Eve 2016 when I attended a wedding ceremony at a Baptist church in a remote part of Harlan County. The preacher took to the pulpit at around 10:00 p.m. and evangelized right up to the crack of midnight. On what one would have expected to be a doubly celebratory night, he delivered a fatalistic two-hour sermon full of damnation and hellfire. The congregation, which included several young children, took it all in, and despite the late hour and heavy subject matter, remained glued to their seats the whole time.

Religious fervor motivated Chris Fugate to give up his job with the Kentucky State Police to become a preacher. By the time he left law enforcement in 2013, Fugate and several officers at the police post in Hazard were openly promoting Christianity as a balm for Eastern Kentucky's social ills. "God is the one who can change our communities," he said at a 2011 prayer meeting in Hazard.[16]

Fugate leased a spacious building in Hazard that used to house "T.J.'s Hillbilly Palace Bar," a weekend hot spot that Fugate regularly patrolled for illicit activity. The Gospel Light Baptist Church sat across a parking lot from a bustling methadone clinic that served about five hundred people a week.

At his church, Fugate welcomed in some of the same people he had once arrested or investigated, including a criminal court judge who got caught up in opioid addiction. "I realized I could do a lot more good for people if I started preaching the Lord," he recently told me.[17]

*

About a month before the Graham crusade, I had attended a very different outdoor celebration in Louisville. One of the perks of working for the *Courier-Journal* was the opportunity to attend the state's most famous event, the Kentucky Derby, held annually on the first Saturday in May, except during times of world war and pandemic. For the newspaper's executives, the Derby experience consisted of sitting in luxury suites and hobnobbing over mint juleps with men in busy plaids and women in garish hats. For reporters, the Derby meant bringing a pen and notepad and writing a "color" story about the Derby to help fill the pages of a special section about the race that the paper put out every year.

The trip to Louisville meant more time in the company Ford Explorer. In an average week, I probably spent twenty hours behind the wheel of the Explorer, a vehicle that served me well on the wooded and mountainous roads of Eastern Kentucky. I got used to the amount and degree of difficulty of the driving, with the car radio serving as my constant companion, except for the moments when I was out of range of any stations or needed silence to navigate icy, flooded, or otherwise treacherous routes. WKCB, 107.1 on the FM dial, played a mix of the awful rock hits of the day (Train, Creed, Nickelback) and classic rock songs that were more to my liking. The station had an afternoon DJ named Sam Neace, nicknamed "The Killer Neace," whose between-song banter about pop culture and the news of the day remains among some of the best and funniest stuff I've ever heard. It was radio the way it was supposed to be, locally produced and totally improvised. The other primary soundtrack of my afternoons was the Richmond, Kentucky–based NPR affiliate, WEKU, which, at the risk of sounding like a public radio pledge drive, kept me plugged into the world, especially in the aftermath of the 9/11 attacks. Occasionally, I'd land on a station airing conservative radio hosts Rush Limbaugh or Michael Savage and I'd listen for a while. Those shows kept me plugged into a different world, one full of the right-wing and evangelical talking points that were influencing political discourse in the country. When my work travels between November and March kept me out at night, I took in a lot of University of Kentucky basketball. If I was still on the road during coach Tubby Smith's normally victorious postgame interview, I knew it had been a long day, probably one in which I had to scramble to find a place with Internet access to file my story.

For the Derby, I drew infield duty, an assignment pulled off to gonzo perfection three decades earlier by Louisville native Hunter S. Thompson in an essay entitled "The Kentucky Derby is Decadent and Depraved." About 80,000 people gather on the 26-acre Derby infield every year to thumb their noses at the gentility of "Millionaire's Row" and make that section of Churchill Downs into a spring break bacchanalia. I went into the assignment thinking the infield denizens would do a ton of drinking but also pay at least some attention to the horse race. That was before I realized that the racetrack wasn't even visible from the infield. It wasn't until 2014 that Churchill Downs installed a jumbotron that allowed the drunkards on the infield to actually see the Run for the Roses.

There wasn't really much to say about the Derby infield that Thompson hadn't already captured, but I gave it my best shot. The copy editors at the *Courier-Journal* titled my 243-word dispatch, "The female anatomy gets lots of attention," a headline that accurately captured the misogynistic climate of the infield. All over the infield giddy men cheered as inebriated women bared their breasts on a scorching eighty-six-degree day. An 18-year-old high school student told me it was his goal to hoist 250 women up on his shoulders for everyone to see. I hope he has daughters now who find the article and give him hell over it. At least I was able to get a sane female perspective into the story, a woman who told me, "It's way wilder than I thought it'd be. But if they want to show their hoo-has, that's fine, I guess."[18]

It was a long hot day, and I was relieved when horses stepped onto the racetrack and the band struck up the opening notes of Stephen Foster's "My Old Kentucky Home." Monarchos won the Derby that year in the second-fastest time in race history. I won a few dollars when Invisible Ink, the horse I bet on to win, place, or show came in second. My biggest takeaway from watching the hooved competitors go through their paces that day was that it didn't look like a lot of fun to be a racehorse.

*

On the day of the crusade, I arrived in Fleming-Neon not long after sunrise to see about fifty of my sleepy-looking travel companions milling around the parking lot. Rev. Winston McCarty of the Fleming Baptist Church introduced me to the group and let them know that whatever they told me on the bus or at the stadium might end up in the Louisville newspaper the next day. Fortunately, he said it with excitement, not caution, which made my job that day a lot easier. There was going to be plenty of room on the buses. A group twice the size had been scheduled to make the trip, but several dozen visiting missionaries from Mississippi had opted at the last minute to skip the crusade in favor of visiting Dolly Parton's Tennessee theme park, Dollywood—perhaps not a mortal sin, but certainly a brush with temptation.

I stood back with the pastors as the bus engines revved up. Most of the older parishioners in the parking lot headed toward one of the buses. I decided to board the other bus that looked to have more of a family vibe. For the first hour or so, the bus remained quiet. But once we got out of the familiar mountains and onto the interstate, it seemed to hit everyone at once that this was a special trip. The bus spontaneously came to life with song. And the religious hymns continued uninterrupted as we rumbled up Interstate 75. It felt weird to be the only person on the bus who didn't know the tunes that everyone was singing. But unless they had decided to have a Steely Dan (or even a Creed and Nickelback) sing-along, I was out of luck. Nearly three hours into the trip, all I knew about the others on the bus was the respective quality of their singing voices, which ranged from pretty impressive to quite poor.

Finally, at a rest stop near Lexington, I found an opportunity to have some conversations. Most of the people on my bus it turned out were recipients of a food-distribution program run out of the Fleming Baptist Church. None had ever been to Louisville before. Others on the bus included Betty Sparkman and her nine-year-old grandson, Michael King, who had passed up an opportunity to see a Backstreet Boys concert in Lexington the previous night so that he could attend the Graham revival. Take that, Dollywood crew! King wore a black T-shirt with a turtle-like creature on it. I've asked dozens of people of all ages to help me identify the image, but none could. Then there was Brian Tackett, eighteen, who told me he had overdosed three times on nerve medication during his teenage years before being sent to rehab in Lexington. He was attending McCarty's church and trying to stay clean. He hoped for "spiritual enlightenment" from the crusade.[19]

It was raining buckets when the buses rolled into Louisville. McCarty told us to try to stick together and instructed anyone who got separated to meet up with the group at Gate 1 of Cardinal Stadium after the event. Because of our early arrival, we had no trouble finding a large cluster of empty seats with a prime view of the end-zone stage. Graham wasn't scheduled to go on until 7:00 p.m. One of his opening acts was Christian rock superstar Michael W. Smith, a Grammy Award winner who has sold more than 18 million albums during his career. As the rain subsided, Smith warmed up the crowd with a lengthy set of songs that many in the stadium seemed to know by heart. It was like my bus experience multiplied by a thousand, but at least this time the song lyrics flashed on four giant screens throughout the stadium. Most of the people didn't look up at the screens, though. They sang along with their eyes closed. My eyes stayed open, and as I looked at the scene around me, I started thinking about the incredible power of music. The crowd waiting for Billy Graham was singing along rapturously, swaying in unison and cheering at the sound of the first notes of Smith's biggest hits. In terms of audience response, it looked much like what I had seen at regular concerts. Tweak a lyric here and there, substitute "God" for "baby," and many classic rock songs become Michael W. Smith tunes.

Smith finished his set, giving my group time to hit the restrooms and concession stands and me time to finish banging out my story on my laptop. Shortly before seven, I called in and dictated it to the news desk. Thunderous applause greeted the eighty-two-year-old Graham as he strode toward the stage, slowed by Parkinson's disease. A chair had been placed on the stage in case he needed it, but he seemed determined to remain on his feet during his sermon. I immediately recognized his distinctive North Carolina drawl from the times as a kid when I momentarily stopped on a UHF channel that was broadcasting one of his services.

Graham captivated the crowd that evening, making the most of each of his twenty minutes of speaking. He started by addressing the role that God can play in fighting racism, poverty, and other social ills. He then veered away from the humanistic and talked about the choice between embracing Jesus Christ and spending an eternity in hell: "You can only find forgiveness of sins through what Jesus did at the cross."[20] He concluded his sermon by inviting people to come forward and accept Christ as their savior. I watched as a procession of thousands heeded the call. Almost everyone who came on the buses from Eastern Kentucky, including King and Tackett, made the long walk down to the infield area. I was relieved that McCarty had told us where to meet if we got separated from the group. I got up and slowly headed down to Gate 1.

As we boarded the bus, some of the congregants told me they had just experienced the greatest day of their lives. Unfortunately, my story had already been put to bed and couldn't reflect that widespread sentiment. The ride back was quiet. We pulled into the church parking lot in Fleming-Neon at four in the morning.

The *Courier-Journal* had sent a small fleet of reporters and photographers to the revival. The headline of the paper's A1 centerpiece story about the event came directly from Graham's sermon: "The Only Answer to the Race Problem Is Love."[21] Graham had warned of the racial intolerance that was "smoldering underneath" American society due to a recent string of police shootings. My story ran on an inside page and featured a smiling photo of young Michael King with the quote, "It's OK to think God is cool."[22]

*

Before the summer was over, 9/11 happened. And some of the country's most high-profile Christian leaders used the tragedy as an excuse to divide. On September 13, 2001, Falwell blamed "abortionists," "feminists," "the gays and lesbians," and other secular forces for bringing God's wrath down on the United States.[23] He made those comments on *The 700 Club*, a show hosted by Pat Robertson on the Christian Broadcasting Network, which Robertson founded in 1960. In response to Falwell's opinion that morning, Robertson said, "I totally concur."[24] And it didn't stop there. In 2002, Falwell referred to the prophet Muhammad as "a terrorist."[25] Robertson, who had been making anti-Muslim statements long before the 9/11 attacks, ratcheted up his rhetoric against Islam following the attacks. He called Muhammad, among other things, "an absolute wild-eyed fanatic."[26] Once again, Graham stood in contrast to Falwell and Robertson. In the days, months, and years after 9/11, he refused to criticize Islam or secular Americans for the attacks. But the voice of restraint that he maintained until his dying day got drowned out by hate and divisiveness—on the airwaves, from the pulpits, and in the halls of Congress.

Falwell and Robertson's business models had long depended on using wedge social issues to stoke controversy. That made their comments about the terrorist attacks and their aftermath extremely troubling, but not entirely surprising. A far more telling sign that Graham's brand of moderation was losing appeal in the evangelical community came through the words of the heir to his empire, son Franklin Graham. The younger Graham remarked in the days following the attacks that Islam was "a very wicked and evil religion,"[27] a broadside that he would launch in varying forms in the coming years. Forsaking his father's reputation for compassion and conciliation, Franklin Graham gave a ringing endorsement to the idea that religion should be a contact sport. This came at a time of fraught emotions when a portion of the country wanted an enemy on which to vent its anger. Muslims fit the bill, as did any group of people that opposed profiling or a ratcheting up of problematic surveillance programs. Franklin Graham fed that animosity, and, by doing so, helped profoundly influence American electoral politics by pushing evangelical voters toward Islamophobia and the political party that convinced them that it was committed to defending the Christian cause, a stand-in for whiteness and Western heritage.

Prior to 9/11, the most distinguishable characteristics of the Eastern Kentucky homes I visited were the University of Kentucky banners and the large plasma-screen television sets tuned to Jerry Springer or reruns of *Law & Order*. Following the terrorist attacks, I noticed a change in decor and viewing habits. The basketball paraphernalia still hung, but it ceded space to American flag displays. The TVs still blared, but the channel of choice became Fox News, which aired continuous updates on the global war on terror, adding a jingoistic angle to whatever news was unfolding.

Franklin Graham and Jerry Falwell, Jr., became fervent supporters of the Republican Party and vocal backers of Donald Trump before and after the 2016 presidential election. Falwell, Jr., the president of Liberty University, an evangelical school that his father cofounded in 1971, claimed that COVID-19 stay-at-home orders in early 2020 had no basis in public health concerns but rather served as another ploy by Trump's political opponents to bring him down. He also speculated that North Korea had created the coronavirus as a biological weapon. In August 2020, Falwell, Jr., took an indefinite leave of absence from Liberty amid controversy over a provocative photo he posted on his Instagram account of himself and a woman on a yacht. Two weeks later, details emerged of a sex scandal involving Falwell, his wife, and a former business partner of theirs, prompting Falwell to resign his posts at Liberty.[28]

Franklin Graham expressed disgust at a June 2020 ruling by the US Supreme Court prohibiting workplace discrimination against gay and transgender people, and went on to be a featured speaker at the August 2020 Republican Convention.

Billy Graham died at the age of ninety-nine in 2018. Two years after he passed away, *Christianity Today*, a publication he founded in 1956, published an essay entitled "Trump Should Be Removed from Office." The column, written by outgoing editor-in-chief Mark Galli, endorsed the House Democrats' case for removal based on Trump's problematic dealings with the Ukrainian government. But Galli also name-checked Billy Graham in offering a scathing critique of how the Ukraine affair offered a window into Trump's character.

Galli wrote, "In our founding documents, Billy Graham explains that *Christianity Today* will help evangelical Christians interpret the news in a manner that reflects their faith. The impeachment of Donald Trump is a significant event in the story of our republic. It requires comment . . . [Trump] has hired and fired a number of people who are now convicted criminals. He himself has admitted to immoral actions in business and his relationship with women, about which he remains proud. His Twitter feed alone—with its habitual string of mischaracterizations, lies, and slanders—is a near perfect example of a human being who is morally lost and confused."[29]

Franklin Graham slammed the editorial and attempted to distance his father from the anti-Trump rhetoric. "My father believed in Donald Trump, supported Donald Trump and he actually voted for Donald Trump, and if he were here today he would tell you that himself," the younger Graham said.[30]

But as Stephen Prothero, a professor of religion at Boston University, wrote in *Politico*, "The qualities of temper and judgment that made Billy Graham so singularly successful are almost entirely lacking in his son, who now imperils his father's legacy. Thanks to Franklin Graham and his cronies on the Religious Right, American evangelicalism has now become first and foremost a political rather than a spiritual enterprise. The life of Billy Graham helped build it up. And his death may well have ensured its demise."[31]

Whenever I think about the role of religion in American society and politics, my mind turns to the day I went to the Graham crusade. I wish I had had an opportunity to write more stories like that one. Too often, newspaper journalism uses people as props, strategically inserting their quotes into a story to break up the monotony of exposition. The Graham story felt different. It involved getting to know some of the people on the bus and trying to convey what mattered most to them at that moment in time.

Wanting to know what mattered today to the boys on the bus brought me back to the parking lot of the Fleming Baptist Church. Pastor McCarty fondly recalled the day we spent together. He informed me that only a few of the people who went to see Billy

Graham remained members of the church. Many had lost their way, he said. Despite doing a lot of asking around, he couldn't tell me what had become of Michael King or Brian Tackett.[32] I didn't have any luck tracking them down, either. King's grandmother, who brought him to church, has since passed away. His father told me he has lost touch with his son and that the last he knew he was working at a Walmart in Lexington.

Religion can provide comfort and inspiration, especially in times of personal turmoil or national grief. It also has the power to divide. I don't think that my Billy Graham companions strayed from the church because they felt Christianity had become too politicized. They likely had other things going on in their lives that pushed religion to the side. Neither Billy Graham nor the local pastor could do anything about that. And that is fine. I didn't expect the day at the crusade to transform their lives. But I hoped to at least find them, if for no other reason than to ask King about the character on his T-shirt. Instead all I got was a message to pass along to him from his father. "If you find him, tell him he owes me money for the guns he took," he said.[33]

Pastor McCarty has made peace with the fact that he and his church can't save everyone. In September 2020, a drug-addicted woman he was trying to help burglarized his home. But he's learned to savor the victories when they come. A few weeks before the burglary, a former congregant of his whom he hadn't seen since childhood popped into the church. The man, whose parents had drug problems, came from Tennessee with his own young children to thank McCarty for what he had done for him and his two siblings. "If it hadn't been for you all, we would have gone to school hungry day after day," the man said.[34]

But the church is only able to reach so many people. With jobs scarce and families and local governments in crisis, many others move on and look elsewhere for something to keep them going.

CHAPTER 6

Bad Nerves

The daily challenges of poverty, addiction, and war that defined Eastern Kentucky in the early days of the new millennium made its inhabitants ideal pawns for a social security attorney who would scam thousands of clients and the US government out of hundreds of millions of dollars. Like so many changes in the region, the story starts on the morning of September 11, 2001.

As was my weekday habit, I was sitting on the couch of my Hazard apartment sipping a cup of morning coffee and flicking back and forth between ESPN's *SportsCenter* and NBC's *Today* show. From my isolated perch, I had come to view both shows as vital lifelines to the outside world. The previous night's sports scores have always been national unifiers. And, silly as it sounds, I liked it when Matt Lauer and Katie Couric broadcast from a set outside of Rockefeller Center, because it gave me a connection to the rhythms of East Coast cities, which had begun to feel like faraway places. On that sunny morning, Al Roker gushed about the beautiful late summer day in New York City. I felt a twinge of nostalgia.

When the first plane hit the World Trade Center, I shared Matt and Katie's confusion. But I was alarmed enough by the oddness of this occurrence to put down the remote control and keep watching. The image seventeen minutes later of a second plane crashing into New York's tallest buildings left little doubt about the sinister intent of the acts. A third plane hitting the Pentagon and a fourth going down in a field in rural Western Pennsylvania confirmed our worst fears.

After checking in with family, I spent the day on the phone with officials from Fort Campbell, home to the Army's 101st Airborne Division, which would play a significant role in the eventual occupation of Iraq. But on 9/11, Fort Campbell was just trying to protect itself against whatever forces had attacked us. The story I contributed to on 9/11 carried the unsensational headline, "Fort Campbell Lockdown Brings Traffic Jam."[1]

In the days that followed, the wire services and newspapers with national reach focused on the grim death toll, the unfolding investigation into who committed the attacks, and the other most consequential parts of the story. Newspapers like mine ran that copy on the front page, but we also looked for ways to localize the tragedy. On my beat, that put me in Eric Conn's Floyd County law office on September 12, as he fought back tears while he reflected on what had happened to the country. He told me that he felt he had a patriotic duty to do whatever he could to help. And he had come up with a plan. He said he was going to indefinitely close his law office so that he and his employees could travel to New York to help with the cleanup effort. "The idea to help came instantly," Conn told me. "I want to let people in New York know that we're part of the same family."[2] Conn, a doughy, fair-haired man of about forty, had already boxed up food and clothing and had chartered a bus. He appeared ready to head north.

This is the kind of story you want to believe, especially during a time of national mourning, and when you're on a tight deadline to produce a feel-good newspaper piece. It captured the anger and sadness of the moment and fit the emerging narrative of American togetherness. And why would anyone fib about wanting to do something benevolent *on the day after* the worst terrorist attack ever on US soil? Nonetheless, I tried to do some fact-checking. I spoke to someone at the American Red Cross who said that the organization did not encourage inexperienced volunteers to go to areas in crisis. In theory, however, nothing could stop Conn and his group from making the trip.

The story ran on page A10 of the paper on September 13. The lead sentence read, "A large iron replica of the Statue of Liberty stands proudly in Eric Conn's office, and the huddled masses that the Floyd County attorney saw on the streets of New York City on Tuesday beckoned him and 17 employees."[3]

My editors asked me to keep tabs on Conn's travel plans. Three months after my trip on the school bus to a Billy Graham crusade, I think they were considering putting me on the bus with Conn to New York, or at the very least documenting the group's departure from Eastern Kentucky. I called Conn's office every day for the next week seeking updates. Someone always answered the phone. But Conn was never available to speak. When I asked if the trip was still happening, I was told that I would need to talk to Eric, who never called me back. I drove to his office a couple of times. Eric was never there.

As far as I could tell, Conn never made the trip. Maybe, as he said, he had made all the arrangements and then common sense kicked in. The people of New York didn't need food and clothing. They needed a sense of security. They needed bodies excavated from the site where the World Trade Center once stood. They needed assurances that the air that they were breathing was clean. And above all, they needed comfort. A busload of Eastern Kentuckians, as well-intentioned as they might have been, would only have gotten in the way of cleanup and recovery efforts. It is also possible, however, that Conn never planned on making the trip and merely saw an opportunity for free publicity in the state's largest and most influential newspaper. If that was the case, shame on him for pulling the hoax . . . and shame on me for falling for it.

As news emerged that many of the 9/11 hijackers had been part of a sleeper cell based in Hamburg, Germany, I couldn't help but feel for the first time since moving to Eastern Kentucky that I was in the wrong place. If I had still worked in the Berlin bureau of *The New York Times*, I would have been in Hamburg digging up information on the movements and activities of Mohamed Atta and his cohorts. Instead I was chasing scraps in the Appalachian Mountains—and misleading ones at that.

But, of course, there were real stories of 9/11 heroism and heartbreak in my extended backyard that emerged as time mournfully carried on. A few days after the attacks, I traveled to Morehead, Kentucky, to attend a vigil for an Eastern Kentucky sailor who was unaccounted for following the attack on the Pentagon. Navy Petty Officer First Class Edward Thomas Earhart, twenty-six, a weather-mapping and computer specialist, didn't have to be in the Pentagon that morning. He had returned early from leave to make sure that some of the Navy's meteorological websites were functioning properly. He was working in a first-floor office when American Airlines Flight 77 crashed into the building. More than 200 people turned out in Earhart's hometown of Morehead to pray for the missing sailor and the nation. Later that week, they found Earhart's body. Another 1,200 people came to his memorial service.[4]

By the time Earhart was laid to rest, President George W. Bush had already declared his war on terror, setting the stage for military intervention in Afghanistan and then Iraq. As is always the case in America's foreign wars, young Eastern Kentuckians rushed off to fight in disproportionally high numbers. For instance, I wrote about Sgt. Leigh Ann Hester, a Kentucky woman who became the first female soldier since World War II to be awarded the Silver Star for heroism. Hester and two other members of her company received the honor for the actions they took when their convoy came under attack from fifty insurgents southeast of Baghdad. But many of Kentucky's sons and daughters didn't make it home alive, including twenty-two-year-old Sgt. Joseph Tackett of Whitehouse, Kentucky, who was killed during his second tour in Iraq in June 2005.

I got to know Tackett's family well as I tried to unravel the circumstances of his death in Baghdad. I read his letters to his mother, Kathy, in which he talked about the war experience and requested that she send him every Chuck Palahniuk novel she could put her hands on. She told me that Joe loved to skateboard and had become pen pals with students at his former elementary school. All the Army would say at first was that he died of a noncombat injury. It took months to get the military to confirm that Joe Tackett wasn't killed on the battlefield, but rather by a US Army officer while the two sat in the "safe haven" of Baghdad known as the Green Zone waiting for a debriefing. The officer who shot Tackett pleaded guilty at a court-martial to negligent homicide and other charges and got eighteen months in the brig.[5] Tackett's parents buried Joseph at a plot in a small family cemetery in Johnson County.

Kathy Tackett died from lung cancer in 2008. Joe's older brother, Sam, has taken over responsibility of the family home. Sam Tackett remembers the day that an Army casualty notification officer came to inform his family about his brother's death. His mother was inconsolable, screaming and pounding her fists on the officer's chest. It stung that the Tacketts never got an apology from the man who took Joe's life, Sam says. He remains bitter about losing his brother during a confused war effort, but he remains a "die-hard Republican" who supports the troops, if not always the higher-ups who oversee the internal investigations. When his teenage stepson recently announced that he wanted to join the Air Force, Sam was thrilled. "My brother went to basic training a baby and came back a man," Sam Tackett says.[6]

*

Amid the triumph and tragedy of war stories, the Eric Conn episode started to fade from memory. Years passed before I even thought about him again. When Conn reentered my consciousness, he left no doubt that he was practiced at the art of deception—on a scale that went far beyond duping newspaper reporters. To understand Conn's most name-worthy con, it is essential to understand the specific local conditions that made it possible for him to get away with his crimes for so long.

A reporter needs to get several basic pieces of information from every interview subject: name, age, occupation, and place of residence. It is important to be able to write that Mary Smith, a thirty-four-year-old accountant from Memphis, said whatever it is that she said. In Eastern Kentucky, I spoke to a lot of people who had jobs but more who didn't. Interestingly, among the latter group, hardly anyone ever referred to themselves as unemployed. Almost always they said that they were disabled and collecting Supplemental Security Income, or as they put it, "SSI." If I was talking to a former coal miner or other worker who I knew got hurt on the job, I let the answer stand because I knew how they had become disabled. But most of the SSI recipients that I encountered had neither suffered a workplace injury nor had any visible signs of infirmity. Among my least favorite tasks as a reporter was getting back in touch with someone I had interviewed to ask a follow-up question from my editors. Having to call someone to ask what was wrong with them most definitely didn't appeal to me, so I got in the habit of addressing the matter while I had the interview subject in front of me.

"What is the nature of your disability?" I would ask, opting for the most direct approach.

And dozens of times the answer came back the same: "Bad nerves."

In terms of frequency, the "bad nerves" response ranked up there with ailing coal miners telling me that their dying wish was to go back in the mines and people commenting that I "talked proper." That is why it surprised me to find that not a single story I wrote featuring people on disability mentioned the term "bad nerves." But then I realized why I had avoided it. Bad nerves isn't a subject that you can just drop into a story. Saying that Mary Smith is an accountant gives us a quick sense of who she is. Saying Mary Smith has bad nerves would only trip up the reader. You either do a deep dive on the subject of bad nerves or you leave it alone. Here is my belated deep dive.

Most of us associate "bad nerves" with adverse reactions to high-stress situations, nothing that a long bath or a little meditation won't cure. But in some pockets of the country, bad nerves are an essential part of local culture, a shorthand way of referring to clinical anxiety or depression. Anyone with a case of bad nerves can go to a doctor for a medical diagnosis and a prescription for a sedative like Valium. Or they can take the process a step further by hiring an attorney like Eric Conn to present the diagnosis to an administrative law judge in the form of a claim for permanent disability benefits.

The number of low-income people and former workers receiving disability nearly doubled in the years following an overhaul of

federal welfare policy in 1996.[7] And in Eastern Kentucky, SSI benefits remain the primary source of income for many people.

The programs are a bureaucratic alphabet soup. There is SSI
and there is also SSDI, Social Security Disability Insurance, both
of which come with Medicaid or Medicare eligibility. To get SSDI,
also known as DIB, or disability insurance benefits, a person needs
to have participated in the workforce for a certain period of time,
and one's level of benefits is based on the number of accrued work
credits. SSI, on the other hand, isn't tied to a person's work history.
In fact, having been employed at any time can actually hurt one's
chances of collecting SSI. A low level of education, little or no work
history, and a diagnosed mental disorder is the most common combination of qualifiers for SSI, which simply put, is Social Security
for people under the age of sixty-five and with a disability. Well
over half of all SSI recipients qualify for benefits because of mental
illness. Children, too, can receive SSI, which had a maximum individual monthly payout of around $800 in January 2020. That year,
more than 8 million people received an average of $577 a month in
SSI benefits. SSDI payments, which go to about 10 million Americans, average nearly twice as much. Nationally, these programs pay
out benefits of close to $200 billion. President Donald Trump's fiscal
year 2021 budget proposed cutting SSI and SSDI spending by about
$45 billion, a line item that, as far as I can tell, didn't get much play
in the Eastern Kentucky media.[8]

Kentuckians, especially Eastern Kentuckians, receive disability
benefits at an alarmingly high rate, a fact that caught the attention
of state regulators, who studied the issue in a 2017 report entitled
*Social Security Disability in Kentucky: The Evolution of Depen-
dence, 1980–2015.* The foreword of the study is a quote from Kentucky's then-acting commissioner of the Department for Income
Support: "This work is offered as a labor of love on behalf of all
Kentuckians. We hope its legacy will contribute to a future wherein
we all live together on our feet rather than survive on our knees."[9]
That is the entire foreword. Pointed language for a numbers-laden
government report.

The study found that Kentucky had the nation's second highest rate of residents receiving some form of disability. In the thirty-five years covered in the report, the state's disability enrollment grew by 249 percent, while the state's population grew by only 21 percent.

The twelve counties in the state with the highest percentage of disability recipients were all in Eastern Kentucky. In some of those counties, close to a quarter of the entire adult and youth population had qualified for disability. The report also found that once Kentuckians go on disability, they tend to stay on it: only one in every thirty people on SSDI and one in every twenty people on SSI return to the workforce after receiving their first disability payment.[10]

The forty-seven-page report falls short of alleging rampant abuse of the system, though its authors do conclude that the disability system has drawn in many people without the type of "genuinely disabling conditions" that would preclude them from working. There is also no mention of "bad nerves." I would like to think that if the authors had actually spoken to anyone receiving disability in Eastern Kentucky that they would have devoted an entire section of the report to the topic.

The "bad nerves" diagnosis is no doubt emblematic of more pervasive emotional and physical health problems in Eastern Kentucky. That is not just an image that is projected on the region by outsiders. A 2014 national survey showed that the congressional district covering Eastern Kentucky ranked last among all 434 districts in people's perception of general health and outlook on life.[11] Many Eastern Kentuckians who have been beaten down physically or mentally don't feel well enough to work. So they turn to the SSI system.

Anxiety and depression are real disabilities. But in Eastern Kentucky, SSI benefits are irreverently (and offensively) known as "crazy checks." I've heard about parents discouraging their children from learning to read so that schools will classify them as mentally disabled. There are also stories about people in Eastern Kentucky who know the SSI system so well that they host sessions at which they counsel friends and neighbors on how to file successful disability claims. Most Appalachian Kentucky counties don't have state unemployment offices, because there isn't enough demand for their services. But I have never seen a Social Security Administration office in Eastern Kentucky without a full parking lot.

Eastern Kentucky's dependence on disability is a symptom of the problem, not the problem itself. I'm not willing to dismiss "bad nerves" as a racket, especially considering that researchers recognize it as a phenomenon that impacts societies with a long history of trauma.

In a 1989 journal article about the high rate of "bad nerves" in Northern Ireland, Jeffrey Sluka wrote, "Although this problem derived from multiple causes—political, economic, and social—terror stands out as the single most important causal factor."[12]

Using a broad definition of "terror," all four of those characteristics apply to poor America, from the mountains of Central Appalachia to the streets of North Philadelphia.

Writing on the website The Root, Dr. Karen Reynolds, a Birmingham, Alabama, physician, discussed the link between urban poverty and bad nerves. "[P]atients frequently complain to me that they have 'bad nerves,' which can sound very nebulous and unspecific. But with some prompting, they will go on to describe anxiety, irritability, insomnia and—very often—a desire to isolate themselves. Sometimes they are tearful, describing losses, fears, persistent stressors. They recount reactions to these issues that sometimes lead to problems with family, relationships, even legal problems."[13]

*

Eric Conn and "bad nerves" are inseparable.

After glorifying him in my first post-9/11 story, Conn's name didn't appear again in the pages of the *Courier-Journal* for another ten years. By that time, he was polishing his reputation as one of the most prolific Social Security disability lawyers in the region. The self-proclaimed "Mr. Social Security" was working on a self-published sixty-page *minimum opus* called *The Social Security*

Disability Code: Cracked. He was also fishing for a presidential appointment to the Social Security Advisory Board, an agency that advises the federal government on Social Security matters. To that end, he enlisted the help of another *Courier-Journal* reporter. This time around, the paper ran a full-blown, front-page profile of Conn in which he made his pitch. "Social security is all I personally do as far as my practice, and it would be nice to be recognized in that capacity," he told the reporter.[14]

Conn tried to get President Barack Obama's attention by releasing a video featuring bluegrass legend Ralph Stanley performing a version of the classic song "Man of Constant Sorrow" alongside Amber Lee Ettinger, who had achieved a modicum of fame back then with her viral Internet persona, Obama Girl. The article gave Conn another platform to promote himself. But thankfully it also included a voice of dissent in the form of a quote from a fellow Eastern Kentucky lawyer who called Conn "a narcissist's narcissist."[15]

Conn didn't get the board appointment. But he did find another way to attract the spotlight. I write about his downfall not out of schadenfreude but because what brought it about is the single best case study of the frustrations and shortcomings of the disability benefits system. But don't take my word for it. Just refer to the 2013 United States Senate committee report entitled *How Some Legal, Medical, and Judicial Professionals Abused Social Security Disability Programs for the Country's Most Vulnerable: A Case Study of the Conn Law Firm.*

As Conn was lobbying Obama, a team of Senate investigators was looking into his growing monopoly on SSI and SSDI cases in Eastern Kentucky, where he had come to represent two out of every three people in the system. The federal government's Social Security Disability Trust Fund was quickly being depleted and the Senate wanted to know if fraud had anything to do with it. The examination of Conn's law practice answered that question with a resounding yes.

The resulting Senate Committee on Homeland Security and Governmental Affairs report[16] was damning. It alleged that Conn used phony medical records to support claims that his clients were unable to work, and that he colluded with a West Virginia–based administrative law judge responsible for a regional docket of cases to get favorable rulings in his cases.

From 2005 to 2011, according to the two-year Senate investigation, Judge David B. Daugherty overturned previous rulings denying lifetime benefits to Conn's clients in all but 18 of the 3,143 appeals cases that came before him, churning through the cases at one of the fastest rates of any administrative law judge in the country.[17] The national approval rate for disability appeals during this period was 60 percent. The Senate report found that Daugherty used a government computer system to ensure that he got assigned as many of Conn's cases as possible. In monthly phone calls between the two men, the judge let Conn know what cases he planned to approve and what documents he needed to make it all look legitimate. Daugherty refused to explain to Senate investigators the origin of tens of thousands of dollars in cash deposits to his bank account between 2005 and 2011.[18]

SSI lawyers work on contingency, receiving a portion of the money awarded to each client. They don't get paid for losing cases. Thanks in large part to Daugherty's intervention in his cases, Conn collected more than $22 million in attorney's fees from the Social Security Administration between 2001 and 2013.[19] Daugherty's favorable rulings for Conn's clients didn't go unnoticed by employees of the Social Security Administration's Huntington, West Virginia, office, Daugherty's home base. Over the course of a decade, some of them took their concerns to Charlie Paul Andrus, the office's chief judge, but Andrus showed little interest and even took steps to silence them. He was rewarded with a promotion.[20]

The scheme, according to the 166-page report, also involved doctors, including Bowling Green, Kentucky–based orthopedist Dr. Frederic Huffnagle, who died before the Senate investigation wrapped up. Huffnagle had a history of malpractice and a lengthy disciplinary record that included revocation of his medical license in New York state. Former Conn employees told investigators that

Conn sought out doctors with troubled histories because they cost less and were more pliable. Huffnagle became Conn's physician of choice when he needed a medical opinion on the decisive question of whether his clients could physically handle holding down a job. Conn paid Huffnagle nearly $1 million in consulting fees from 2006 to 2010 to say time and again that the applicants were unable to work. Huffnagle's evaluations, which took place in a "medical suite" at Conn's law office, varied only slightly from patient to patient.[21] And Daugherty's stamp of approval of those applications differed even less. Almost all included the paragraph, "Having considered all the evidence, I am satisfied that the information provided by Dr. Huffnagle most accurately reflects the claimant's impairments and limitations. Therefore the claimant is limited to less than sedentary work at best."[22] If Daugherty told Conn that he needed a mental evaluation to approve a claim, Conn got in touch with Dr. Brad Adkins, a clinical psychologist in Pikeville. The Senate investigation uncovered evidence that Adkins routinely signed forms filled out by Conn or his employees about a person's medical impairment without performing an examination.

A 2011 *Wall Street Journal* article about Daugherty put Conn and his cohorts on notice that they were being watched, and prompted the group to try to cover its tracks. [23] Emails between Conn and Daugherty went missing. The two men started talking on burner cell phones. Conn hired a shredding company to destroy more than three million pages of documents. And during a multi-day bonfire, a Conn employee burned office computers and hard drives. Meanwhile, over at Daugherty's Huntington office, the Social Security Administration approved the purchase of personal shredders, items that the inspector general's office seized before they could be put to further use.[24]

The Senate committee convened a hearing on the day of the report's release. In an opening statement, Senator Tom Coburn of Oklahoma, the ranking Republican on the Homeland Security and Governmental Affairs committee, lashed out at Conn and his accomplices. "While lawyers (and) doctors were getting rich by exploiting a broken program, the real victims were the claimants and the American taxpayer," Coburn said. "The claimants suffer because we don't do any favors when we wrongly award benefits. While the disability programs have tremendous upside, there is a real risk we needlessly sentence someone to a lifetime of dependency."[25]

Conn asserted his Fifth Amendment rights and declined to testify at the hearing. Despite receiving a subpoena to appear, Daugherty didn't show up at all. Adkins gave a statement in which he claimed to have conducted thorough examinations and that any suspicion that he had acted inappropriately came down to a paperwork problem.

Former Conn employee Jamie Slone told the panel about the cozy relationship between Conn and Daugherty. She said that Conn would ask everyone to leave the room whenever Daugherty called. After the *Wall Street Journal* article ran, Conn allegedly told Slone that he was scared of going to jail. He talked to her about fleeing to Cuba to avoid extradition.

Following the Senate hearing, the Social Security Administration's inspector general concluded that Daugherty had ruled inappropriately in roughly half of Conn's cases. Based on that finding, the agency immediately stopped making payments to about a thousand of Conn's former clients.

Floyd Countian Leroy Burchett was one of the people who lost his SSDI benefits. Burchett had helped work the printing press at a small Eastern Kentucky newspaper before two spinal surgeries made it difficult for him to work anymore. The man nicknamed "Big Daddy" went to see Conn, whose office was located just a few miles from his home, to make a disability claim based primarily on mental illness. Until he received notice that he would no longer receive benefits, Burchett had collected a monthly disability check of $1,063 for five years. It amounted to just enough for him, his wife, Emma, and their three minor children to get by. When the letter from the federal government arrived in May 2015, the forty-one-year-old Burchett became despondent and stopped taking his antidepressants, according to attorney Ned Pillersdorf, the veteran attorney who took on Massey Energy after the devastating Martin County slurry spill, and who has represented Burchett and hundreds of other former Conn clients. Concerned about the emotional well-being of Burchett and others who had their benefits cut off, Pillersdorf took to Facebook. "Very concerned about some of the extremely distressed messages I have been receiving," he wrote. "Don't hesitate to contact medical professional if feeling too overwhelmed. Fully realize how serious this is."[26]

Two days after Pillersdorf's post and ten days after opening the letter from the Social Security Administration, Burchett went into the front yard of his home and shot himself in the chin as his wife and children looked on. He died instantly.[27]

Pillersdorf told me that around three-quarters of his clients collected disability for mental health reasons. "Bad nerves equal significant mental illness," he said. "It's depression and schizophrenia."[28]

In neighboring Martin County, former Conn client Melissa Jude, forty, received the same letter as Burchett. The day after Burchett's suicide, Jude, who had been on SSI for six years for mental health issues, put a gun in her mouth and pulled the trigger.[29] Following news of these suicides, the Social Security Administration abruptly reversed course and reinstated benefits to everyone who received the letter and allowed every former Conn client the right to a hearing at which they would have a chance to show that they had legitimate disability claims.

Conn and Daugherty denied any wrongdoing, but the Senate committee's findings gave criminal investigators a lot to work with. A host of federal agencies, led by the FBI, dove into the case and found that Conn and his associates had pulled off what they believed to be the largest Social Security scam in American history, a series of actions that cheated the federal government out of up to $600 million. The precise dollar figure depended on how many of Daugherty's approvals turned out to be for baseless claims.

According to the April 2016 federal indictment against him, Conn pulled the same swindle over and over again, with the help of Daugherty, Adkins, and the late Huffnagle. The indictment accused

Conn of paying Adkins up to $450 per patient to fraudulently sign forms attesting to a patient's claimed disability. It alleged that in exchange for kickbacks of around $600,000, Daugherty saw to it that any of Conn's clients who were initially denied benefits would gain approval on appeal. Conn was also accused of destroying clients' medical records and other evidence of the scam after he learned of the federal investigation.

In a separate legal action, a federal grand jury indicted Judge Andrus on one count of conspiracy to retaliate against a witness. The charge stemmed from Andrus hiring a private investigator to surveil the Social Security Administration employee who blew the whistle on Daugherty and Conn. Andrus pleaded guilty and was sentenced to six months in federal prison.

Notably, not a single one of Conn's clients was accused of knowingly participating in any crimes. Congressman Hal Rogers later referred to them as the victims of a scheme by Conn "that preyed on disabled residents, manipulated their trust, and turned their plights into his own financial gain."[30]

It was going to take years to sort through the disability claims of Conn's former clients, to clean up the unholy mess that the lawyer, doctors, and judge had made. But the prosecution of the main players in the conspiracy moved briskly and appeared to be heading toward a tidy resolution.

A year after the indictment, Conn, whose defense team included a former chief justice of the Kentucky Supreme Court, entered a guilty plea that called for twelve years in prison and a promise by Conn to cooperate with prosecutors in securing convictions against Daugherty and Adkins. A few weeks later, Daugherty also took a plea deal and received a four-year prison sentence. In his plea, Daugherty admitted to soliciting bribes from Conn starting in 2004.[31]

Adkins took his chances by going to trial. He ended up paying for it. A jury found him guilty in June 2017 of signing bogus mental-health evaluations for Conn's clients and pocketing about $200,000 for doing so. The psychologist's sentence? Twenty-five years.[32] Questions of fairness aside, the cases illustrate the realities of the United States justice system. There is a reason that more than 95 percent of federal criminal cases end in guilty pleas. Adkins rolled the dice on an acquittal at trial and lost.

Conn didn't testify at the Adkins trial, but not because prosecutors made a strategic decision to exclude him from the proceedings. They didn't call him because they couldn't find him. No one could. Two months after his guilty plea and a few days before the start of the trial, the fifty-seven-year-old Conn cut off his ankle bracelet, escaped house arrest, and went on the lam. The FBI tracked him as far as New Mexico, where agents found an abandoned getaway vehicle and surveillance photos of Conn at a gas station near Albuquerque and at a Walmart less than an hour's drive from the US-Mexico border. Disappointed, the agents realized that all Conn had to do was ride like the wind to be free again. A nationwide search turned into an international manhunt.

Back in Kentucky, Conn was sentenced in absentia to twelve years in prison and ordered to pay $72 million in restitution to the government for his involvement in the disability scam.[33] Time would tell how many more years would get tacked onto his sentence for becoming a fugitive from justice. But first, authorities had to locate him. The FBI offered a $20,000 reward for information leading to Conn's capture.

Almost anyone else in Conn's situation would have tried to remain out of sight. But ever the showman, Conn couldn't resist dropping bread crumbs for the police and media to follow. He sent a cryptic email to newspaper reporters and others in which he negotiated the terms of his surrender but also complained about having received a longer prison sentence than either of the two judges charged in the case. Far from showing contrition, he expressed indignation about the way he had been treated.

"Tell me how it is reasonable that the federal government takes such good care of its own corrupt federal judges and aggressively goes after me demanding a protracted sentence," Conn wrote in the email sent to the *Lexington Herald-Leader*. "I fail to see any justice in this. On the contrary, I see patent injustice."[34]

Conn accused federal prosecutors of giving preferential treatment to the "country's political class" while treating the "politically powerless" with disdain. The email quoted the Roman philosopher Seneca: "For nothing is more common than for great thieves to ride in triumph while small ones are punished."[35]

For the next six months after that, Conn went quiet. How he ended up in the depths of Central America remains a mystery. But that is where a Honduran SWAT team surrounded him and took him into custody outside of a Pizza Hut restaurant in December 2017. If Conn had managed to hop the border to less extradition-friendly Nicaragua, he might still be on the run.

At his sentencing in September 2018, Conn finally admitted to his mistakes, sounding like a man who was angling for as lenient a sentence as possible. "For a man who wanted to do a lot of good in life, I've done a lot of wrong," he said. "An apology can't right the wrongs I've done, but I think it's a good start."[36]

US District Judge Danny Reeves sentenced Conn to an additional fifteen years in prison, bringing the total number of years he would serve behind bars to twenty-seven. It emerged that someone helped Conn flee Kentucky. Curtis Lee Wyatt, of Raccoon, Kentucky, pleaded guilty to aiding Conn's escape by scouting security measures along the US-Mexico border and providing Conn with an escape vehicle purchased with cash in Montana. Wyatt was convicted for his role in the escape and served seven months in jail.[37]

Conn's replica of the Statue of Liberty, the one I mentioned in my post-9/11 article, went up for auction. So did a nineteen-foot-tall statue of a seated Abraham Lincoln that Conn commissioned to be placed outside his office in 2009.

Attorney Pillersdorf, whose many tangles with polluting coal companies and other wrongdoers had heightened his fighting spirit, appreciated the symbolic value of the seizure of Conn's items. "There's always been a lot of consternation around here because you have the greatest Kentuckian, Abraham Lincoln, linked to Eric Conn, who is not the greatest Kentuckian ever," Pillersdorf said in a television interview. "Finally we will be able to free Abraham Lincoln from Conn's law office."[38]

Conn is scheduled to be released from a federal prison in Bruceton Mills, West Virginia, in November 2040. I wrote him a letter in 2020 reintroducing myself and included a copy of the article I wrote about him. I didn't ask him about the series of events that landed him in prison. I just wanted to know if he ever intended to go to New York in the days after 9/11. He didn't respond.

*

Pillersdorf's fight to permanently restore disability benefits to Conn's former clients has been draining, but he has never wavered in his assertion that these people are victims of a crime. "There is zero evidence that any Conn client knew what was going on," he says.[39] Congressman Rogers has been a helpful advocate. Kentucky Senator Mitch McConnell has declined to get involved, despite being asked to do so.

Pillersdorf has the bravado of a skilled trial lawyer, but it is much easier to take what he is saying as the truth considering that much of the time he isn't receiving a dime for his legal services. He and legendary Eastern Kentucky attorney John Rosenberg recruited pro bono lawyers from the firm WilmerHale and volunteers to help sift through more than 3,000 of Conn's cases. When the task proved too immense for the group, Pillersdorf turned to law students from Vanderbilt University, his undergraduate alma mater, and other schools to comb through clients' medical records to prove they suffer from the conditions they sought benefits for.

I know that Pillersdorf took Conn's actions personally. Not only because Conn screwed over thousands of vulnerable people, but also because he besmirched the legal profession in the process. Enriching the rich and impoverishing the poor runs antithetical to everything Ned has stood for during his decades-long career in Eastern Kentucky, where he has a reputation as an attorney who does more than just take depositions, file briefs, and make arguments in court. He realized that the disability debacle had further imperiled the physical and mental health of an already at-risk population. Following the suicides of two former Conn clients, a psychologist friend told Pillersdorf that more tragedy could be prevented if others seeking to regain their benefits received messages of support, and not just ominous letters from the US government.

Pillersdorf took that advice to heart. Through almost-daily Facebook posts with the heading "Eric Conn fiasco update," he kept his clients informed about any and all developments in the case. A sample post from February 2018: "Eric Conn fiasco update-out of a deep concern that the additional 2000 former Conn clients who are receiving letters from the SSA and are not submitting medical evidence within 30 days - I have purchased advertising time WYMT to get the word out. Send in your medical records-you might avoid a hearing and save your benefits!"[40] Other posts warned former Conn clients of telephone scammers who were trying to take advantage of the situation by posing as Social Security Administration officials. An attorney billing by the hour likely wouldn't have taken this step, let alone one offering his services at no cost.

Case by case, he led the effort to help get benefits restored to all that deserved them. Between 2015 and 2018, around 1,500 of Conn's former clients participated in the Social Security Administration's "redetermination hearings." Less than half of those people had their benefits restored. But Pillersdorf remained on the offensive and got those hearings ruled unconstitutional on the grounds that the applicants were denied the opportunity to show that their original disability claims had merit. That set off another round of litigation that returned benefits to several hundred more people. Meanwhile, these more thorough redetermination hearings continue to take place.

Was every single one of Conn's clients an unwitting pawn in what went down? I'm not so sure. The criminal enterprise he took part in was a logical extension of the "pill mill" culture in Eastern Kentucky that flooded communities with prescription drugs. The people who went to Conn's "disability mill" certainly needed help, but some needed more than the kind that a monthly disability check could provide.

Eric Conn painstakingly cultivated a larger-than-life persona, but a true accounting of his legacy shows that he is Eastern Kentucky in miniature. While companies like Purdue Pharma could take advantage of the region's desperation, an Eric Conn or a corrupt local politician could capitalize on the resulting instability. While this type of grift is all too common in Appalachia's most troubled region, it is merely a symptom of its larger problem: too few advocates in positions of power, acting too late, in bad faith, or not at all.

CHAPTER 7

Poison Politics

It almost sounds like a joke:

Did you hear the one about the US senator who cared about unsafe working conditions in Eastern Kentucky coal mines?

Yeah, he was from Minnesota.

But anyone with a historical knowledge of Kentucky's congressional delegation, the power structure of the state, and the influence of money in politics could distinguish a punchline from a strange reality.

Kentucky has never elected anyone from the state's coalfields to the US Senate. John Sherman Cooper, a Republican who spent two full terms and three partial terms in the Senate between 1946 and 1973, came from just beyond the mountains in Pulaski County. Cooper had the poverty of the region on his mind when he sponsored legislation that created the Appalachian Regional Commission in 1965. But ever since Cooper left the Senate to become the US ambassador to East Germany, the coal miners and other working people of Eastern Kentucky have lacked a true voice in the upper house of Congress. In the early 2000s, that voice came from an unlikely source: Senator Paul Wellstone, a Minnesota Democrat who represented a constituency more than a thousand miles away.

Wellstone was a forty-five-year-old political science professor at Carleton College in Northfield, Minnesota when he mounted an insurgent bid for the Senate in 1990. He campaigned on the cheap, traveling around the state in a broken-down green school bus with a speaker mounted on top. Despite being massively outspent by incumbent Republican Rudy Boschwitz, Wellstone rode a wave of grassroots support to victory.

Wellstone's affinity for Eastern Kentucky developed after he met his future wife, Sheila, whose family came from the community of Kingdom Come in Letcher County. Sheila Wellstone was born an Ison, one of the handful of last names that heavily populate the local phone book there. Sheila's parents moved from Eastern Kentucky during her childhood, but she never lost her connection to the area. And what she told her husband about its struggles left an impression on him.

Though it wasn't going to win him any votes in Minnesota, Wellstone traveled to Eastern Kentucky once he became a senator to tour non-union coal mines, talk with residents at town hall meetings, and get an up-close look at what his wife had observed growing up. While Kentucky Senator Mitch McConnell was asking coal operators for political donations, Wellstone was listening to what coal miners had to say about working conditions. Wellstone's trips to the region convinced him that the national Democratic Party needed to do more outreach to a forgotten group of Appalachian voters.

Wellstone's advocacy for Central Appalachia grew in response to the *Courier-Journal*'s award-winning 1998 *Dust, Deception and Death* series that found evidence that the mining industry was cheating on coal-dust tests. Speaking at a Senate hearing on the subject, Wellstone said, "This alleged cheating, of which there appears to be nearly incontrovertible evidence, apparently has led to much unnecessary suffering in thousands of American families. It likely also has led to the unnecessary death from black lung disease of thousands of American coal miners."[1]

In 2001, Wellstone became the chairman of the Senate panel that oversees coal mine safety. In that capacity, he questioned why so few disabled miners were qualifying for black lung benefits and battled with the US Mine Safety and Health Administration when it whitewashed its investigation of the Martin County slurry spill. McConnell and fellow Kentucky Republican Senator Jim Bunning remained silent on these issues.

Then, just like that, Wellstone's voice was lost forever. In October 2002, less than two weeks before his potential reelection to the Senate, he, his wife, their daughter, and five others were en route to an election debate when their plane went down in Eveleth, Minnesota. All eight died.

Writing in the Whitesburg *Mountain Eagle* a few days after Wellstone's death, Tony Oppegard, Kentucky's most prominent mine-safety advocate, memorialized Wellstone:

> He understood that miners must work in dark, wet and cramped conditions, and worry about the mine roof falling or methane or coal dust exploding. And, keeping his pledge to the miners he had met, he worked diligently to make the mines safer. Determined that coal miners should not have to risk their lives in order to provide for their loved ones, he repeatedly spoke out for better mine safety and health protections and for greater accountability from both coal companies and the federal mine safety agency. Indeed, Paul Wellstone was the only true champion of the coal miner in the U.S. Senate.[2]

Senators Amy Klobuchar and Elizabeth Warren are among the politicians who consider Wellstone a mentor.

*

Born in the mountains of Eastern Kentucky on the Fourth of July, 1960, Daniel Mongiardo was no Paul Wellstone, but he, too, had aspirations of toppling Kentucky and the nation's political establishment.

Like a lot of states, Kentucky has had its share of highly influential political families: the many Breckinridges (one vice president, two senators, six representatives, one cabinet member), the three John Y. Browns (one representative, one governor, one Kentucky secretary of state), Happy and Ben Chandler (one governor, one representative), and more recently, Steve and Andy Beshear (both governors). The Pauls don't make the list because, despite benefiting from his father Ron's presidential run and time in Congress, Senator Rand Paul is a Kentucky transplant.

Even in the absence of close family ties, there is often only a degree or two of separation between Kentucky's political elites.

Mongiardo didn't come from anything close to a powerful or well-connected family. His grandfather, Vincent Mongiardo, was an Italian immigrant who came to Eastern Kentucky in 1910 to work as a stonemason. Vincent Mongiardo's brother, Frank, also immigrated to the United States around this time and "shortened" his surname to what he believed was the more American sounding "Majority." Vincent returned for a time to Italy where he met his wife. They had a son named Jimmy, who left Mussolini-era Italy with his mother when he was in the fifth grade to join Vincent in Eastern Kentucky. As a high school student, Jimmy Mongiardo bought a small grocery store in the Hazard area that he and later his wife, Katherine, whom he met in Italy in the 1950s, owned for many decades. Along the way, Jimmy Mongiardo became a pioneer in the cable television business in Eastern Kentucky.[3] For most of his ninety-three years on earth, Jimmy spoke English with an improbable Italian-Appalachian accent.

Jimmy and Katherine Mongiardo had four children, including a firstborn son named Dominick, who died when he was just twenty-nine days old. A doctor who examined Dominick a day before his death sent the family home with a lazy diagnosis. The infant's constant crying, the doctor said, was a result of his parents spoiling him.[4]

Dominick's death from suspected heart problems weighed heavily on his younger brother, Daniel. Though his grieving parents didn't share their feelings with him, he knew they blamed their son's death on poor medical care in Eastern Kentucky. Every day he saw a framed photo of his late brother and wondered what he could do to save other parents from what his went through. Before the age of ten, he made it his goal to become a doctor.[5]

After receiving his medical degree from the University of Kentucky, Mongiardo returned home and embraced the role of country doctor, or in his case, ear, nose, and throat surgeon.

In Hazard, he helped launch a free health clinic and served as chief of staff of the local medical center. He found fulfillment in treating patients and being involved in hospital administration, but the death of his mother from colon cancer at the age of forty-seven prompted him to reflect on whether he might have a second calling in life. Suspecting that her cancer was caused by contaminated well water in Eastern Kentucky, Mongiardo resolved to find a way to influence public policy related to rural healthcare and other issues. He started by reaching out to local elected officials. But they didn't call him call back. This irritated Mongiardo, who came to the conclusion that most politicians only show an interest in others when asking for donations and votes. He had no mentor or political role model. He didn't follow politics. He was a Democrat only because his father served on a local Democratic committee. But he thought he could do better than the politicians who wouldn't return his calls. His father's only advice to him was, "Be careful. In politics, your best friend will stab you in the back."[6]

In 2000, Mongiardo, bumping up against forty years old, launched a bid for the Kentucky state Senate. He dumped $100,000 of his own money into the campaign, an exorbitant amount for that type of race, saturating the local airwaves with political ads promising better education, health care, and early childhood programs. Mongiardo beat the Democratic incumbent in the primary and went on to win the seat.

The president of the Kentucky Senate, a Republican named David Williams, assigned Mongiardo to a pair of key health-care committees. As one of his first official acts, Mongiardo requested a study into the need for a cancer research center in Eastern Kentucky.

Feeling he was owed a political favor in return for the committee appointments, Williams thought he could count on Mongiardo to work with Republicans. Then came a highly partisan debate over a campaign financing bill that Williams wanted Mongiardo to support. But the Hazard doctor had reservations about the wording of the bill.

"I'll vote for it if you make the changes," Mongiardo told him.

"No, I'm not going to change anything," Williams shot back. "I've invested a lot in you and I expect a return on my investment."[7]

Mongiardo wouldn't budge. The two men never had a kind word for each other after that.

Mongiardo had barely had a chance to familiarize himself with the inner workings of state government when a bizarre redistricting plan put his nascent political career in jeopardy.

The Hazard physician still had two years left on his four-year term when Williams and Senate Republicans pushed through a plan that resulted in Mongiardo automatically representing a new constituency, one that was hundreds of miles north of his home town of Hazard. And now this newly drawn district that included his own county in Eastern Kentucky would be holding an election. This raised the prospect of a loophole in which he might end up holding two seats and casting two pivotal votes in the state Senate if he won the new gerrymandered seat and decided to hold onto the existing one. Mongiardo said at the time that he had every intention of doing just that, prompting Williams to complain, "One of him is quite enough."[8]

*

Prior to his 2002 state Senate campaign, I knew Mongiardo from his involvement in efforts to educate the public about the addictive nature of prescription painkillers and for his advocacy for a small Eastern Kentucky town called Saul that had been cut off from the rest of the region by an Army Corps of Engineers project that created a popular local lake. I would run into him from time to time around Hazard, usually at the Food City supermarket or at Applebee's. He was an unassuming guy, not the type you imagined would be interested in mixing it up with adversaries in the cutthroat world of state politics. He was never going to win office on the strength of his personality or with rousing stump speeches. In fact, he confessed he had a fear of public speaking. But beneath the placid surface, he clearly had a sense of purpose. And his antagonistic relationship with Williams fed his ambition. "If David had left me alone, no one would have known who Daniel Mongiardo was," he says.[9]

I had an opportunity to study Mongiardo the politician during the bizarre 2002 post-redistricting campaign that he never expected having to mount. He was running against a good ol' boy from Harlan County named Johnnie L. Turner, an attorney who was considered the odds-on favorite to win the race. Turner was finishing up his first term as a state representative and seemed poised to benefit from the redrawing of the Senate district to include Republican-dominated Leslie County.

As a state rep, Turner had cosponsored important legislation that eased draconian rules for receiving state black-lung benefits. But I had known him in his role as the attorney for the Harlan County school board. It was Turner who gave legal advice when a Harlan County high school transformed the teacher's lounge into a prayer chapel. In reporting that story, I could tell that Turner, the private citizen, had no problem with the chapel. But Turner, the attorney, had to be mindful of potentially costly litigation being threatened by the American Civil Liberties Union. The chapel ultimately closed. I don't think Turner liked being put in a position where he had to choose between a popular local cause and constitutional law. And he resented me and my big-city newspaper as much as he did the ACLU for meddling in Harlan County's business.

Due to its unusual circumstances, the Mongiardo-Turner race received significantly more attention than it would have otherwise. That helped raise Mongiardo's profile, and established him as an irritant to the state Republican Party. The most memorable moment of the campaign came when Turner ran a provocative television ad criticizing Mongiardo for opposing a bill in the state legislature that would have made it more difficult for non-US citizens to obtain Kentucky driver's licenses. It was an odd line of attack considering that Turner had also voted against the bill, arguing that it would unfairly punish noncitizen military members and their families. But logic aside, there was a clear strategy at play. The ad, which ran a little more than a year after the September 11 terrorist attacks, noted that the 9/11 hijackers had obtained licenses from various states, and it featured out-of-context quotes from Mongiardo that included, "The acts of

9/11 were probably the most brilliant act of war ever conceived." The ad concluded with Mongiardo saying, "9/11 will pass."[10]

If the ad had merely invoked Mongiardo's words, it would have generated controversy. The country was still in the process of healing and making an effort to put up a united front that crossed party lines. No politicians anywhere dared use 9/11 imagery in political ads, especially not to attack an opponent. But Turner's TV spot went a step further by showing a photo of Mongiardo and playing his words before cutting to an image of 9/11 ringleader Mohamed Atta. The message seemed apparent. Mongiardo's dark hair, dark eyes, and olive skin gave him a passing resemblance to a very bad person who represented what some Eastern Kentuckians felt was a wicked religion. Mongiardo felt the ad crossed a line of decency, but what most wounded him about it was how it affected his father, who as child had endured his share of xenophobia after moving from Italy to Kentucky. The elder Mongiardo cried when he saw the spot.[11]

The *Courier-Journal's* ace political reporter Al Cross and I co-wrote a front-page story about the ad. Al and the other reporters on our state capital desk excelled at covering all aspects of Kentucky politics, including the dirty side. And who doesn't enjoy a little drama and theater in their politics? Mindful of his competitor's dilemma involving the high school chapel, Mongiardo, a Catholic, punched back with a television ad touting his own support of prayer in public schools and the posting of the Ten Commandments in public buildings. Score one for Mongiardo and his consultants, who answered a slick piece of xenophobia with a clever bit of religious pandering.

As I said, Daniel Mongiardo was no Paul Wellstone, nor did he present himself as a progressive of any stripe. He supported mountaintop removal mining with comments like, "Let's not call it mountaintop removal. Let's call it what it is, mountaintop development."[12] He, like most of his constituents, was pro-life. He twice voted against Bill Clinton because of concerns over Hillary Clinton's approach to health-care reform.[13] And in the most politically calculated move of his career, he cosponsored legislation in 2004 that led to a state constitutional amendment banning same-sex marriages.

The amendment and others like it were later invalidated by the US Supreme Court.

In most other parts of the country, Mongiardo would have been considered a moderate Republican—but he never seemed the dogmatic type. He struck me as an independent thinker who cared about the needs of the people of Eastern Kentucky. During his race against Turner, the soft-spoken physician from Hazard demonstrated a knack and an affinity for the hand-to-hand combat of electoral politics.

After doing the math and realizing that he could defeat Turner as long as he didn't get trounced in Leslie County, Mongiardo made it his goal to personally introduce himself to all 10,000 people in that county. Traversing the rural community by foot was out of the question, so he bought a four-wheeler to zoom up and down the hollers to meet voters. In an appeal for votes, he promoted the idea that Eastern Kentucky could become the ATV trail capital of America because it had leveled its mountains. Despite a rising number of ATV deaths in Kentucky, owning one or more off-road vehicles helped mark one as a real Eastern Kentuckian. Turner owned four of them and had sponsored a bill to allow the vehicles to travel on public roads.

Mongiardo's ATV tour helped. To the surprise of many, he handily defeated Turner, by a two-to-one margin, in November 2002. Mongiardo came up short in Leslie County by only a handful of votes while performing strongly in the more populous Harlan and Perry Counties. Following his victory, Mongiardo made the Republican-controlled Senate sweat by renewing his threat to hold onto both the Seventeenth and Thirtieth District Senate seats, at least until he went up for reelection in his Northern Kentucky district in two years. He let his adversaries stew over that possibility for a month before announcing he would resign the Northern Kentucky seat. Turner, for his part, kept at it, finally winning a state Senate seat in 2020. A few weeks after his victory, a disgruntled tenant burned down an apartment building in downtown Harlan owned by Turner and that housed his law office.

The victory over Turner elevated Mongiardo's stature within the Kentucky Democratic Party and thrust his name into the mix of potential candidates for higher office. Mongiardo wasn't the party's first choice to take on US Senator Jim Bunning in 2004. Far from it. Two-term governor Paul Patton had been the presumptive Democratic challenger until becoming mired in scandals, most notably an extramarital affair that included an accusation that he had abused the power of his office by helping his mistress get state approval on a business matter. That allegation resulted in a conviction for the mistress but no charges against Patton.[14] Still, the scandal all but ended Patton's political career. Two other prominent state Democrats, including an incumbent congressman, passed on the race, leaving Mongiardo as the next best option, even though he remained a relative unknown outside of Eastern Kentucky. Up until his name was thrust into the US Senate conversation, Mongiardo says he had never considered seeking federal office. He figured it would be enough of a challenge to work to get health-care reforms on the state level. But when proposals like creating a state network of electronic medical recordkeeping got rebuffed in the Kentucky legislature, he decided he might as well try to take his ideas to Congress.[15]

Mongiardo faced scant opposition in the Democratic primary, but that didn't prevent the race from being tinged with a dose of quirkiness. The only other candidate running in the primary was a businessman named David L. Williams, a "perennial candidate" who ran time and again for various offices but never came close to winning. But in the lead-up to the Senate primary, Kentucky voters could have been forgiven for thinking that Williams was someone else altogether given that his first name, last name, and his middle initial matched that of the Republican president of the state Senate. Granted, it didn't make a lick of sense that a Republican would be running in a Democratic primary, but it also defied logic that Mongiardo could have simultaneously held two state Senate seats. A *Courier-Journal* poll conducted before the primary showed that Mongiardo and the "other" David L. Williams had the same level of name recognition.

Despite any confusion over the names, Mongiardo easily defeated Williams and moved on to face Bunning, a Northern Kentucky Republican with an impressive resume that included one term in the US Senate, six terms in the US House of Representatives, and election to the National Baseball Hall of Fame. Bunning, a stalwart pitcher for teams in both the American and National Leagues, was perhaps best known as a ballplayer for pitching a perfect game on Father's Day in 1964. He was an early leader in the baseball players' union, though later in life he would become a bitter foe of organized labor. Before he retired from the game, he showed a proclivity for politics by heading up a group of like-minded jocks called "Athletes for Nixon."

It was an inauspicious year to be challenging a Republican incumbent in a down-ballot race, especially in Kentucky. Patton's scandals had hurt the Democrats. And George W. Bush, a wartime president of a country still addled by the attacks of 9/11, appeared well positioned to defeat the Democratic challenger, Senator John Kerry. The implausibility of Mongiardo's candidacy prompted a writer at the *Cook Political Report* to comment, "It's like one day playing Pop Warner football and the next day trying out for the Washington Redskins."[16] Like the nickname of Washington's football team, the print version of the *Cook Political Report* is no longer with us.

On paper, the Bunning-Mongiardo race screamed mismatch. Bunning's extreme conservatism played well in most parts of the commonwealth. And a right-leaning, Eastern Kentucky Democrat like Mongiardo didn't seem like a candidate who could drive the vote in Kentucky's urban centers of Louisville and Lexington. On top of that, the Bunning campaign had an impressive war chest. By the summer of 2004, Bunning had raised $6 million, a record amount at the time for a US Senate race in Kentucky.[17]

The national Democratic Party had largely written off the race, creating cash problems for Mongiardo. He kicked in some of his own money to keep the campaign afloat, and like he did two years earlier in Leslie County, he started barnstorming for votes, this time in a Chevy Suburban, attending picnics, cookouts, and any other public gatherings he could find.

Out on the road, Mongiardo found an opening he could exploit. The physician from Hazard began contrasting his relative youth and energy with Bunning's increasing lack of lucidity and vigor. To put it in baseball terms, as the 2004 campaign wore on, it became apparent that the seventy-three-year-old Bunning had lost his fast-ball. Taking a page from Johnnie L. Turner's playbook, Bunning commented publicly that Mongiardo resembled one of Saddam Hus-sein's sons. Bunning's campaign manager gave a proto-Trumpian non-apology apology for the comment: "We're sorry if this joke, which got a lot of laughs, offended anyone."[18] Bunning's blunders and odd statements continued. He seemed unaware of major current events and admitted that he hadn't read a newspaper in many weeks. He got extremely agitated when a Rotary Club member in the town of Paducah challenged him about the nation's military preparedness. He accused Mongiardo staff of trying to physically abuse his wife at a political event. He became increasingly reliant on teleprompters. It got to the point where he enlisted a fleet of bodyguards to physically come between him and reporters in public, cementing a contentious relationship with the press that dated back to his baseball-playing days.

"He was the pitcher, the guy in charge, the man in command, but there was a reason that the Veterans Committee, and not the writ-ers, voted him into the Hall of Fame," says Al Cross, the dean of Kentucky political journalism.[19]

As his 2004 Senate campaign entered the late innings, Bunning decided to skip a televised debate, allowing an abbreviated version of the event to go on anyway with Mongiardo getting thirty minutes of free airtime to further introduce himself to voters.

A *Courier-Journal* editorial questioned Bunning's mental compe-tence: "Is he, as he ages, just becoming a more concentrated version of himself: more arrogant, more prickly? . . . Or is his increasing belligerence an indication of something worse? Has Sen. Bunning drifted into territory that indicates a serious health concern?"[20]

By 2021 standards, none of Bunning's actions seem all that out of the ordinary. Every one of the above behaviors, with the exception of skipping out on a televised event, is Trump-like. A comment about an opponent's physical appearance that is weaponized for political purposes? Check. Getting information exclusively from right-wing media and condemning all other sources as "fake news"? Check. Heated exchanges with reporters and other adversaries? Check. But by the political rules of 2004, Bunning's behavior struck even Republicans as abnormal. And some started taking a closer look at Mongiardo.

Sensing trouble ahead, Bunning's surrogates joined in the attacks on his Democratic challenger. Kentucky Senate President David L. Williams (the "known" one) used homophobic dog whistles when referring to Mongiardo, who was forty-four and unmarried at the time. In praising Kentucky's Republican duo of Bunning and McConnell, Williams said, "We don't want to trade that one-two punch for a limp wrist." Williams also referred to Mongiardo as a political "switch-hitter." And another GOP state senator questioned whether "the word 'man' applies to him." [21]

Bunning continued to play up Mongiardo's otherness and tried to tar him as a "Medicaid millionaire" who had profited from treating poor patients in Eastern Kentucky. Bunning's lead in the polls, which stood at 17 percent in September 2004, dwindled to just six points the week before the election. Mongiardo, the political novice in the race only because no other higher-profile Democrat chose to run, seemed to have a chance to pull off a shocking upset.

If that came to pass, I was going to be there—sort of. On election night, which is always an all-hands-on-deck event for newspapers, my editors assigned me to cover the Kentucky Republican Party's rally at the Marriott Cincinnati Airport in Hebron, Kentucky. The hotel was a little ways down Interstate 275 from where Bunning had tossed his first baseball as a kid. When I entered the hotel ballroom shortly after polls closed at 6:00 p.m. it was just me, a smattering of well-dressed Republicans, and a pack of TV camerapeople setting up equipment. A muted cheer rippled across the room when early returns indicated that Bush would win going away in Kentucky. Over the next couple of hours, the room started to fill up with a lot of young operatives carrying Bunning signs and a lot of older people wandering around looking for hands to shake. I felt a pang of nerves, probably a reaction to all of the pent-up energy in the room, but also because I knew there was a lot at stake that night for Kentucky and the nation.

Throughout the event, I kept my eyes glued to the big-screen televisions that were broadcasting results. The early returns from Louisville, Lexington, and some southeastern Kentucky counties pushed Mongiardo out to an early lead. The restlessness at the hotel turned into a discernible sense of angst as a growing line of people stood at the cash bar looking for an elixir to take the edge off. The presidential race between Bush and Kerry was also shaping up to be tight. After the election night debacle of 2000, when all of the major TV networks projected Al Gore winning Florida before later retracting the claim, the media were treading carefully with their pronouncements this time around. In 2004, Ohio stood in for Florida. The winner of Ohio, where the race was too close to call, would win the White House.

As we waited for the final tallies, I talked to some Republican dignitaries who told me they felt optimistic that Bunning would pull out a victory once a more complete set of results came in from his home region of Northern Kentucky and from conservative Western Kentucky. They were right. At close to midnight, Bunning had pulled out to enough of a lead to claim victory. He received 50.7 percent of the vote. Mongiardo got 49.3 percent.

That day, Kentucky voters overwhelmingly approved the amendment banning same-sex marriages and invalidating civil unions. Al Cross says that Mongiardo, who cosponsored the state bill that put the amendment up to a vote, might have defeated Bunning if it hadn't been on the ballot.[22] The amendment helped drive Republican turnout to the polls, he says. Mongiardo later came to regret his involvement with the issue. "I did it with an eye toward running for the Senate, and I'm ashamed of it," he says.[23]

In his concession speech the night he lost to Bunning, Mongiardo reflected on an election in which he received more votes than any Kentucky Democrat in state history. "Only in America can a skinny kid with a funny last name from the mountains of Appalachia do anything close to what I have done in the past year," Mongiardo said from a subdued Lexington hotel ballroom.[24]

In Northern Kentucky, a loud roar went up after the announcement of the results. A short time later, a victorious Bunning strode to the stage to address his supporters. My most important task of the night required me to try to get a quote from him for the morning paper. I slipped by one of his bodyguards but was intercepted by another who carved out a path for Bunning to the podium. Not wanting to disappoint my editors, I stepped up on the front of the stage. Bunning was there hugging supporters and waving to others when I came face to face with him. He asked me who I was. I told him I was a reporter for the *Courier-Journal*. His smile turned to a scowl and he nudged me aside.

The Republicans had much to celebrate that night. Bush won Ohio and a second term as president. And the GOP kept its majority in both the House and Senate.

*

I had been an avid follower of electoral politics since the Reagan era, and the 2004 Senate race in Kentucky gave me a lot to think about, especially when considering it alongside that year's presidential election which solidified the blue/red divide in America. Political campaigns have always been ugly, but it seemed that the tone and tactics employed in 2004 brought the country several steps closer to the death of civility in politics, to a place where a unified vision for the future took a back seat to divisiveness and personal smears.

It was the year that three-time Purple Heart recipient Kerry, a former swift-boat captain in Vietnam, had his character assassinated in a series of political ads created by a group called "Swift Vets and POWs for Truth." In the spots, fellow veterans accused

Kerry of inflating his war record and questioned his patriotism for engaging in antiwar activism after completing his tour of duty. Bush, who had his own Vietnam-era service record to defend, criticized the ads, but only after they had repeatedly run on network television. Before Kerry got "swiftboated" in the summer of 2004, he led Bush in most polls. The war in Iraq wasn't going well and the economy was struggling. By summer's end, however, Bush had regained a solid advantage over his Democratic opponent. Kerry chose not to dignify the attack ads by directly responding to them. And by the time he went on the offensive, it was too late. There were other factors working against Kerry. He was wooden, too aristocratic to appeal to working-class voters, and, of the two candidates, came up on the short end of the latest litmus test for White House aspirants: He wasn't someone that Americans wanted to have a beer with. But polls show that the swiftboat ads hobbled Kerry, especially among independent voters.

Bush's victory was fueled by gains he made among white evangelical Protestant voters. In 2004, Bush got 78 percent of their vote, compared to 68 percent four years earlier against Gore.[25] Bush also benefited from increased conservative turnout caused by Ohio and ten other states, including Kentucky, having same-sex marriage amendments on the ballot in 2004. Despite rhetorical attempts to differentiate law-abiding Muslims from international terrorists and the governments that support them, Bush's performance among American Muslims dipped dramatically between 2000 and 2004, a period during which the Bush administration expanded government surveillance of Muslims and other groups via the Patriot Act.[26]

In retrospect, the 2004 elections further revealed the country we were becoming. Writing in the *Courier-Journal* on the Sunday after Bush and Bunning's victories, columnist David Hawpe noted:

> [Bush] won by appealing to the fears and prejudices of an intol-
> erant minority, for whom the concept of Christian love does not
> extend to those who, by God's hand, have a different sexuality

than most of us. And by scaring the rest of America into (1) ignoring the fact that he has made the nation less safe from militant Islamic terrorism and (2) believing that John Kerry wouldn't protect us. In Kentucky, the Republicans not only put the anti-gay-marriage amendment on the ballot to boost the conservative religious turnout but also resorted to gay innuendo, stereotype and caricature in order to assassinate the character of Democrat Daniel Mongiardo.[27]

In the Kentucky coalfields, the 2004 presidential election represented a turning point for a constituency that was quickly moving toward a full embrace of Republican Party candidates. In 2000, six of the eight largest coal-producing counties in southeastern Kentucky counties went for Gore. In 2004, only three remained in the Democratic column. By 2008, there were none, a trend that continued for the next three presidential cycles.[28] A less extreme version of this scenario played out across Central Appalachia.

After his near-defeat of Bunning in 2004, Mongiardo's political star continued to rise. He returned to the Kentucky legislature for two years before running for lieutenant governor on a ticket that had veteran politician Steve Beshear at the top. Beshear hailed from the western part of the state, and choosing an Appalachian running mate provided strong geographic balance. Beshear easily defeated incumbent Governor Ernie Fletcher, sending Mongiardo to a high-profile position in the state capitol.

"Lieutenant governor has been a stepping stone to governor," Al Cross told me. "The thought was that Beshear would seek a second term and after that, Mongiardo would be set up to run for the big job, as long as he was a cooperative partner for Beshear."[29]

As lieutenant governor, Mongiardo flashed a maverick streak by being one of the few Democratic officials in Kentucky to endorse Barack Obama in the 2008 Democratic primary against Hillary Clinton. In doing so, I wondered if he was preparing to make an ideological pivot to the left. He made the endorsement knowing that

Obama would struggle to win votes in Kentucky, which turned out to be a major understatement.

The eye-popping result of the 2008 Kentucky Democratic presidential primary is one of the things that motivated me to write this book. It just amazes me. Though Obama was just days away from securing the Democratic nomination when the Kentucky primary rolled around in May of that year, Clinton beat Obama by more than a two-to-one margin statewide. No real surprise there. But in many Eastern Kentucky counties, Clinton took home more than 90 *percent* of the vote. To put that figure in perspective, eighteen of the twenty-four counties in the United States where Obama received less than 10 percent of the vote against Clinton were in Eastern Kentucky. And the other six were all in Central Appalachia.[30] The recipient of this largesse is the same candidate who lost some Eastern Kentucky counties by equally large margins to Donald Trump eight years later.

I see three reasons why Clinton trounced Obama in Central Appalachia in '08.

The first is undeniable racial bias among some voters. Fortunately, organized factions of the white nationalist movement have been largely nonexistent in Eastern Kentucky. The Southern Poverty Law Center map that tracks hate groups has a cluster of dots in nearby parts of Central Appalachia, but only one in Eastern Kentucky, the League of the South, a neo-Confederate group based in the town of McKee.[31] Al Cross has traversed the Bluegrass State more than any reporter I can think of, and by his estimate, there are hundreds of thousands of Kentuckians who don't know a person of color. In the absence of sheer hate, there is wariness of urban culture, as well as antiquated ways of talking about race. It is still common for older Eastern Kentuckians, even those in leadership positions, to refer to Black people as "colored." Before Republicans jumped on the "birther" bandwagon, Clinton supporters first floated questions about whether Obama was actually an American citizen. And the false narrative about Barack Hussein

Obama being a secret Muslim also started to gain traction in some circles during the primary.

Secondly, Eastern Kentucky's residual affection for Bill Clinton was a key factor, though it would completely evaporate in the years that followed. By the time Clinton journeyed to Hazard in the final year of his presidency to promote economic development in the region, he had already been pummeled by right-wing media for the behavior that led to his impeachment, as well as for other alleged activities that fell into the realm of conspiracy theory. As the 2000s progressed, he became something even worse: Hillary's husband.

And lastly, Obama alienated a lot of people in Appalachia and elsewhere with comments like the one he made at an April 2008 fundraiser about working-class voters clinging to "guns or religion or antipathy to people who aren't like them . . . to explain their frustrations."[32]

These factors turned what would have been a decisive loss in Eastern Kentucky into the type of result that we usually only see when undemocratic nations hold sham elections. In terms of the Kentucky primary, Hillary Clinton was the unlikely beneficiary of an early manifestation of what we would later come to know as Trumpism, which partly capitalized on white working-class fear of liberals who were coming for their guns and religion.

Paul Matney, the longtime TECO Coal executive who I got to know while reporting mining stories, agrees with what Obama said about working-class people, but he doesn't view it as a negative. "Eastern Kentuckians are proud of how they cling to their Bibles and to their guns and to their beliefs," he says. "Trump was protecting Christian values and protecting Second Amendment rights. Maybe he doesn't live all of it, but as far as politics go, he was the much better choice."[33]

While the rise of Trump was an improbable political story, it did not happen without warning. Trump didn't place some kind of spell on voters in Eastern Kentucky and elsewhere. His election to the White House can largely be explained by national political shifts that started in the 1990s and accelerated in 2004. But a sea change happened during Barack Obama's run for the presidency in 2008. And its effects would hit Eastern Kentucky harder and last there longer.

Never before had a candidate of color commanded such a high level of support in a primary. And that got the conspiracy theory machine working overtime. Obama's general election opponent, Senator John McCain, forcibly pushed back on baseless claims about Obama, but some in the Republican Party interpreted McCain's defense of Obama as a sign of weakness. Obama inherited a disastrous economy and the country sank into the Great Recession. Around this time, the Tea Party movement emerged and, with the help of the rising tide of social media, took toxic politics to new levels.

During Obama's second term, political scientist Norman J. Ornstein wrote, "Polarization itself is not new in America, but the divisions with which we now contend have become almost tribal in nature. And a new media dynamic, with its own tribal divisions, only accentuates the problems—including a coarsened political and social culture. It seems we are moving further every day from the ideal of a public square, where citizens share a common set of values and facts and can debate and deliberate to find the common good."[34]

I'll take it a step further: The very idea of the "common good" has been destroyed by ideological tribalism. We do not just disagree with our ideological adversaries on policy and direction. We believe the other side is loathsome and deranged and determined to destroy the foundations of family and democracy. Though we've never met, we know each other so well. Back in 2009, I wrote about a right-wing group called the Oath Keepers, a collection of current and former law enforcement and military members who vowed to disobey any orders they deemed to be unconstitutional. The virulently anti-Obama Oath Keepers created quite a stir at the time. A decade later, in the QAnon era of mind-bogglingly wild conspiracy theories or the Proud Boys era of physical violence, the Oath Keepers re-emerged as key players in the January 6, 2021 riot at the US Capitol.

Hillary Clinton is another perfect nemesis. Her 2016 comments about putting coal miners out of work represented the latest in a long line of broadsides that prompted *The Washington Post* back in 1999 to comment on her "us-against-them instincts."[35]

"They do not have names or faces, but Hillary Clinton knows Those People are out there, and she attacks Them almost every time she speaks in New York," the story opened.[36] The *Post* took this jab at Hillary on the same day that her husband stood on Main Street in Hazard pledging to help lift up historically impoverished communities.

Seventeen years later, with those promises still unfulfilled, Clinton gave "Those People" a name: Deplorables. And in doing so, she underestimated the size of the movement and the degree to which insulting Trump's supporters would galvanize them.

Former Kentucky Coal Association president Bill Bissett punches back at the idea that Trump used racist dog whistles and anti-Clinton rhetoric to fool Central Appalachians into voting for him in 2016. "We understood he wasn't like us. He doesn't talk like us. He doesn't act like us. He can be seen as a parody. But he had a swagger that was appealing."[37]

Shane Barton, an economic development coordinator in Eastern Kentucky, believes Bernie Sanders would have performed far better than Clinton in Appalachia.

"There is a polarization of ideology where there is no middle ground," Barton says. "A lot of voters were looking for a candidate to destroy the system, to provide a second chance, a restart. A lot of those people were potential Bernie supporters."[38] In Eastern Kentucky, like in a lot of places, "the system" is a hazy concept, holding different meanings for different people. To some, blowing up the system centers on reducing corporate influence in politics. To others, it means cleaning up all manners of political corruption. But to most, it means exactly what Barton said, an individual restart, a new beginning, a chance at making good.

A few days after Trump's victory in 2016, the *Harvard Business Review* published an essay entitled "What So Many Don't Get

POISON POLITICS · 201
POISON POLITICS · 201

About the U.S. Working Class."[39] The author of the piece, Joan C. Williams, a professor at the University of California's Hastings College of the Law, outlines the combustible factors that ignited into a Trump conflagration that swept through many parts of rural America. One of her points that resonates with me as I think about the 2016 vote tally in Eastern Kentucky concerns the role that machismo played in the election.

"Manly dignity is a big deal for working-class men, and they're not feeling that they have it," Williams wrote. "Trump promises a world free of political correctness and a return to an earlier era, when men were men and women knew their place. It's comfort food for high-school-educated guys who could have been my father-in-law if they'd been born 30 years earlier. Today they feel like losers—or did until they met Trump."[40]

Trump time and again promised he would lift up working-class white voters and return to them what they had lost. He would bring back jobs in coal mines and factories. He would guarantee freedom from oppressive government by "draining the swamp." He would restore overall dignity. His meek attempts to reach out to Black voters by asking them what the hell they had to lose by voting for him rung hollow because they came without even a kernel of an idea about economic and social advancement. His words were meant to deflate. Trump encouraged disenfranchisement long before his attempt to suppress and then discount large voter turnout.

Trump won in 2016 because he convinced enough working-class white voters that they deserved more than they were getting. Shortly after Trump's election, fifty-five-year-old Barbara Puckett of Lee County, Kentucky, told CNN, "I voted for Trump 100 percent. It's the most hopeful I've been in a long time now that he's in there."[41] In 2016, more than 80 percent of Lee County, population 6,500, pulled the lever for Trump, 5 percent more than voted for Mitt Romney against Barack Obama in 2012, with similar turnout levels in both elections.[42]

If Puckett and others like her had responded to Trump's racial and ethnic dog whistles (Build that wall!), they didn't let on to it. They instead expressed confidence that a man who had built an entire career on crass self-interest understood them like no politician ever had.

So how did that work out for these voters in Eastern Kentucky? Did Trump deliver on his promise of creating jobs? Did he drain the swamp? Did he restore dignity to working-class Americans?

I was driving through a remote part of Lee County on the November morning that the 2020 election was called for Joe Biden. I had planned to stop in on Puckett to ask her these questions. But when news of Biden's victory came over the radio, I reconsidered the idea. In 2020, Trump carried Lee County and most other Eastern Kentucky counties by even wider margins than four years earlier. The people there had spoken and I saw no value in pulling up in a rental car with Pennsylvania plates to further ruin their weekend by talking politics.

During Trump's term, Kentucky's McConnell—the Senate majority leader—made sure the Republican political machine focused on a limited slate of legislation while churning out judicial appointments that would impact the nation for decades to come. In 2020, nearly three hundred bills passed with bipartisan support in the House of Representatives had yet to come to a vote in the Senate, including an amended version of the Abandoned Mine Lands bill that McConnell originally cosponsored.[43] McConnell has never cared much about Eastern Kentucky, because he hasn't needed to care much about Eastern Kentucky. All the same, his support in the region has only grown, thanks to clever campaign slogans—like 2014's "Coal Guns Freedom"—and resentment among many Eastern Kentuckians over the Democratic Party's anti–fossil fuel platform. Alison Lundergan Grimes, McConnell's Democratic opponent in 2014, slammed Obama's "war on coal" and vowed to fight environmental regulations that hurt the coal industry. Positioning herself as a pro-coal Democrat didn't help her one bit. She was still a Democrat. McConnell handily defeated Grimes in Eastern Kentucky en route to a blow-out win statewide.

McConnell's standing in the region was further helped by his loyalty to Trump. In 2020, McConnell benefitted from a "Trump bump" in Eastern Kentucky, winning the region by a wider margin than ever before. Statewide, McConnell defeated challenger Amy McGrath by nearly 20 points.

"Eastern Kentucky has been a gift to McConnell in the last decade," Cross says. "He never ran all that well there. He just wanted to keep from losing the coalfields too badly. Once Obama was elected, there was a reaction among a lot of rural Kentuckians that was partially race driven, but not entirely. The UMW [United Mine Workers] wouldn't even endorse Obama in 2012. He was bad for the Democratic brand in Kentucky."[44]

And so was Hillary Clinton. In 2016, Kentucky House Speaker Greg Stumbo, an Eastern Kentucky Democrat and Clinton supporter, lost his bid for re-election and the Republicans took control of the Kentucky House of Representatives for the first time since 1921.

McConnell's 2020 campaign benefited from millions of dollars in "dark money," political donations from shadowy non-profit groups that aren't required to reveal their donors. A dark money group called One Nation put around $75 million into 2020 elections nationwide. The Senate Leadership Fund, a super PAC aligned with McConnell, shares staff and offices with One Nation.[45]

I have to hand it to McConnell—he's a smooth political operator. I remember the day that I opened my PO box in Hazard to find a letter from him. He wrote to tell me that he had met my mother, a university president, at an education conference and that they had talked about my work at the *Courier-Journal*. He didn't compliment or even comment on that work in his note, but he tried to win me over in a different way. "Your mother is a very impressive woman," he wrote. As a proud son, I admit he scored some points with me.

McConnell has tried to shake the perception that he is a coal industry shill who has neglected the needs of working people in Eastern Kentucky. The *Courier-Journal* gave this point of view the full treatment in the fall of 2019. McConnell fought back in an opinion piece in the paper, writing, "Once again this shrinking newspaper has confused its news and opinion pages . . . I regularly meet with coal miners. They want good jobs, which coal has provided for generations in Kentucky. They motivated my fight against President Barack Obama's deliberate 'war on coal' and its job-killing consequences. Hillary Clinton was clear about the Democrats' plan when she proudly said, 'We're going to put a lot of coal miners and coal companies out of business.'"[46] McConnell is no dummy, either. His column was a knowing nod toward Trump's war on journalism and the struggles of the newspaper industry, a topic that I will examine in the next chapter.

*

Daniel Mongiardo had a chance to shake up the Kentucky political establishment, but instead, his bright political career abruptly burned out. Despite having one of the most powerful positions in state government, he still felt like he belonged in Washington. For a while, it looked like there might be a Bunning-Mongiardo rematch in 2010. But under pressure from McConnell and other prominent Republicans, Bunning retired from politics following his second Senate term. Political newcomer Rand Paul, a Bowling Green eye doctor, emerged as the Republican candidate for the seat, upsetting the party's establishment candidate in the primary. Paul wasn't your average ophthalmologist. As the son of libertarian icon, congressman, and Republican presidential candidate Ron Paul, the younger Paul tapped into the deep vein of Tea Party sentiment that arose after Obama's election. Mongiardo vied with Kentucky attorney general Jack Conway for the Democratic nomination. A turning point came when Conway gained the support of one of Kentucky's most admired Democrats, Wendell Ford, who spent twenty-four years in the US Senate before serving as governor of the state. Up until three weeks before the election, it still looked like Mongiardo's race to lose. But his unwillingness to say that he supported every element of the newly passed Affordable

Care Act didn't sit well with Democratic voters, who viewed his tepid support of Obamacare as a repudiation of health care for everyone. "I said I would have voted for it if and only if there were cost control measures," he says. "The problem we have, and it's the one that no one wants to confront, is that our system is broken."[47]

Then, at a time when undecided voters were relying on television ads to make up their minds, his campaign ran into money problems. The charismatic and urbane Conway, who ran to the left of Mongiardo on most issues, pulled out a narrow victory before losing big in the general election to Paul. Adding insult to injury, Governor Steve Beshear dumped Mongiardo from his reelection ticket.

Nearly a decade after I covered his 2004 race, I bumped into Bunning again, this time at a baseball game in Philadelphia. I had recently cowritten a book with a close friend of his, former Phillies teammate Dallas Green, and Bunning and Green were hanging out together at a reunion event at the ballpark. I told Bunning that I used to work for the *Courier-Journal*, figuring we might bond a little over our shared Kentucky connection. The face of his wife, Mary Catherine, lit up at the mention of the paper, but Bunning's attention remained focused on the action on the field, odd considering it was a midweek night game in the middle of a terrible Phillies season. I decided to try to bring Bunning out of his trance.

"I actually covered your election night victory in 2004," I told him. "I tried to interview you after you won."

I don't think he remembered our election-night run-in. And why should he have? But I did get a response from him. He smiled politely and told me he had forgiven the *Courier-Journal* for treating him so unfairly. Bunning died in 2017 at the age of eighty-five.

Ten years after winning state office, Mongiardo quit politics and returned to the full-time practice of medicine. He was married by this time, with a daughter and plans of further growing his family. "The center of my universe has shifted," the father of three says.[48] Each week, he splits his time between four patient centers, three of which are in Eastern Kentucky.

Mongiardo wasn't going to single-handedly reverse Eastern

Kentucky's fortunes if he had defeated Bunning. But it would have been empowering for the people of the region to have the guy who once pulled up on a four-wheeler to say hello as an advocate in Washington. It would have also provided a check on McConnell.

Mongiardo remains concerned about the future of his home region. "The leaders of Eastern Kentucky have done a terrible job of diversifying the economy," he says. "It was coal or nothing, and now it's pretty close to nothing."[49] And he still worries about the future of health care in the country, warning that the system is on the verge of collapse.

His experiences in politics soured him to the point where he doubts he'll ever venture back into that world. So who out there has the platform to amplify the voice of Eastern Kentuckians? In the tumultuous days of 2020, a new hope would emerge from an unlikely place—but not before the means of informing the public and building community would change in this country forever.

CHAPTER 8

The Day the News Left Town

After my first year in Eastern Kentucky, Gideon Gil, the editor who hired me at the *Courier-Journal*, left his post to return to reporting. This was disappointing. During those eventful months, I developed a strong working relationship with Gideon and came to trust his news judgement and overall instincts. He had been at the paper for a long time and knew how to prioritize coverage. I can't say the same about the two regional editors I worked with for the remainder of my time at the paper. Both came from other Gannett-owned properties. Neither ever bothered to come to Eastern Kentucky to get a feel for the place.

Gideon's immediate successor came from an entertainment and lifestyle background and did not last long in the new role. The next person to step in arrived from a Gannett paper out West. Years later, long after I left the *Courier-Journal*, I met some of his former charges at a journalism conference. We bonded over the misery he had caused all of us. They told me that when he left for Louisville that they printed up T-shirts to celebrate having survived his reign. Based on my experience with him, I could definitely relate. In my eyes, he was the middle manager from hell. In his eyes, I could do no right. I didn't like him, and he didn't like me.

There was a lot of that going around back then. By the mid-aughts, the existential crisis facing newspapers put everyone a little bit on edge. An industry that for decades had enjoyed a stable business model based on a steady stream of subscriptions and advertising revenue was now staring down an enemy from within: the World Wide Web. No longer just print products sold at stores and newsstands and delivered to homes, newspapers were residents of the infinite

Internet. That meant advertisers no longer felt beholden to the local newspaper to promote their wares. And readers had many other places to go to quickly access news, usually at no cost. The idea of hiding content behind paywalls hadn't taken off yet.

In corporate newspaper offices across America, executives offered the same refrain: times change and so will we. Gannett, with the most holdings of any news company, took a lead role in the industry's efforts to remind the public that newspapers still mattered, whether consumed in paper or electronic form. But beneath that surface coolness, there was panic. I could hear it in the voices of the editors responsible for implementing the latest industry-saving plans. Innovation is a great thing. Ill-conceived change that smacks of desperation is not. Eager to appeal to a younger generation of readers who grew up getting information off of screens, newspapers used the digital revolution as an excuse to gut parts of their traditional news operations. It was disconcerting to see the column width and number of pages of the newspaper melt away, but as long as there remained a place for important journalism, whether in print or online, I could live with it.

Like so many other reporters, I was at the mercy of the people entrusted with digitally and spiritually transforming the dusty old newspaper. I'm not sure how many of these executives had journalism backgrounds or any clue what had made newspapers great in the first place. I didn't envy them. It was a tall order in a time of transition to retain existing readers, court new ones, and maintain the integrity of the product. Was journalism the top priority of most newspaper executives at Gannett and other media companies? Despite a lot of lip service paid to the importance of watchdog journalism, I would argue that putting out a high-quality newspaper became even more of a secondary concern than before. They were businesspeople looking to sell a good. That meant the difficult responsibility of putting out quality papers fell to the newsroom leaders in cities across America. As many newspaper chains scrambled to find ways to stay relevant and profitable, others simply gave up trying. In 2006, the country's second largest newspaper company, Knight Ridder, sold its thirty-two daily newspapers to the McClatchy Company.

One of Gannett's earliest twenty-first-century initiatives focused on newspapers providing content that could not be found anywhere else and getting those stories online as quickly as possible. This comprised part of the ill-fated "hyperlocal" strategy, engineered to fend off a new crop of websites specializing in local and community news. My good friend Chuck Myron, whom I met in Eastern Kentucky when he was an editor for the *Harlan Daily Enterprise*, became the face of the hyperlocal movement after taking a job for a Gannett paper in Fort Myers, Florida. In a 2006 front-page profile in the *Washington Post*, we learned that Chuck was a "mobile journalist," or in Gannett parlance, a "mojo." He worked out of his car, combing the streets of North Fort Myers for any morsel of news.

"The mojos have high-tech tools—ThinkPads, digital audio recorders, digital still and video cameras—but no desk, no chair, no nameplate, no landline, no office," the *Post*'s Frank Ahrens wrote. "They spend their time on the road looking for stories, filing several a day for the newspaper's Web site, and often for the print edition, too. Their guiding principle: A constantly updated stream of intensely local, fresh Web content—regardless of its traditional news value—is key to building online and newspaper readership."[1]

That mandate forced Chuck to stretch the definition of "news" to its breaking point. A small group of people at a strip mall getting their "Hunks of North Fort Myers" calendar signed by the hunks? News! A sixteen-year-old with preternatural hair-styling skills? Definitely news!

Two months after Ahrens's story ran, Chuck had so soured on being a mojo that he left journalism altogether and never returned. As he puts it, he had become "Gannett's ill-fated bridge to the future of newspapers," and he found the task soul-crushing.[2]

*

I hoped that the *Courier-Journal*'s reputation as one of Gannett's best-quality papers would help shield it from at least some of the company's misguided new directives. Bennie Ivory, the paper's top editor, had received a fistful of Gannett-awarded President's Rings in recognition of the paper's meritorious work. He embraced public-service journalism and was always willing to go to court if necessary to pry loose public records. But he also knew how to follow instructions from his higher-ups. Still, there was reason to be optimistic that the paper would maintain its commitment to in-depth journalism. I spent the better part of 2003 working on a series about deficiencies in the Kentucky court system that nearly won the paper a Pulitzer Prize. As it stood, the reporting team settled for being one of three nominated finalists in the public service category.[3] I missed a few juicy stories on my beat while reporting and writing "Justice Delayed, Justice Denied," but the trade-off was worth it, considering our stories led to much needed reform of the state's criminal-justice system. As we learned from the flawed investigation into the death of Breonna Taylor in 2020, more reform is needed.

When not out in the field, I spent an increasing amount of time in conversation with colleagues about the future of what we did. As the "ink-stained wretches" on the front lines of journalism, we had a different perspective than the executives in corporate suites and even the editors giving us marching orders. But that didn't mean we had answers, either. Those of us on the *Courier-Journal*'s state desk wondered what might happen to our positions if the paper started veering sharply toward prioritization of local (or even hyperlocal) news.

Sure enough, in early 2005, I started hearing rumblings about a newsroom shake-up at the *Courier-Journal*. I had no idea if the rumors of change had any factual basis, but I tried to brush them aside by reminding myself that the Hazard bureau meant a lot to the paper. And though slashed print runs had made it next to impossible to buy a copy of the *Courier-Journal* anywhere in Eastern Kentucky, that was what the Internet was for.

Season five of HBO's *The Wire*, whose story arc borrowed heavily from show creator David Simon's real-life experiences as a crime reporter at *The Baltimore Sun*, captured the zeitgeist of what news-paper journalists were experiencing in the early 2000s. In one scene, the top editor of the Baltimore paper summons everyone into the newsroom for an important announcement. "It's a bad time for newspapers. As you all know," the editor begins. "The news hole is shrinking as advertising dollars continue to decline. Our circula-tion numbers are also down as we compete with a variety of media. Technology is driving distribution. And the Internet is a free source of news and opinions. Seeking a balance in this new world, we're now faced with hard choices."

The editor goes on to announce an upcoming round of buyouts as well as the demise of the fictionalized *Sun*'s foreign bureaus in Beijing, Moscow, Jerusalem, Johannesburg, and London, closures that happened at the real *Sun* between 2005 and 2008. The briefing ends with words heard at one time or another, and usually more than once, in newsrooms across America.

"We're going to have to find ways to do more with less," the editor says.[4]

As the occupant of the closest thing that the *Courier-Journal* had to a foreign bureau, I wasn't privy to the newsroom chatter in Lou-isville, nor could I try to curry favor with editors by obsequiously dropping by their offices to talk sports or whatever else they were into. Not having to do that kind of thing helps explain why I wanted the Hazard job in the first place. All I could do was pick up on any clues about possible changes on the horizon. I got a big one on the day in May 2005 when I returned from two weeks of paternity leave following the birth of my first child. During my time off, I had made my first appearance on *Comment on Kentucky*, the long-running political affairs show that aired on public television. It was a rite of passage for any Kentucky reporter and a further sign that I was making my mark.

On my second day back at work, I drove to Louisville at the request of the state editor. Maybe, I thought, he wanted to talk about a new project, or perhaps he felt it was an opportune time to talk about coverage goals for the coming months. At the very least, I expected that he would congratulate me on the arrival of my daughter. Instead, after arriving bleary-eyed to the main office, I walked into a workplace ambush. There were no best wishes. I don't think the baby even got mentioned. No, the purpose of the meeting was to discuss my *productivity*. While out on leave, I didn't write any stories. That is true. And the last week or so before the birth hadn't been a period of stellar output, either, as I tried to avoid straying too far from my home base in case my girlfriend went into labor. Prior to that, except for the time that editors gave me to work on "Justice Delayed, Justice Denied," I had been filing stories at a rate that well surpassed that of any previous Eastern Kentucky reporter. I consistently met the paper's arbitrary "A1 quota" of producing six front-page stories per month in addition to any other published stories that didn't make it onto A1.

And yet, the regional editor and the assistant managing editor wanted more. More of what they didn't say. The timing and non-specific nature of the conversation irritated the hell out of me. And it made me wonder about the motivations behind it. But eager to please, I returned to Eastern Kentucky with the intention of giving my editors what I thought they wanted. Along with the usual fare of hard news articles, I was going to seek out stories that make people talk, and more importantly in the Internet age, make people click. In an attempt to steer readers to websites, Gannett had started religiously tallying "page views" and compiling lists of the "most viewed" stories of the day, week, and month. This metric gave the company a direct line to readers, at least the ones consuming the online version of the paper. The articles that received the most clicks were the ones that busted out nationally and "went viral," a term that, along with "clickbait," wouldn't get coined until years later. Based on their clicking habits, readers seemed most drawn to provocative and easy-to-digest stories. I remembered my editor telling me during a previous conversation that I should write more in the tabloidy style of the *New York Post*. I blew off his advice, concluding that stories out of Eastern Kentucky shouldn't be in the "Headless Body in Topless Bar" mold.

But I challenged myself to find a story that would get clicks. And I struck gold with my article about an Eastern Kentucky judge who gave convicted defendants the option of going to jail, to drug or alcohol rehabilitation . . . or to church.[5] The president of the National Judicial College said he had never heard of this type of alternative sentencing before. The judge's conduct, which appeared to be a textbook violation of the separation of church and state, raised the hackles of the American Civil Liberties Union. It was the perfect clickbait story, offbeat and culturally polarizing at the same time. Fox News called and requested an in-studio interview. I passed. The online story got more traffic than all of the coal mining, prescription drug, and poverty stories I had done that year put together.

While I should have been focusing on the rise of the dubious Internet pharmacies flooding Eastern Kentucky with prescription pills, I was instead chasing dubious clickbait. And it was a particularly inopportune time for the nation's journalistic priorities to be anything besides serious news coverage. I remember sitting in the downtown Hazard home we rented after the birth of our daughter watching live video of the levees breaking down in New Orleans. What happened during Hurricane Katrina was a quintessential American tragedy caused by a combination of poor preparation and inadequate response, the same brand of neglect that had menaced Appalachian Kentucky for so many years. As a journalist, I found the news coverage of the disaster fascinating. The correspondents on the ground in New Orleans, most memorably Anderson Cooper of CNN and Shepard Smith of Fox News, helped usher in an era of op-ed journalism that has since spun out of control. Though a place remains for Katrina-style reporting, it distresses me to see the constant blurring of the lines between news reporting and opinion pieces. But there is a reason that bloviating pundits, both on the left and right, far outnumber reporters on cable news channels. Opinions don't cost a dime. Going out and reporting a story does.

During Katrina, America saw the people stranded on rooftops, heard about the bodies floating in the streets, and felt the journalists' outrage at an inept and uncompassionate federal response to the disaster. Some of the worst of the flooding took place in the Lower Ninth Ward of New Orleans, an isolated, almost entirely African-American enclave in one of the most segregated cities in America. The traditional tenets of journalistic objectivity and detachment were appropriately suspended. People were dying, and the Federal Emergency Management Agency didn't seem to have a clue what to do about it. The journalists there shouted to us about a forgotten America.

The greatest tragedy of all was that the worst of the suffering didn't need to happen. Three years before Katrina, the New Orleans *Times-Picayune* warned about the potentially catastrophic consequences of a powerful hurricane.[6] In the immediate aftermath of Katrina, as the national TV networks conveyed the horrors of the storm, the reporters from *The Times-Picayune* provided an invaluable public service to locals stuck in the middle of the disaster. The paper never stopped publishing online and resumed its print edition just a few days after Katrina struck, printing information about where to find essential items like food and water and how to locate missing loved ones. It was a moment that all newspaper journalists could take pride in. Under the worst of circumstances and when its readership needed help most, the local New Orleans newspaper shined.

The Times-Picayune wasn't around to cover COVID-19. Its descent into nonexistence started in 2012 with the announcement of a limited three-day-a-week print run, a digital-first strategy, and massive newsroom layoffs. The Baton Rouge *Advocate* responded to its competitor's cutbacks by launching a daily New Orleans edition of the paper. *The Times-Picayune* eventually resumed its daily print run up until the day it was bought by *The Advocate*'s parent company. The newspapers combined forces and more layoffs ensued.[7]

*

My conversation with the editors in Louisville continued to nag at me. It not only affected my news judgement, but also my general sense of well-being. I didn't trust my bosses to be straight with me about the paper's plans for the Hazard bureau, so I had to rely on coded messages and passive-aggressive signals. And if my instincts were right that something was up, I couldn't afford to be caught off-guard. I was a father now and had more than myself to think about. I hoped everything would work out, but in case it didn't, I needed a back-up plan. So I started applying for other newspaper jobs. Pretty soon, I had an offer from the *Las Vegas Review-Journal*, which was creating a five-member investigative reporting team. The job seemed like an ideal fit, and one that paid $20,000 a year more than my current position. I decided to tell my editors about the opportunity in Nevada, hoping that the possibility of losing me would lead to a vote of confidence. That was all I needed in order to tell Las Vegas "no." But that was not what I got. Instead the regional editor dryly observed, "As you consider your options, remember there's no state income tax in Nevada." A couple of weeks later, the editors doubled down on their criticisms of my work, telling me that if I remained at the paper I would be placed on a dreaded PIP, or performance improvement plan. I knew other reporters who got "pipped" and it was rarely for legitimate reasons. Most people in my position would have accepted the Las Vegas offer then and there, but I felt like I needed to figure out why, all of a sudden, I had come under such scrutiny.

The answer revealed itself a couple of weeks later, in mid-December 2005, when the *Courier-Journal* announced that it would be shutting down all of its state bureaus except for the capitol bureau in Frankfort early the following year. Gone would be the Western Kentucky bureau in Paducah, a central Kentucky bureau in Elizabethtown, and the Eastern Kentucky bureau in Hazard. The Bowling Green bureau, which had been without a reporter for a while, was also gone. I got the news by phone while working on a story about efforts to make Kentucky the first state in the nation to require drug tests for coal miners.

Coverage of Eastern Kentucky was no longer considered local enough for the Louisville paper. The *Courier-Journal*, like many other big city papers across the country, had made a strategic decision to retrench from covering the entire state and to post local news items online as frequently as possible.

Courier-Journal publisher Ed Manassah gave his reasoning for the decision in the next day's paper. "We want to continue to focus on local news and better utilize our resources," he said, adding that he wanted to bolster the paper's coverage of the Louisville suburbs.[8] A few weeks later, Manassah announced his retirement.

The paper offered the bureau reporters affected by the decision other positions. If I had chosen to stay on, I would have been relegated to the Neighborhoods department, covering the suburbs of Louisville. At least it wasn't a mobile journalism gig. Unlike my "mojo" friend Chuck, I'd have a desk. But the Eastern Kentucky job was the only one I had ever wanted at the paper. I called the investigations editor at the *Las Vegas Review-Journal* and accepted his offer.

One of the reporters who preceded me in the Hazard bureau was Gardiner Harris. Shortly after winning a national award for coauthoring *Dust, Deception and Death*, the acclaimed series of stories on falsified coal-dust tests in underground mines, Gardiner landed a job at *The Wall Street Journal* as a pharmaceuticals reporter before moving on to *The New York Times* as a public health correspondent. When Gardiner got wind of the closure of the Hazard bureau, he pitched a story to the *Times*'s national desk. It would have been a conflict of interest for him to write it himself, so the paper assigned it to another reporter, who came to Hazard to interview me.

I didn't care much for the resulting *Times* article, "The Day the News Left Town." The reporter quoted me in the opening paragraphs of the article as saying there was little point in keeping the bureau open because the print version of the *Courier-Journal* didn't circulate in Eastern Kentucky anymore.[9] As someone not used to being asked the questions, it's possible that I didn't phrase my answers artfully enough. Or maybe the reporter took liberties with what I said and stitched together a quote that expressed what I believed to be the prevailing view of Gannett executives. I didn't think it was pointless at all to keep the bureau open. I also resented that after recounting the *Courier-Journal*'s long history of holding the coal industry accountable for its misdeeds, the writer quoted the Kentucky Coal Association president as saying that I had treated the industry fairly. That is like saying a reporter has been fair to the asbestos or tobacco industries. I thought maybe the sting of the bureau closure caused me to read too much into the story. But all these years later, my interpretation of those parts hasn't changed.

I've never claimed to be God's gift to journalism. In Kentucky, I inadvertently racked up significant roaming charges on my company cell phone back when that was a thing. I didn't treat the company car particularly well. And I didn't have a trusting relationship with my editors. Above all, I was still young and honing my skills. But if I had been the problem, the *Courier-Journal* would have simply replaced me. I wouldn't have agreed with the decision, but at least the paper would still have had a presence in Eastern Kentucky.

Hazard mayor Bill Gorman, one of the first people I met after moving to Eastern Kentucky, lamented the closure of the state bureaus. "The *Courier* has had such an impact in eastern Kentucky," Gorman told the *Times*. "They've pulled their horns in, and closing the bureaus will hurt the regions they've been serving more than it will hurt the *Courier-Journal*."[10] He compared the paper to the Bible in terms of its importance to the region and its people.

The mayor was going to be one of the people that I missed most. When friends or journalism colleagues came to visit, I'd take them by his office to hear him hold court and maybe make them a Duke or Duchess of Hazard. It was a better introduction to Eastern Kentucky than I could have ever provided. To the mayor's credit, he never called to complain about *Courier-Journal* stories that didn't portray the city, county, or region in the most flattering light. He respected the paper and its journalists enough to know that just having a reporter there was a boon.

The photo that accompanied *The New York Times* story showed me packing up my belongings in the company Ford Explorer in preparation for one final trip to Louisville. During some recent house cleaning, I found a little silver *Courier-Journal* clock that the newspaper gifted me on my five-year anniversary. I decided to hold onto it, because despite how things ended for me at the paper, I will always be grateful I had the opportunity to cover Eastern Kentucky. Reflecting on my time there, I think of the scene from the movie *Almost Famous* where the young rock critic tells the even younger rock critic that he has to make a name for himself in the industry by being honest and unmerciful. I prided myself on always being honest, but maybe I wasn't unmerciful enough. It's difficult to take no mercy and convey important subtleties at the same time.

*

After the big announcement, I stayed on the job for another few weeks, knowing that my next few stories would be my last. I had arrived in Hazard just before Christmas 2000 and would be leaving town a few weeks after Christmas 2005. The symmetry of the dates gave me an opportunity to reflect on all that I had learned about the area. During those first freezing weeks in Hazard, I felt every bit the foreign correspondent that my first editor had asked me to be. But over time, I stopped viewing my environs as foreign and recognized that life in Central Appalachia is a part of the American experience too often brushed aside or reduced to caricature.

I covered a few more tragic reminders of the dangers of coal mining before leaving the *Courier-Journal*, writing a story about Cornelius Yates, an Eastern Kentucky miner who was crushed to death by a huge slab of rock that fell from a mine roof. Less than two weeks earlier, twelve miners lost their lives in an explosion at a West Virginia mine. In all, thirty-eight Kentucky miners were killed on the job during my five years at the paper. Like so many of them, Yates only became a miner because other work was difficult to come by. "That's really the only thing there is around here," his brother-in-law Don Coleman told me. "If you're not willing to work in the mines, you have to leave."[11]

I also got in one last story about economic hardship, set mostly in Owsley County, the poorest and most isolated county in Eastern

Kentucky. Unlike other counties in the region that thrived during coal booms, sparsely populated Owsley County has never had an economic base of any kind. Owsley County is Eastern Kentucky at its most extreme, making it an easy target for stories about economic marginalization. I had gone there previously to cover a triple murder and a major drug roundup, but I waited until my final weeks at the *Courier-Journal* to pick the lowest-hanging piece of fruit that the county had to offer.

My article introduced readers to families seeking to break out of the cycle of generational poverty. I interviewed a woman named Paula Thomas, whose two school-aged sons sat by us busily doing homework. After they shut their books, they told me they were trying to make good grades so that they could be the first in their family to go to college. But even at a young age, the boys knew that the odds were against them. At the time, only 8 percent of Owsley County residents had any kind of college degree. That number has risen only slightly in the past fifteen years.

The Thomas family was living paycheck to paycheck off of Paula's husband's $27,000-a-year salary as a truck driver. Paula told me that she hoped to help put her sons through college by opening a craft store, where she could sell handmade dolls, blankets, and other wares.

"That's my dream," Thomas said. "I don't know if it will ever happen, but it's my dream."[12]

I didn't know what to expect when I attempted to get back in touch with the people I interviewed back then. The boys on the Billy Graham bus had drifted away. A young woman from Clay County who had vowed to stay in school despite being a teen mom has been caught up in the criminal justice system for the past decade.

It was gratifying to learn that Paula Thomas did in fact turn her passion for crocheting into a moneymaking venture, selling her work online and at local markets. One of her sons, Stephen, attended Eastern Kentucky University, where he made the dean's list. Following the sudden death of her husband in January 2018, she lost interest in crocheting and just about everything else. But she regained her spirit and was back displaying her goods at the 2019 Owsley County Christmas Bazaar. Both of her sons still live in the area.

The Owsley County industrial park that I highlighted in my story as a sign of economic hope for the area is still all but empty. The only business located in the park is Wolf Creek Metal Fabrication and Cement. A $2 million, privately funded golf course built on the site of a Civil War cemetery has given people a place to whack around little white balls but little in terms of economic development. The Dollar Tree and Dollar General in the county seat of Booneville are among the top local employers. The few underground mines that used to operate in Owsley County are no more.

From Couch Town to Whoopflarea, the county is moribund. But it has its lore. Whoopflarea? According to the late Robert M. Rennick, who authored a book about unusual Kentucky place names, this tiny Owsley County community was likely named after a skilled moonshiner named Larry who lived so far up in the hills that customers would have to "whoop for Larry" once they got within shouting distance of his home. And Owsley County native Earle Combs, who played on a 1927 New York Yankees team that featured Babe Ruth and Lou Gehrig, is memorialized with a huge photo that adorns the county courthouse. The longtime mayor of Booneville, who died in 2019 at the age of ninety-nine, held that office for sixty years and never ran in a contested election. In terms of longevity, he bucked the odds. Between 1980 and 2014, Owsley County had the biggest drop in life expectancy of any county in the nation.

Today, the new sign of hope for its economic future is the technological revolution that has taken place in Owsley County. Through a combination of foresight and savvy, the local telecom company in the area created a broadband network that provides Owsley and neighboring Jackson County with some of the fastest Internet speeds in the entire country.[13] The Peoples Rural Telephone Cooperative used loans and grants from the American Recovery and Reinvestment Act of 2009 and other federal loans to complete the five-year project that featured a team of mules to lay cable on the most rugged terrain. The feat is even more improbable when you consider the hundreds of millions of dollars that got poured into a state-wide broadband project called KentuckyWired, an initiative widely viewed as an abject failure. The dreams of transforming Eastern Kentucky into "Silicon Holler" might never be realized, but in one of the most impoverished counties in America, a noble experiment is playing out. Owsley County is hoping a sense of adventure and a low cost of living will attract work-from-home urban transplants who only need fast Internet service to do their jobs.

*

It's a shame that too few journalists are left in Eastern Kentucky to tell these stories.

For anybody who grew up reading newspapers, and especially for those of us who went on to write for them, the decline of print journalism has been hard to accept. Where is the newspaper industry going? I don't know for sure, but it's safe to say that the future will continue to be uncertain.

In November 2019, Gannett merged with GateHouse, another large chain, firming up its sizable place in the media landscape, or what was left of it. By the time of the merger, Gannett was a shadow of its former mighty self. The total value of Gannett's more than 250 papers in early 2020 was $261 million, less than the company paid to buy the *Courier-Journal* and a sister publication back in 1986.[14]

Because of its large network of metropolitan dailies, Gannett papers have reduced newsroom costs by sharing content and other resources. The company has survived. Others haven't. In February 2020, McClatchy filed for bankruptcy protection, a move that ended 163 years of family ownership and paved the way for hedge fund Chatham Asset Management, LLC, to become the majority owners of the company, whose holdings include the *Lexington Herald-Leader*.[15] Compared to some of the other entities running newspapers today, Gannett doesn't look so bad anymore. A few months after the sale, McClatchy announced a controversial plan to tie reporters' pay to the number of clicks their stories get.[16]

In its own story on the bankruptcy filing, McClatchy cited the numbers behind the decision: "Between 2006 and 2018, McClatchy's advertising revenue fell by 80 percent and daily print circulation fell by 58.6 percent. While the company has worked over three years to achieve a more sustainable 50-50 split of print vs. digital advertising, those gains couldn't outpace the approaching pension and debt obligations."[17]

The past two decades in journalism have also featured some positive developments, including the emergence of outstanding non-profit news collectives like New York-based ProPublica and the California-based Center for Investigative Reporting's California Watch project. The ProPublica approach to investigative journalism, which involves a content-heavy website and collaborations with local newspapers, has developed into a model for the future. In 2017, ProPublica expanded its operations to Illinois, and the following year, the organization created a Local Reporting Network to bolster statehouse coverage across the country. Meanwhile, newspapers with national reach like *The New York Times*, *The Washington Post*, and *The Wall Street Journal* have managed to use the Internet and technology to create web features that augment the traditional print product. They have attracted digital advertising and brought in revenue through online subscriptions. All of these news outlets are setting new standards for the use of data in journalism. *The Washington Post*, for example, used Drug Enforcement Administration data to create a database that allows the public to see which businesses distributed, manufactured, and dispensed the most prescription drugs in every US county over a recent nine-year period.[18] From that database, I learned that between 2006 and 2014, nearly 50 million pain pills were prescribed in Perry County, population 26,000. Meanwhile, Fayette County, which includes Lexington and has twelve times more people than Perry, had 100 million pills prescribed from its pharmacies. It's no coincidence that, in 2017, a Hazard doctor was sentenced to fifteen years in prison for illegally prescribing opiates from 2006 to 2014.[19] (Full disclosure: as a member of the *Post*'s freelance talent network, I occasionally contribute stories to the paper.)

Since I left the Hazard bureau, there has been a lot of outstanding reporting from Central Appalachia, much of it from Bill Estep and Lee Mueller of the *Herald-Leader* and Ken Ward Jr. of the Charleston, West Virginia *Gazette*. But with so much ground to cover and stories to tell, the *Courier-Journal*'s retrenchment from the region left a void that was difficult to fill, especially now that some small Eastern Kentucky papers have gone under. *The Big Sandy News*, a paper serving a number of Eastern Kentucky counties, closed its doors in 2019 after a 134-year run.[20] As more and more local newspapers struggle to stay in business, a slew of faux-local-journalism websites have sprouted up. With reputable sounding names like Des Moines Sun and Ann Arbor Times, these sites represent themselves as legitimate news outlets, when in fact their content is paid for by political groups and other entities.[21]

Occasionally, a local Eastern Kentucky paper has bravely bucked the power brokers of a community and stepped up to produce a stellar piece of journalism. I'm thinking specifically of the tiny Corbin *Times-Tribune*, which, in 2010, published a series of stories that brought down a corrupt local sheriff, this time before any violence took place. In order to free up a reporter to work on the stories, managing editor Samantha Swindler had to cut back on the paper's coverage of the fluff that usually helped fill the pages of the community paper. Swindler tasked cub reporter Adam Sulfridge, a college sophomore who was earning eleven dollars an hour at the *Times-Tribune*, to help her on the project. Working seventy-hour weeks, the two journalists exposed a drugs-and-gun racket being operated by Whitley County sheriff Lawrence Hodge, who as a result of the investigation, lost his re-election bid and then got convicted of crimes that landed him in federal prison for fifteen years.[22] Out of fear for their safety, both journalists left the paper soon after the stories ran. Swindler went on to publish a weekly newspaper in Oregon before getting a job with the state's largest paper, *The Oregonian*. Sulfridge, who wanted to stay closer to home, left journalism altogether. He eventually got involved in local political and advocacy work. Swindler and Sulfridge serve as examples to small-town journalists everywhere that pluck, passion, and a skillful use of open-records requests can yield important results.

Courier-Journal opinion page editor David Hawpe had repeatedly told me that he would leave the paper if it ever closed the Hazard bureau, but he didn't follow through on that promise. Perhaps Gannett convinced him it was for the best. When the bureau closed, executive editor Ivory said the paper would still cover the big stories in Eastern Kentucky. He cited mine-roof collapses as an example. The *Courier-Journal* still occasionally sends reporters to the region to cover breaking news like the Blackjewel mining protest that took place in Harlan County in 2019. But most of its in-depth coverage there has focused on the poor health of Eastern Kentuckians, a series of superficial offerings that bring to mind the infamous 20/20 episode about the region's dental woes. And since Hawpe's retirement in 2009, there have been far fewer editorials about the struggles of the coalfields. David passed away in July 2021, leaving behind an amazing legacy of public service and journalistic achievement.

The much-ballyhooed hyperlocal movement proved to be a fad. The *Courier-Journal* doesn't even have a suburban desk anymore. Like many of its urban counterparts, it has become, true to Mitch McConnell's taunt in his 2019 guest column for the *C-J*, the incredible shrinking newspaper, both in terms of width and number of pages. When I started at the paper in 2000, you could count on seeing five or six stories on the front page. By 2010, you generally got only three stories on A1, with enlarged photos and graphics making up for the decrease in content. Some esteemed papers, like *The Rocky Mountain News* in Denver were shrunk completely out of existence.

An already-struggling industry faced further setbacks as a result of the COVID-19 pandemic. One of the outbreak's many economic victims was the media industry, and newspapers in particular, whose perennial pursuit of advertising dollars became that much more challenging in a time of widespread economic shutdown. At a time when local news needed to play a more vital role than ever, news organizations made cuts. At the end of March 2020, Gannett took steps to avert financial freefall by enacting a three-month furlough plan that cut the pay and hours of most newsroom employees by 25 percent.[23]

As *Vanity Fair* noted in late March 2020, "Coronavirus has led to a surge of readership—and an existential threat."[24] Margaret Sullivan, a media columnist for *The Washington Post*, suggested that federal stimulus money go toward helping news organizations stay afloat.[25] Sullivan's idea was seconded and fleshed out by a number of media insiders. The idea had merit considering the abundance of federal funds that went to help other struggling industries cope with the economic impacts of the outbreak. But it was also a nonstarter for a president with a deep disdain for a free press that he dubbed "truly the enemy of the people."

It is far more difficult these days to find out what is going on in Eastern Kentucky. During the first weeks of the COVID-19 outbreak, for example, I was curious to know whether coal mines in the region were still operating. I couldn't find a story that answered the question. All I could find was a *Huffington Post* story about how the high rate of respiratory disease in coal-mining regions put the population of Central Appalachia at even higher risk during an outbreak. Another story, in *The Washington Post,* revealed that the coal industry was seeking a pandemic-related reprieve from paying into the Department of Labor's trust fund for black-lung victims.

I'm glad these stories got reported from afar. But they are no substitute for persistent and daily coverage of a region. In the absence of well-funded newspapers establishing bureaus throughout each state, I root for the success of such initiatives as Report for America, a nonprofit organization that seeks to place journalists in under-covered corners of the country. One such reporter covered Eastern Kentucky for the *Lexington Herald-Leader.*

I was also happy to see that the *Courier-Journal* was awarded a Pulitzer Prize in April 2020 for its breaking news coverage of controversial pardons issued by Kentucky governor Matt Bevin during his final days in office. Two of the pardons went to a child rapist and a man who beheaded a woman. The paper found that some of the convicted felons who received pardons came from wealthy, politically connected families. It was a solid piece of journalism that the paper's reporters executed on tight deadlines. One of the lead reporters on the story tweeted that he was in the middle of a two-week unpaid furlough when he got the Pulitzer news.[26]

Hopefully the prize and national acclaim for coverage of the 2020 social justice protests in Louisville will help stave off another round of layoffs at the paper, which put its downtown building up for sale in 2021. In the first half of 2020, newsrooms across the country shed a staggering 11,000 jobs.[27] An industry that was in crisis before the pandemic now faces an even less certain future as the news continues to leave town—at a moment in which the town is undergoing more nuanced and unforeseen realignments than ever.

CHAPTER 9

From the Hood to the Holler

Back in my Hazard days, I would get pizza a couple of times a week from Giovanni's, the gas station–pizzeria down the road from where I lived that served up, improbably, some of the best pizza I've ever had. I recently went to pay homage to Giovanni's. On the occasion of that visit, I learned that even pizza had become partisan. Somewhere along the way, Giovanni's turned into a shrine to Donald Trump and Friends of Coal politics. You couldn't miss it. The front entrance door was plastered with about two dozen stickers, featuring familiar pro-Trump, pro-gun, and anti-Obama messages. One of the stickers stood out more prominently from the rest. It read, THE FEDERAL EMPIRE IS KILLING THE AMERICAN DREAM. Oh, and according to another sticker on the door, Giovanni's now serves a pizza with a cauliflower crust. In a bit of liberal influence, the anti-gluten movement has also hit the mountains.

Perhaps the part-time Appalachian regional wrestler Daniel Harnsberger has found the most inventive way to comment on the political divisions of our time. To appreciate the genius of Harnsberger's alter ego, "The Progressive Liberal," you first need to understand the exalted history of pro wrestling's "heels," broadly drawn characters that play to the raw emotions of a live audience and viewers at home. When I was a kid, in the 1980s, two of the main villains of the World Wrestling Federation were Nikolai Volkoff and "The Iron Sheik," tag-team partners who strutted to the ring waving the flags of their respective homelands, the Soviet Union and Iran. At the height of the Cold War and amid tensions between the United States and Iran, this act of geo-political provocation brought the angry crowd to life with chants of "U-S-A! U-S-A!" A match commenced only after Volkoff belted out the Soviet national anthem and The Iron Sheik grabbed a microphone to disparage and spit on the USA. The men who played these characters were actors and the matches they fought were staged, but that hardly mattered to fans who devoured the "us versus them" narrative that culminated in 1984 when Hulk Hogan became the first WWF wrestler to escape The Iron Sheik's "camel clutch" en route to winning the championship belt.

Harnsberger had knocked around the regional wrestling scene for years, using monikers including "Dynamite Dan Richards" and "Big Dan" before finding inspiration for The Progressive Liberal late in 2015, just as the presidential primary race was heating up. His schtick at his early bouts consisted of spouting generic liberal talking points. But it wasn't until he started bashing Donald Trump and praising Hillary Clinton that the character really took shape. "I did it at a small little show in West Virginia, and it got a palpable reaction," he says. "Trump was becoming a thing at that point."[1]

I interviewed Harnsberger in the spring of 2020, six months after his most recent bout on a pre-Thanksgiving card in Kingsport, Tennessee. Just as his wrestling career was taking off, his body was giving out. His knees and neck ached from more than a decade of physical punishment in the ring. Right before his character started getting widespread media attention, he obtained his real estate agent's license with an eye toward cutting back on wrestling and opening his own property management business. He followed through on that goal but loved wrestling enough to continue making regular appearances on cards in small towns throughout West Virginia, Tennessee, and Kentucky.

Appalachian Mountain Wrestling, headquartered in Eastern Kentucky, is the low minor leagues of professional wrestling, a world and hundreds of millions of dollars away from the WWF (later WWE) empire built by Vince McMahon. But Harnsberger, a native of the Richmond, Virginia, area gave the fledgling company a major publicity boost.

In high school gyms and dirt fields in Hazard and other Eastern Kentucky towns, The Progressive Liberal, standing an imposing 6 feet 5 inches, weighing 237 pounds, and usually wearing blue tights and a T-shirt emblazoned with dozens of airbrushed images of Hillary Clinton, came to do battle with both his opponents and a decidedly pro-MAGA crowd. Instead of "U-S-A! U-S-A!" the crowd chanted "Don-ald Trump! Don-ald-Trump!"

Harnsberger took a page from more recent wrestling stars like "Stone Cold" Steve Austin and Dwayne "The Rock" Johnson by playing The Progressive Liberal as an exaggerated version of himself. When he talks about "zombies to the Fox News talking points," he is quoting a line from his act, but it is one that he wholeheartedly believes. When he gets into the political weeds and complains that Trump violated the emoluments clause by having foreign dignitaries stay at his hotels, he is not speaking in character. When he delivers a pro-choice monologue, he is expressing his own strongly held opinion.

Clutching a microphone to his mouth before bouts, Harnsberger took rhetorical jabs at the all-ages crowds. He might bash Trump, condemn Russian interference in the 2016 presidential election, or chastise the working-class audience for voting against its own economic self-interests. Or he might brandish one of his favorite attack lines about the death of coal and the virtues of the progressive "Green New Deal." Sometimes it got deeply personal. Before one bout in an Eastern Kentucky town where a coal mine had recently reopened, Harnsberger lashed out at the townsfolk: "There's nothing to be proud of! There's nothing to be happy about! You're just following in the footsteps of your ignorant fathers and grandfathers!"[2]

It's professional wrestling, where the matches are choreographed and everyone is supposed to be in on the joke. And I'm sure most people who came to see Harnsberger insult them took the barbs in stride. But in the low-budget world of Appalachian Mountain Wrestling, security isn't particularly tight and little stood between the wrestler and the insulted, possibly armed fans. In the years that

Harnsberger played the character, it never got violent, however. And the people who came out to jeer the heel usually received validation by seeing The Progressive Liberal get pinned by his opponent.

Still, I wondered whether seeing The Progressive Liberal go down to defeat was enough to keep some fans from seeking him out in the parking lot after the match. It's one thing to criticize Trump or even call someone a hillbilly, quite another to say their family is ignorant. With a combustible mix of alcohol and machismo at these events, I imagined Harnsberger had to be prepared for the worst. He told me that someone on social media threatened to bring a gun to one of his matches, but it didn't deter him from showing up and wrestling, unarmed, and goading fans by telling them the government was going to confiscate their guns.

"If somebody wants to kill me, go ahead," he told me. "I never carried a weapon. If I could, I'd take every single gun in the world and melt them down to scrap."[3]

*

The Progressive Liberal's bit about firearms was well-calculated. Guns are important to places like Eastern Kentucky, and Republicans like Trump understand their value to the party's base. In a December 2019 tweet lashing out at an anti-Trump editorial in the Billy Graham–founded *Christianity Today*, Trump spoke of an unnamed "Radical Left nonbeliever, who wants to take your religion and guns."[4] That same month, the Harlan County Fiscal Court made the county one of a growing number of communities around the region that have voted to declare themselves "Second Amendment sanctuaries" that are determined to resist any state or federal efforts to restrict gun ownership.

Being called a "gun nut" in Harlan isn't a pejorative term. It's a badge of honor.

"Any time you see gun crimes occur, you're not seeing law-abiding citizens involved in those crimes," Harlan judge/executive Dan Mosley, a supporter of the resolution, said at the fiscal court meeting,

adding, half-jokingly, that he was fairly certain that guns outnumbered people in Harlan County.[5]

No one at the fiscal court meeting rose to speak about gun violence. The attendees were only concerned with what they perceived
as an ongoing assault on their right to bear arms.

In separate incidents the same week that Harlan became a Second
Amendment sanctuary, a twenty-five-year-old local man was shot
several times in the head and a sixteen-year-old was wounded by a
gunshot blast to the head.[6] But a month later, the "good guys with
guns" narrative got a major boost on the national stage when an
armed parishioner neutralized a gunman who had shot and killed
two people at a West Texas church. The death toll likely would have
been much greater without his intervention.

The unanimously adopted resolution in Harlan, the first of its
kind in Kentucky, was modeled on a series of such measures enacted
in more than a hundred Virginia counties, cities, and towns[7] ahead
of the passage of stricter gun laws in 2020 by a state legislature
that flipped Democrat thanks in part to $2.5 million in spending by
a group affiliated with gun-control advocate Michael Bloomberg.[8]
In Kentucky, Republicans have held firm control of both the state
House and Senate since 2016, with no end to their rule in sight, leaving little chance that the Bluegrass State will follow Virginia's lead.

So what was Harlan County thinking? Probably the same thing
that my current hometown in New Jersey was thinking when its
elected officials voted in 2017 to declare the tiny town a sanctuary
city for undocumented immigrants. Both sanctuary votes represented
quintessential Trump-era gestures of the middle-finger variety, conservatives flipping off liberals for being feckless and liberals flipping
off conservatives for being intolerant. The former sentiment isn't limited to Harlan County. In January 2020, a year before pro-Trump
forces stormed the US Capitol, a cadre of armed gun owners from all
over the region entered the Kentucky capitol building without incident
to protest what they believe is a slow encroachment on their rights. As
Mosley put it on the day the gun resolution passed, "We want to pass
this resolution because our country is in a pivotal time."[9]

232 · TWILIGHT IN HAZARD

Mosley was a lifelong Democrat who became a registered Republican in February 2021. He is quick to differentiate between "Eastern Kentucky Democrats" and "Washington, D. C., Democrats."

"I'm a Democrat who voted for Donald Trump, because he was the candidate who didn't say he was going to put my family and friends out of jobs," he told me before he switched parties.[10]

Mosley and Daniel Mongiardo, the Hazard doctor who nearly won a US Senate seat in 2004, represent different types of Eastern Kentucky Democrat. Mosley was a classic "John L. Lewis Democrat," that is to say a Democrat in name only whose party identification is a part of family and cultural legacy. Mongiardo, though moderate to conservative in many of his political views, was one of the few Kentucky politicians to endorse Barack Obama for president. During his nascent political career, Mongiardo flashed a maverick streak that is difficult to find in Congress today. What both share is a love for Eastern Kentucky.

Mosley grew up in Harlan County, the son of a coal miner who got laid off from the mines in the 1990s and never went back. Like a lot of men in Eastern Kentucky who are seeking a life after mining, Mosley's father became a long-haul trucker. Mosley is careful not to speak critically of the coal industry. That is still risky for politicians in communities where coal has enjoyed economic and cultural dominance for well over a century. But Mosley is too young to have lived through a coal boom, and that makes him less nostalgic and more realistic about the industry's future. He is a believer in the area's potential to broaden its economic base and takes every opportunity to meet with business leaders to tout Harlan as a potential landing spot. On many days, however, he answers his own phone at the county government building, fielding questions and complaints from residents about flooded roads, drug houses, or county dumpsters. To stay in office, he has to please his constituents, most of whom are more concerned about daily problems than about trying to grow Harlan's economy.

Some in the community wanted a judge/executive less focused on commerce and more on God, a sentiment that his Republican opponent ran on when Mosley was seeking reelection in 2018. "I am led and believe in God's word," the opponent said on the campaign trail. "I believe the Scripture is very clear in Proverbs 29:2 when it says the righteous grow more powerful . . . It is time we seek God's will for our country and move in the direction He would have us to go."[11]

That kind of talk can go a long way in Harlan County, a place that values a good religious awakening—at least in theory. I'm thinking of the local businessowner there whose baptism prompted him to turn the only adult entertainment store in the area into a Christian bookstore in 2003. He had an ulterior motive in doing so. The conversion led authorities to drop an obscenity charge against him. But when his Bibles didn't sell as briskly as his vibrators, he was forced to close shop again.[12]

Despite his opponent's religious pandering, Mosley handily won a second term.

In April 2020, Eastern Kentucky's ardent churchgoing population faced a moral quandary in light of COVID-19 restrictions on attending Easter Sunday services, especially considering that as of that day, there had been almost no reported cases of the virus anywhere in the region.

Three days before Easter, US attorney general William Barr, in a Fox News interview, questioned the constitutionality of banning or limiting in-person religious services. Kentucky Republican senator Rand Paul backed this view, tweeting, "Taking license plates at church? Quarantining someone for being Christian on Easter Sunday? Someone needs to take a step back here."[13] Meanwhile national figures on the religious right were encouraging the faithful to view the virus from a biblical perspective that emphasized worshiping, fasting, and praying over social distancing. I was certain that the words of these politicians and evangelical leaders would serve as a rallying cry in an area that often found itself in battles over government overreach and First Amendment religious rights.

But I was happy to be wrong. Mosley urged local residents and religious leaders to abide by Kentucky governor Andy Beshear's

order against mass gatherings. On Facebook, Mosley wrote, "To the
10 churches that I am aware of in our county that are proceeding
with in-person gatherings inside a building, just know you are putting your members in harm's way unlike the hundreds of churches
in our county that are doing it the right way and having virtual or
drive-up services."[14] Only a couple of the churches carried through
with the planned in-person services.

One Kentucky church made national news that Easter Sunday for
flouting the state order, but it wasn't in the eastern part of the state.
In Hillview, a town fifteen miles south of Louisville, about fifty
worshippers showed up for Easter service at the Maryville Baptist
Church. Police jotted down plate numbers in the parking lot and
left notices on windshields advising everyone inside the church to
self-quarantine for fourteen days or face the possibility of "further
enforcement measures."[15]

As I said earlier, Eastern Kentucky has its saints and sinners. But
any place that has communities with hundreds of churches of all
conceivable denominations certainly values its faith. The decision
by most churches in the region to obey the stay-at-home orders on
the holiest day of the Christian calendar represented an act of patriotism, as well as an indication that amid the acrimony that has
always plagued the region, there is a strong and admirable sense of
community there. Whether it is the anonymous benefactor who paid
the Christmas 2020 layaway balances at the Hazard Walmart or the
nonprofit called With Love from Harlan that galvanizes community
support for those in need, people in Eastern Kentucky tend to look
out for each other.

*

Even the most creative minds would have been hard-pressed to
create a foil for The Progressive Liberal as flamboyant as Donald
Trump. But the man does have a history in the ring. Back in 2007,
when he was still just a reality TV star with questionable morals,
he played his carnival barker role to a hilt during a "Battle of the

Billionaires" bit at the WWE's annual WrestleMania. He clearly reveled in the spectacle, though the crowd seemed unsure whether to treat Trump as a heel or not. Years later, as president, Trump tweeted out an altered GIF from the event showing him pummeling a person with a CNN logo superimposed on his face.[16]

Donald Trump was the Great American Rorschach Test, a hero to many, a heel to even more. Trump brought his wrestler's bluster to the most powerful office in the world, and other upstart politicians, including Kentucky's Matt Bevin, tried to emulate that style. Bevin, a venture capitalist and a New England transplant, made a sport of clobbering Obama and the media on his way to winning the governorship in 2015.

When Bevin ran for reelection in November 2019, political observers looked to Kentucky for clues about Trumpism's future. And despite having Trump's full support, Bevin lost his reelection bid to Democrat Andy Beshear, in the process losing some of the Eastern Kentucky counties that Trump had won handily. Those results, but more importantly, the high rate of Democratic voter turnout in Louisville and Lexington and a blue wave in the Cincinnati suburbs of northern Kentucky, helped vault Beshear to victory.[17] Bevin was an unpopular governor for, among other reasons, his attacks on Medicaid and public education. There was no chance that Trump would lose Kentucky in 2020, but in battleground states like Pennsylvania and Michigan, Joe Biden's urban turnout and performance in the suburbs ended up being pivotal.

The 2020 Democratic Senate primary in Kentucky had an even more compelling backdrop. In March of that year, twenty-six-year-old Breonna Taylor, an African-American emergency medical technician, was shot and killed by plainclothes Louisville police officers who served a no-knock warrant at her apartment. It turned out they were looking for someone who didn't live there. Taylor's death, which preceded the police killing of George Floyd in Minnesota by two months, helped spur the racial-justice demonstrations that took place that spring. The national outcry gave a little-known state representative from Louisville named Charles

Booker traction in the Senate race. Booker, who is Black, surged in the polls until he was running even with establishment candidate Amy McGrath for the Democratic nomination and a chance to unseat Mitch McConnell.

Booker could have spent his last day on the campaign trail stumping anywhere in the state. He chose to go to Eastern Kentucky. In Hazard, he told a socially distanced crowd of fifty that he would fight for communities like theirs "that have been abandoned and ignored."

"From the hood to the holler, we need to stand together because we've all been getting screwed," Booker said.[18]

Daniel Mongiardo was impressed by the attention that Booker paid to Eastern Kentucky. While more progressive than Mongiardo on most issues, Booker had qualities that won over the Hazard doctor. "I look at a person's character, if they're authentic, and whether they think from the head and the heart," Mongiardo said.[19]

On primary day in June 2020, most Kentucky counties opened only a single polling place due to COVID-19 restrictions, though all Kentuckians had the opportunity to vote by mail in the weeks leading up to the election. The hashtag #AllEyesonKentucky trended on Twitter that day, with celebrities including Reese Witherspoon, Sheryl Crow, and Samuel L. Jackson tweeting out support for Booker. Mindful of how abysmally Barack Obama performed in Eastern Kentucky in 2008, I was eager to see how Booker would do. In Hazard, voting took place at Perry County Central High School, right across from a revitalized Perry County Park, which twenty years earlier had carried the nickname Pillville. On election day, Booker got about as many votes as McGrath in most Eastern Kentucky counties. But his push came too late. By the time all of the mail-in ballots were tallied, McGrath won a narrow victory statewide, aided by comfortable but not outrageously large margins in the mountains.[20]

Booker, who endorsed Senator Bernie Sanders in the 2020 Democratic primary, had a lot more riding on the votes of Appalachian Kentuckians than Barack Obama or Hillary Clinton did in their bids for the presidency. But it was still refreshing to hear Booker attempt to expand the Democratic playbook by making a pitch for rural votes.

"When I talk about the hood to the holler, I'm talking about people who are often treated as invisible, forgotten about, talked at but not listened to," Booker told me in an interview a few months after his primary loss. "I often have this image in my head of waking up in the West End of Louisville and of all the experiences I have throughout my day. A lot of people waking up in Appalachia experience those same struggles. People are looking for leaders who will treat them like they exist, and not just play politics with them."[21]

Booker talks passionately about a permanent underclass of people who have been mired in generational poverty. He believes a national reckoning on race should include a reckoning with poverty.

The last president to successfully woo both urban and rural constituencies was Bill Clinton, who, once elected, didn't always back up his lofty promises with fruitful policy. The 1996 welfare reform bill that Clinton signed into law gutted the Aid to Families with Dependent Children program and ended up hurting the poorest of the poor. I would also argue that it made tens of thousands of Appalachian Kentuckians more dependent on Social Security disability benefits. The Eric Conn fiasco discussed earlier illustrates this point.

In 2005, Virginia Senator Jim Webb envisioned a future in which a politician brings the urban and Appalachian poor together under one umbrella. In an opinion piece in The Wall Street Journal, Webb wrote that "the greatest realignment in modern politics would take place rather quickly if the right national leader found a way to bring the Scots-Irish and African-Americans to the same table, and so to redefine a formula that has consciously set them apart for the past two centuries."[22]

Yes, not all communities in "white America" are doing well. No, the Appalachian experience is in no way comparable to that of the African-American experience. But Webb still has a point, even if the strategy didn't work for him when he made a brief bid for the Democratic presidential nomination in 2016.

Booker is striking many of those same notes. He says he will likely

seek the Democratic nomination for US Senate again in 2022. If he
secures it, he'll go up against incumbent Rand Paul. Booker wants
to build a coalition of urban and rural voters in his home state that
he believes can serve as a regional model.

"When I go places where Trump said the system was broken, I tell
people that he's right about that but that he was BS'ing you about
how we can fix things," Booker told me. "He was just selling snake
oil and exploiting people's pain."[23]

There are others in leadership positions who also seem to grasp
the idea that the country needs a comprehensive plan to help the
economically disadvantaged. Illinois senator Tammy Duckworth is
onto something with her Marshall Plan for coal country, a package of proposed legislation introduced in 2020 that would provide
Medicare coverage for laid-off miners and free college for coal workers and their families. The bill also aims to boost the economy of
coal communities through a combination of stimulus programs.

These are the type of discussions that we should be having, but
instead we remain mired in what separates us.

In the view of many rural Americans, cities are scary, godless,
and crime-infested places. In the eyes of many urban Americans,
small towns are cesspools of bigotry and cultural and political
backwardness. In a lot of ways, I felt more at home living in Berlin,
Germany, than I did in Hazard, Kentucky. And I don't doubt that
a large segment of Eastern Kentuckians would feel more comfortable in rural Germany than in Chicago. Americans have been
grappling with an inherent urban-rural divide since our nation's
founding.

Trump used this division as a campaign strategy both times he
ran, particularly for reelection in 2020 with his constant attacks
against racial justice demonstrations in cities across America. The
Democrats, Trump said while accepting his party's 2020 nomination, approved of "rioters and criminals spreading mayhem in
Democrat-run cities." He further claimed that Democrats wanted
to "demolish the suburbs" by eliminating redlining and other
unfair housing practices.[24] "If I don't win, America's Suburbs will

be OVERRUN with Low Income Projects, Anarchists, Agitators, Looters and, of course, 'Friendly Protesters,'" he tweeted in September 2020.[25]

McConnell enabled Trump. I would have loved to have seen a Booker-McConnell matchup in 2020. As it stood, the centrist McGrath got the nomination and lost to McConnell by nearly 20 points. It took McConnell until December 15 to recognize Biden as president-elect, and another three weeks to acknowledge that Biden had won the election fair and square. But by that time, the insurrectionists were already at the US Capitol. Congressman Hal Rogers was the only Kentucky representative to vote against certifying Biden's election victory.

As one of the few high-profile Republicans willing to condemn Trump's actions on January 6, McConnell appeared statesmanlike. But by waiting so long to state the obvious, and by voting to acquit Trump at his second impeachment trial, he hoped to avoid the full wrath of Trump and his supporters. Although the strategy didn't work, Senate Minority Leader McConnell remains a cunning political operator.

*

From the hood to the holler, America faces a reckoning with poverty. It will take a momentous effort by our institutions and communities to secure lasting change. This is no time for a lack of will, because the effort will require a fundamental shift in how we think about people and places.

Over the next few years, the Democrats will have a choice. It would be a mistake not to target rural poverty as part of their platform, and an even worse transgression to turn their back on those voters who supported Trump in the previous elections.

It is twilight in Hazard, almost twenty years to the day after I first arrived. The vast, family-owned entertainment center on the outskirts of town that used to welcome me back to Hazard after a long day of reporting is now gone, the victim of tough economic times. Hazard is once again putting its hopes in Sykes Enterprises, the same company that Bill Clinton touted as an engine for economic development over two decades ago. The current mayor of Hazard, who pulls double duty as principal of a local high school, believes the jobs created by Sykes could help keep young Eastern Kentuckians from leaving home to find work. In downtown Hazard, a recently launched arts collective brings a jolt of color and renewal to the city's lagging Main Street. Even a collapsed roof couldn't keep the ArtStation from opening. It now hosts poetry readings and other events in an open-air setting.

There have been a few times when I vowed never to step foot again in Eastern Kentucky. It's too bleak, I tell my wife, too depressing. But I keep returning, not only because that is an unkind thing to say about the place a loved one calls home, but also out of a need to see if this truly unique place can experience a triumphant new dawn.

A few days after the 2020 election, I meet up with John Hansen, the former county prosecutor who still reels at what he saw during the height of the prescription pill epidemic in the early 2000s. I suggest we have lunch at the recently opened Steak 'n Shake restaurant, but he tells me that might be awkward because he prosecuted the former county clerk whose son owns the place. We go to Applebee's instead.

I sit down with Joe Palumbo who just started a new job as a COVID-19 contact tracer in Eastern Kentucky. Palumbo has a lot on his mind these days. About three hundred people came to the Black Lives Matter demonstration that he co-organized in Hazard in June 2020. The thirty-four-year-old Palumbo was so moved by the turnout, and especially by all the young faces he saw in the crowd that day, that he feels a sense of duty to continue bringing attention to issues of inequality. He wants to do that work in Hazard, the town he has called home for all but the two years after high school when he moved to Lexington. The son of a Black father and a white mother, Palumbo was raised by grandparents who were first-generation Americans. He refers to himself as "mixed," using the term he has heard applied to himself his entire life, as if he were a breed of dog or a bag of nuts. The march in Hazard helped spawn a movement that has found a thriving home online with thousands of Facebook followers. The group is set to private, because as Palumbo knows from his previous social media experiences, Facebook becomes a waste of time when it devolves into constant bickering. To amplify his voice, Palumbo plans to run for a seat on the Hazard City Commission, a body that has been revitalized in recent years with the election of other younger members. But before making a run, he wants to better inform himself on the social and economic history of his community so that he comes to the table with ideas for change.

Of the eighty people who graduated high school with him, only a few remain in Eastern Kentucky. The rest ran and haven't looked back, he says.

"I don't want young people to be discouraged from imagining a world where they can stay in Eastern Kentucky, get a good paying job, and raise a family," Palumbo says. "That all revolves around knocking down inequality and the old ways and giving people a voice."[26]

The success of the demonstration buoyed him, but in the months that followed, the realities of what the area's social justice advocates are up against hit home. A banner from the march displaying Breonna Taylor's name and bearing the signatures of many of the event's attendees hung for a short time in Hazard's new arts center. Then came complaints and the banner was removed. A couple of months later, the first meeting of a local equity and inclusion committee hit a snag when one of its members disparaged Black Lives Matters protesters as Marxists and terrorists.

While Ned Pillersdorf sorts out the Social Security disability mess created by a fellow attorney and others, he is defending two former University of Louisville cheerleaders charged with disorderly conduct and unlawful assembly for alleged actions at a justice demonstration in Louisville. As we walk his rescue dogs around Dewey Lake on a warm fall day, he also talks about his continued work on behalf of the former Blackjewel coal company miners who blocked coal trains from leaving Harlan County until they received the pay that the bankrupt company owed them.

Over the mountains in Harlan County, Jerod Blevins, just shy of turning thirty, reflects on life since taking part in the Blackjewel protest. A husband and father of three, with a fourth child on the way, Blevins is finished with coal mining, the only job he's known since leaving high school at the age of eighteen. After Blackjewel's bankruptcy, Blevins found work at mines in Virginia. But after three layoffs, he decided it was time to move on. Without Trump in office, the coal industry has no future, he says. He dumped all of his savings into a car detailing business that he now operates out of his front yard and also received his certification to lay fiber-optic cables, a sought after skill in a region still trying to become wired. He hopes he and his family can stay in Harlan County. "It was my dream to be a coal miner ever since I was eight years old," Blevins says. "My oldest son, who is about to turn eight, isn't going to have that same dream." 27

Some other Blackjewel miners have had an even tougher go of it. Dalton Lewis, who, along with his father, helped lead the protest on the train tracks, left Kentucky for a mining job in Alabama. His dad went with him. The younger Lewis is now back in Harlan, confined to a wheelchair after an accident at the Alabama mine. It is uncertain if he will ever walk again.

I stop in for Sunday services at the Gospel Light Baptist Church in Hazard. Pastor Chris Fugate, the state trooper turned preacher, has added yet another title: state representative. Fugate, a Republican who represents Perry County and part of Harlan County, has just won a third two-year term in a landslide. About a hundred mostly unmasked congregants fill the pews. The service starts with a recitation of the Pledge of Allegiance followed by renditions of "The Star-Spangled Banner" and Lee Greenwood's "Proud to be an American." Fugate's sermon that morning is titled "Why I Love America," and focuses on his hopes for God and country. "America will not be brought back to God through the courthouse, the state-house, or the White House," he orates.[28]

Few Americans would dispute the notion that we are a nation in deep distress. We just come at the issue from dramatically different angles. But I hope that we can all agree that it is not enough to keep talking about reckonings, religious, racial or economic. We've been reckoning with these challenges for a very long time, with relatively little to show for our efforts. Perhaps it's time to have a reckoning with the word "reckoning."

We have a power structure in Washington that is more interested in undoing the actions of "the other side" than charting a course for meaningful change. Persistent poverty persists, while ideas like an economic bill of rights get dismissed as dangerous socialist nonsense. We plod on allowing special interest groups to write legislation as the gap between rich and poor continues to grow. The same week that the Dow Jones Industrial Average hit a record high in November 2020, millions of Americans were lining up at food banks across the country.

Though certainly not an easy or pleasant task, it is time to fundamentally reimagine our idea of Americanism. Rather than touting a return to normalcy after a particularly tumultuous and dangerous period in our history, we have to aggressively rethink what is normal and acceptable. We have to attack the historical and structural forces that keep people in poverty. We have to combat the notion that people and places are irredeemable, by telling their stories. Only then will we have a chance of becoming the most righteous version of ourselves.

Afterword

Appalachian Kentuckians are understandably sensitive about "outsiders" writing about their home. While the hardcover edition of *Twilight in Hazard* received its share of praise in the first year of release, it also received pushback from some people who felt it lacked qualities of hope and redemption and spoke too little about community-level efforts to bring about change. At a book talk on Main Street in Hazard in July 2021, I heard from several civic leaders who argued that they were experiencing the dawn of a new day, not the sun setting on a previous one. I was also grilled by some audience members on why I didn't write at greater length about the businesses that have recently opened on and around Main Street. In an opinion piece that ran a few days before the event, Mandi Sheffel, the bookstore owner who kindly hosted me, discussed her journey from opioid addict to entrepreneur. I'm glad she got a forum to tell her incredibly courageous story and am equally pleased that she provided an open forum to discuss my book.

But where does Eastern Kentucky really stand in its economic development process? The struggles of Appalachian Kentucky were briefly spotlighted in July 2021 when the White House released a series of videos highlighting the region's water, Wi-Fi, and other woes. The social media campaign had the dual purpose of promoting President Joe Biden's national infrastructure plan and needling Senate Minority Leader Mitch McConnell for not doing more to help improve living conditions in his home state.

In one of the videos, Martin County, Kentucky, resident Barbi-Ann Miner's kitchen faucet spews a stream of murky tap water. "People talk about 'Eastern Kentucky is poor and they don't really

246 · TWILIGHT IN HAZARD

have anything,'" Miner says as she drives on her community's battered roads. "Well, how are we ever going to have anything if our government won't invest in our infrastructure?"

Though more slickly produced than politically framed messages of decades past, the videos delivered a familiar refrain: Eastern Kentucky is emblematic of an America that has been left behind. The infrastructure bill spurred discussion about strengthening the nation's core. The bill, it was said, had the potential to bring a level of renewal to Eastern Kentucky not seen since the New Deal era, when the region's physical, educational, and public health infrastructure all received major boosts. While a massive infusion of federal money into the Eastern Kentucky economy would be welcome, history tells us that that what happens to that money isn't always the hoped-for panacea. There is the potential pitfall of state and local officials failing to honestly and effectively administer and utilize funds. A former statehouse reporter for the *Courier Journal* reminded me that Kentucky has a history of waste and corruption when it comes to road building in the eastern part of the state.

It is unfortunate that a legislative companion to the infrastructure bill aimed at expanding the country's social safety net failed to pass the US Senate in 2021 when Democrat Joe Manchin of West Virginia announced he would use his swing vote in the 50-50 Senate to kill the Build Back Better bill. Failure to pass the bill brought an end to a temporary child tax credit that lifted millions of Americans out of poverty. It would have made a difference to Eastern Kentucky.

Ultimately, government can provide resources and direction, but it is up to stakeholders in Hazard, Harlan, and other Eastern Kentucky towns to devise a plan to address the area's most pressing challenges. Another year of observing Eastern Kentucky has further convinced me of the value of a jigsaw approach to economic development. No single industry or major project can replace coal, nor should it.

The prison system has tried to fill the void. Eastern Kentucky is home to three federal correctional facilities, and leaders including

Congressman Hal Rogers were pushing hard to build a fourth, which was to be housed on a mountaintop removal site in Letcher County. But the plan was scuttled in 2019, thanks in part to opposition from local activists.

The opening of the Boone's Ridge nature preserve that I wrote about in Chapter 3 has been delayed to the summer of 2023. The latest transformative idea for the region is a massive solar farm on reclaimed mine land in Martin County.

But the type of development that could have a significant impact is more gradual and won't make headlines, at least not for a while. It involves establishing a patchwork of different industries: green energy, tech, tourism, agriculture, manufacturing, and the arts. There is reason for optimism on this front. It is inspiring to see the people of the region banding together to give a distinctly local flavor to development. Taking a page from the popular television show "Shark Tank," a non-profit called Invest 606 has given Eastern Kentucky entrepreneurs, including Sheffel, an opportunity to grow their businesses through training and mentorship.

Geoff Marietta, the founder of Invest 606, has graduate and doctoral degrees from Harvard and an executive background in software development and artificial intelligence. He too is a small business owner who has hopes of revitalizing downtown Harlan with a coffee shop and, more ambitiously, a brewery and restaurant that has drawn significant investment from the local population.

Marietta's wife's family ties to Eastern Kentucky prompted them to move there in 2015. He sees similarities between Appalachian Kentucky and the region in the iron mining area of Minnesota that he grew up in. He is a proponent of the build-from-within model. "If you open shop and are waiting for outsiders to come in, you'll go out of business," he told me. "You have to build a foundation of livability before you can even think about recruiting outside industries."

On the ground it's heartening that people are talking about their future. And I am pleased that *Twilight in Hazard* has helped contribute to conversations about the past, present, and future of a region seeking to show that its most important natural resource is its people, not its coal, even though, as I write, its price has surged after the United States placed sanctions on Russian coal and oil. I hope this book has helped attack the notion that conditions simply are the way they are there and can never change. Things are most definitely happening there, making the coming years a pivotal time that carries hope of twilight leading to a new day.

Acknowledgments

This book was fifteen years in the making, and I am grateful to the *Louisville Courier-Journal* for the opportunity to run its fabled Hazard bureau and to Melville House for allowing me to reflect on how the events I witnessed in Eastern Kentucky continue to impact both the region and the country at large.

It was immensely gratifying to revisit the people and places I chronicled in the early 2000s and to meet new people who could help tell Eastern Kentucky's stories. Thank you to everyone who took the time to talk to me about their work and life experiences, then and now.

Whenever I needed to hear a friendly voice back in my Hazard days, former *C-J* colleagues Matt Batcheldor and Jason Riley were there for me. I'm grateful that our friendship has spanned the years. For this book, Matt and Jason helpfully shared their memories of the years that we spent together at the paper. An extra thanks to Matt for reading over the manuscript.

Thank you to Chuck Myron, another friend I made during my Hazard days. Chuck has done early reads of all of my books, and he once again came through with excellent suggestions.

Ryan Harrington, my first editor at Melville House, served as a strong advocate for the book. As things took shape, he consistently provided sound guidance and deft editing. Later in the process, Carl Bromley stepped in and offered valuable insight and perspective. Thank you to the rest of Melville House's editorial and production team for turning manuscript pages into a polished book.

Thank you to Lexie Gross, Tony Oppegard, and Mike Saenz for helping to spread word about the book.

Thank you to everyone at Centurion for the amazing work you do. I'm proud to be a part of it.

I knew the biggest challenge that I faced with this book was getting a positive review from my wife, Angela, a Harlan County native who understands the complexities of her home region as well as anyone. Thankfully, she liked what she read, and her input and ideas helped make the manuscript stronger.

The rest of my family has also been amazingly supportive. I am lucky to have parents and a sister who are always available to talk about my work, writer to writer.

I hope this book spurs discussion about our national identity and priorities and illuminates the struggles of a place that deserves better from its leaders and institutions.

Notes

PREFACE

1   "Pivot Counties: The Counties That Voted Obama-Obama-Trump from 2008–2016." Ballotpedia, accessed November 2020. https://ballotpedia.org/Pivot_Counties:_The_counties_that_voted_Obama-Obama-Trump_from_2008-2016.

2   Bycoffe, Aaron. "The Most Durably Democratic County in the Country Could Go for Trump." FiveThirtyEight, October 26, 2016. https://fivethirtyeight.com/features/the-most-durably-democratic-county-in-the-country-could-go-for-trump/.

INTRODUCTION

1   Maimon, Alan. "Doping's Sad Toll: One Athlete's Tale from East Germany." *The New York Times*, February 6, 2000. https://www.nytimes.com/2000/02/06/sports/dopings-sad-toll-one-athletes-tale-from-east-germany.html?searchResultPosition=2.

2   Dalakar, Joseph. *The 10-20-30 Provision: Defining Persistent Poverty Counties* (Washington, D. C.: Congressional Research Service, March 27, 2019). 26. https://fas.org/sgp/crs/misc/R45100.pdf.

3   "Tragic pattern repeated." Southern Illinoisan, January 14, 1971, Newspapers.com. https://www.newspapers.com/image/86711770/.

4   Maimon, Alan. "OSM issues new mine-permit rules." *Courier-Journal*, December 22, 2000, Newspapers.com. https://www.newspapers.com/image/111309026/.

5   McConnell, Mitch. "Tribute to Vernon Cooper." S. Doc. No. 151, pt. 2 at 1521–1522 (2005), govinfo.gov, accessed October 27, 2019. https://www.govinfo.gov/content/pkg/CRECB-2005-pt2/html/CRECB-2005-pt2-Pg1521-2.htm.

6   Hofstede, David. *The Dukes of Hazzard: The Unofficial Companion* (Renaissance Books, 1998).

7   Williamson, Kevin D. "Appalachia: The Big White Ghetto." *The Week*, January 25, 2014. https://theweek.com/articles/452321/appalachia-big-white-ghetto.

8   Lowrey, Annie. "What's the Matter with Eastern Kentucky?" *The New York Times* Magazine, June 26, 2014. https://www.nytimes.com/2014/06/29/magazine/whats-the-matter-with-eastern-kentucky.html.

CHAPTER 1

1   Maimon, Alan. "Rural group builds on TV show fight." *Courier-Journal*, December 30, 2003, Newspapers.com. https://www.newspapers.com/image/361805632/.

2   "Heroes of the Hills | Hidden America: Children of the Mountains PART 4/6." *20/20*, ABC News, aired February 13, 2009, YouTube video, 3:16, posted June 21, 2018. https://www.youtube.com/watch?v=dEcjmV6pjak&list=PLrJopoeegOOo6KqoCuoIu95CO9cLoB6Me&index=5.

3   Moody, Lara N., Emily Satterwhite, and Warren K. Bickel. "Substance Use in Rural Central Appalachia: Current Status and Treatment Considerations." *Journal of Rural Mental Health* 41, no. 2 (2017): 123–35. https://doi.org/10.1037/rmh0000064.

4   Maimon, Alan. "Eastern Kentucky in drug epidemic." *Courier-Journal*, February 7, 2001, Newspapers.com. https://www.newspapers.com/image/361505297/.

5   Yetter, Deborah. "Abuse of pain drug increasingly common." *Courier-Journal*, February 11, 2001, Newspapers.com. https://www.newspapers.com/image/361511734.

6   Maimon. "Eastern Kentucky."

7   Yetter. "Abuse."

8   Mongiardo, Daniel. Interview by Alan Maimon, August 12, 2020.

9   Hansen, John. Interview by Alan Maimon, August 28, 2020.

10 Maimon, Alan. "Governor: Financial crisis hurts drug fight." *Courier-Journal*, November 23, 2002, Newspapers.com. https://www.newspapers.com/image/362128745/.

11 Hansen. Interview.

12 Fugate, Chris. Interview by Alan Maimon, November 8, 2020.

13 Fugate. Interview.

14 Maimon. "Governor."

15 "Kentucky Drug Threat Assessment." National Drug Intelligence Center, US Department of Justice, published July 2002, archived January 1, 2006, accessed January 9, 2020. https://www.justice.gov/archive/ndic/pubs1/1540/index.htm.

16 Sprang, Ginny, Moon Choi, Jessica Eslinger, Adrienne Whitt-Woosley, and Rachel Looff. *Grandparents as Parents: Investigating the Health and Well-Being of Trauma-Exposed Families* (Lexington: University of Kentucky Center on Trauma and Children, 2014). https://core.ac.uk/download/pdf/232564805.pdf.

17 Maimon, Alan. "Lawsuit: Negligence led to shattered lives." *Courier-Journal*, July 26, 2001, Newspapers.com. https://www.newspapers.com/image/361736104/.

18 The Associated Press. "Doctor says police lied to get OxyContin." *Courier-Journal*, January 29, 2002, Newspapers.com. https://www.newspapers.com/image/361900059/.

19 Graves, Chris. "Karma: Pill Mill Doc's Home Gets New Use." *The Cincinnati Enquirer*, June 9, 2016. https://www.cincinnati.com/story/news/2016/06/09/karma-pill-mill-docs-home-gets-new-use/85589732/.

20 *The New York Times*. "Abused painkiller's marketing was lax on warnings, critics say." *Courier-Journal*, March 5, 2001, Newspapers.com. https://www.newspapers.com/image/361479256/.

21 Yetter, Deborah. "Ex-prosecutor became adviser to OxyContin maker." *Courier-Journal*, November 23, 2001, Newspapers.com. https://www.newspapers.com/image/361751203/.

22 Yetter. "Ex-prosecutor."

23 Clark, Katherine, and Hal Rogers. *Corrupting Influence: Purdue & the WHO* (Washington, D.C.: US House of Representatives, May 22, 2019). https://katherineclark.house.gov/_cache/files/a/a/aaa7536a-6db3-4192-b943-364e7c599d10/818172D42793504DD9DFE64B77A77C0E.5.22.19-who-purdue-report-final.pdf.

24 Maimon, Alan. "Ground broken for 'clean-coal' power plant in Eastern Kentucky." *Courier-Journal*, July 3, 2001, Newspapers.com. https://www.newspapers.com/image/361843911/.

25 Maimon. "Ground broken."

26 Maimon. "Ground broken."

27 "Kentucky Mountain Power (EnviroPower)." Beyond Coal, Sierra Club, updated November 2008. https://contentdev.sierraclub.org/coal/environmentallaw/plant/kentucky-mountain-power-enviropower.

28 "The Politics of Energy: Coal, the Bush Administration's Fuel of Choice." The Center for Public Integrity, updated September 25, 2018. https://publicintegrity.org/environment/the-politics-of-energy-coal-the-bush-administrations-fuel-of-choice/.

29 Maimon, Alan. "EPA chief backs clean-coal power." *Courier-Journal*, May 12, 2001, Newspapers.com. https://www.newspapers.com/image/361460815/.

30 MacGillis, Alec. "Before the Blankenship-McConnell Feud, the Senator Aided the Mining Executive." ProPublica, May 7, 2018. https://www.propublica.org/article/don-blankenship-mitch-mcconnell-feud-the-senator-aided-the-mining-executive.

31 Maimon, Alan. "Study says slurry pond was too close to mines." *Courier-Journal*, October 10, 2001, Newspapers.com. https://www.newspapers.com/image/361870782/.

32 Maimon, Alan. "Coal slurry spill still taints E. Kentucky, residents say." *Courier-Journal*, October 8, 2001, Newspapers.com. https://www.newspapers.com/image/361867113/.

33 Maimon, Alan. "Hundreds file legal claims over disaster. *Courier-Journal*, February 2, 2001, Newspapers.com. https://www.newspapers.com/image/110518742/.

34 Maimon, Alan. "Chao calls for end to 'food fight' over slurry." *Courier-Journal*, April 21, 2001, Newspapers.com. https://www.newspapers.com/image/361512764/.

35 Wright, Will. "'A Second Pandemic.' How Kentucky Coal Communities Are Bracing for Financial Crisis." *Lexington Herald-Leader*, April 9, 2020. https://www.kentucky.com/news/coronavirus/article241802611.html.

36 Wright, Will. "Ex-UK Trustee Jim Booth owes his home county more than $2 million in overdue taxes." *Lexington Herald-Leader,* October 25, 2019. https://www.kentucky.com/news/state/kentucky/article236514933.html

37 Wright, Will. "'Lock your doors, load your guns,' sheriff warns. Shortfalls gutting Eastern Kentucky." *Lexington Herald-Leader,* February 11, 2019. https://www.kentucky.com/news/state/kentucky/article225392910.html.

38 Honeycutt Spears, Valarie. "Ky. sees rise in overdose deaths from pills obtained in Fla." *Lexington Herald-Leader,* April 12, 2009, updated November 10, 2015. https://www.kentucky.com/news/state/kentucky/article43996500.html.

39 Maimon, Alan. "Web pills a rising threat." *Courier-Journal,* May 2, 2005, Newspapers.com. https://www.newspapers.com/image/180169848/.

40 Maimon, Alan. "Methadone abuse hits Kentucky." *Courier-Journal,* May 9, 2004, Newspapers.com. https://www.newspapers.com/image/180091891/.

41 Loftus, Tom. "Stivers Says He'll Call for Investigation of Kentucky's Purdue Pharma Settlement." *Louisville Courier-Journal,* September 24, 2019. https://www.courier-journal.com/story/news/politics/2019/09/24/kentucky-purdue-pharma-settlement-stivers-call-investigation/2432455001/.

42 Chakradhar, Shraddha, and Casey Ross. "The History of OxyContin, Told Through Purdue Pharma Documents." *STAT,* December 3, 2019. https://www.statnews.com/2019/12/03/oxycontin-history-told-through-purdue-pharma-documents/.

43 Shraddha and Ross. "The History of OxyContin."

44 Shraddha and Ross. "The History of OxyContin."

45 Shraddha and Ross. "The History of OxyContin."

46 Balsamo, Michael, and Geoff Mulvilhill. "OxyContin maker Purdue Pharma to plead to 3 criminal charges." The Associated Press, October 21, 2020. https://apnews.com/article/virus-outbreak-business-criminal-investigations-opioids-epidemics-5f0679ffee14577b1696a94b64abc9c2.

47 "DEA Database: Where the Pain Pills Went." *The Washington Post,* July 16, 2019. https://www.washingtonpost.com/graphics/2019/investigations/dea-pain-pill-database/.

48 Long, Heather, and Andrew Van Dam. "Why aren't more Americans working? Fed Chair Powell says blame education and drugs, not welfare." *The Washington Post*, February 15, 2020. https://www.washingtonpost.com/business/2020/02/15/powell-labor-force/.

CHAPTER 2

1 Withrow, Michael V. "Broad-Form Deed—Obstacle to Peaceful Co-Existence Between Mineral and Surface Owners." *Kentucky Law Journal* 60, no. 3 (1972): 742–56. https://uknowledge.uky.edu/cgi/viewcontent.cgi?article=2639&context=klj.

2 Roberts, David. "Coal left Appalachia devastated. Now it's doing the same to Wyoming." *Vox*, July 9, 2019. https://www.vox.com/energy-and-environment/2019/7/9/20684815/coal-wyoming-bankruptcy-blackjewel-appalachia.

3 Guilford, Gwynn. "The 100-year capitalist experiment that keeps Appalachia poor, sick, and stuck on coal." *Quartz*, December 30, 2017. https://qz.com/1167671/the-100-year-capitalist-experiment-that-keeps-appalachia-poor-sick-and-stuck-on-coal/.

4 Schmidt, Ann. "Near-abandoned coal town struggles to live past 100 Years." Daily Mail, March 27, 2017. https://www.dailymail.co.uk/news/article-4332054/Lynch-Kentucky-turns-100-year-fights-survive.html.

5 Maimon, Alan. "Service celebrates poet's life." *Courier-Journal*, May 2, 2001, Newspapers.com. https://www.newspapers.com/image/361499173/.

6 *Kentucky Coal Facts: 17th Edition* (Frankfort: Kentucky Energy and Environment Cabinet, Department for Energy Development and Independence, in Partnership with the Kentucky Coal Association, 2017). https://eec.ky.gov/Energy/Coal%20Facts%20%20Annual%20Editions/Kentucky%20Coal%20Facts%20-%20 17th%20Edition%20(2017).pdf.

7 *Kentucky Coal Facts.*

8 "Coal Fatalities for 1900 Through 2019." Mine Safety and Health Administration, US Department of Labor, 2019. www.msha.gov, n.d., accessed September 27, 2020. https://arlweb.msha.gov/stats/centurystats/coalstats.asp.

9 "Mining Gets Safer." *The Messenger,* November 2, 1963, Newspapers.com. https://www.newspapers.com/image/529695242/.

10 "Our Appalachia - Martin County Coal Corporation - Episode 42." Morehead State Special Collections & Archives, originally aired 1984, YouTube video, 25:30, posted March 7, 2018. https://www.youtube.com/watch?v=SpM26vOZX6w.

11 Cross, Al. "Mining Board reform passes in House 93–0." *Courier-Journal,* February 22, 2001, Newspapers.com. https://www.newspapers.com/image/361464400/.

12 "The Politics of Energy: Coal, the Bush Administration's Fuel of Choice." The Center for Public Integrity, updated September 25, 2018. https://publicintegrity.org/environment/the-politics-of-energy-coal-the-bush-administrations-fuel-of-choice/.

13 Harris, Gardiner. "Patton-run mines in '70s had inaccurate tests." *Courier-Journal,* April 21, 1998, Newspapers.com. https://www.newspapers.com/image/110341414/.

14 Caylor, Bill. "Mining board composition, penalties opposed by coal industry." *Courier-Journal,* February 25, 2001, Newspapers.com. https://www.newspapers.com/image/361470894/.

15 TECO Energy. "TECO Energy Subsidiaries." *The Tampa Tribune,* October 8, 2003, Newspapers.com. https://www.newspapers.com/image/341987837/.

16 Matney, Paul. Interview by Alan Maimon, August 10, 2020.

17 Maimon, Alan. "Battle lines forming on mining appointee." *Courier-Journal,* August 22, 2001, Newspapers.com. https://www.newspapers.com/image/361722984/.

18 Maimon, Alan. "Mine-safety prosecutor is known as a fighter." *Courier-Journal,* May 13, 2001, Newspapers.com. https://www.newspapers.com/image/361463251/.

19 Dunlop, R. G. "Families fail to get hearing on mine blast." *Courier-Journal,* July 7, 1982, Newspapers.com. https://www.newspapers.com/image/110839904/.

20 Oppegard, Tony. "A 'fairy-tale' approach to coal-mine safety." *Courier-Journal,* April 11, 1983, Newspapers.com. https://www.newspapers.com/image/109548879/.

21 Maimon, Alan. "Mine safety enforcer is fired." *Courier-Journal,* May 28, 2005, Newspapers.com. https://www.newspapers.com/image/180182653/.

22 Maimon, Alan. "Citizen group to try to protect Kentucky River." *Courier-Journal*, May 7, 2002, Newspapers.com. https://www. newspapers.com/image/364581533/.

23 Maimon. "Citizen group."

24 Maimon, Alan. "Blast supervisor wins $142,500 in suit." *Courier-Journal*, April 15, 2003, Newspapers.com. https://www.newspapers. com/image/361920479/.

25 Maimon, Alan. "Boulder from strip mine rips through Pike home." *Courier-Journal*, August 15, 2002, Newspapers.com. https://www. newspapers.com/image/362134975/.

26 Thornton, Tim. "Southwest Virginia family and A&G Coal settle in 3-year-old's death." *The Roanoke Times*, September 7, 2006, updated September 4, 2014. https://roanoke.com/news/ southwest-virginia-family-and-a-g-coal-settle-in-3-year-olds-death/ article_3b76102b-e8db-5216-a222-00dd61df3f89.html.

27 *Wal-mart Stores Inc. v. Smith.* No. 2007-CA-001469-WC, 2008 KY App. Findlaw (June 13, 2008). https://caselaw.findlaw.com/ky-court-of-appeals/1206760.html.

28 Maimon, Alan. "Mining method assailed in Letcher." *Courier-Journal*, December 11, 2002, Newspapers.com." https://www. newspapers.com/image/362135702/.

29 Maimon. "Mining method."

30 Bissett, Bill. Interview by Alan Maimon, July 15, 2020.

31 Bissett. Interview.

32 Bissett. Interview.

33 Lovan, Dylan. "No union mines left in Kentucky, where labor wars once raged." *The Washington Post*, September 5, 2015. https://www.washingtonpost.com/business/economy/closure-of-kentuckys-last-unionized-coal-mine-may-be-ironic-sign-of-success/2015/09/05/8c1a1a42-5417-11e5-8c19-0b6825aa4a3a_story. html.

34 Davis, Dee. Interview by Alan Maimon, February 5, 2020.

35 Bissett. Interview.

36 Bissett. Interview.

37 Oppegard, Tony. Interview by Alan Maimon, 2020.

38 "Voter Registration Statistics Report." Commonwealth of Kentucky, State Board of Elections, February 15, 2017. https://elect.ky.gov/statistics/Documents/voterstatscounty-20170215-094112.pdf.

39 "Voter Registration Statistics Report." Commonwealth of Kentucky, State Board of Elections, February 15, 2017, and September 15, 2020. https://elect.ky.gov/Resources/Documents/voterstatscounty-20200915-093200.pdf.

40 "Voter Registration Statistics Report." Commonwealth of Kentucky, State Board of Elections, September 15, 2020.

41 Thomas, Jo. "Kentucky Town Plans Proudly for Nixon Visit." *The New York Times*, June 5, 1978. https://www.nytimes.com/1978/06/05/archives/new-jersey-pages-kentucky-town-plans-proudly-for-nixon-visit.html.

42 Maimon, Alan. "Videotaping's role in mine death questioned." *Courier-Journal*, July 18, 2004, Newspapers.com. https://www.newspapers.com/image/180240937/.

43 Maimon, Alan. "Mining practice is standard, but poses dangers." *Courier-Journal*, July 18, 2004, Newspapers.com. https://www.newspapers.com/image/180240966/.

44 "Coal Mining Fatality Statistics: 1900-2013." 2013. www.msha.gov. 2013. https://arlweb.msha.gov/stats/centurystats/coalstats.asp.

45 Lawson, Gil. "Governor would tighten benefits for black lung." *Courier-Journal*, November 21, 1996, Newspapers.com. https://www.newspapers.com/image/111426356/.

46 Schreiner, Bruce. "Patton pushes black lung rules." The Associated Press, in *The Messenger*, January 16, 2002, Newspapers.com. https://www.newspapers.com/image/530747591/.

47 Maimon, Alan. "Strict state law offers miners little hope." *Courier-Journal*, January 22, 2001, Newspapers.com. https://www.newspapers.com/image/361853196/.

48 Maimon. "Strict state law."

49 Matney. Interview.

50 Maimon, Alan. "Fletcher seeks stricter mining enforcement." *Courier-Journal*, January 12, 2006, Newspapers.com. https://www.newspapers.com/image/180654208/.

51 Browning, Paul III. Interview by Alan Maimon, December 27, 2019.

52   Horsley, Scott. "Fact Check: Hillary Clinton and Coal Jobs." NPR, May 3, 2016. https://www.npr.org/2016/05/03/476485650/fact-check-hillary-clinton-and-coal-jobs.

53   Kizziah, Lane. "Inside the Greenbrier's star-studded tennis bubble, where World TeamTennis is staging a season like no other." July 30, 2020, *Richmond Times-Dispatch*. https://richmond.com/sports/professional/inside-the-greenbriers-star-studded-tennis-bubble-where-world-teamtennis-is-staging-a-season-like/article_54f1d98e-d2a8-5223-b9c7-a107a007196e.html.

54   Colman, Zack. "Powerful coal executive edges closer to White House." *Politico*, March 30, 2019. https://www.politico.com/story/2019/03/30/coal-executive-white-house-1282376.

55   Gardner, Lauren. "Trump's U.N. nominee was 'absent' ambassador." *Politico*, June 17, 2009. https://www.politico.com/story/2019/06/17/kelly-craft-trump-ambassador-canada-1366735.

56   Devaney, Tim. "House to repeal Obama coal rule Wednesday." *The Hill*, January 31, 2017. https://thehill.com/regulation/energy-environment/317193-house-to-repeal-obama-coal-rule-wednesday.

57   Krol, Debra Utacia. "Trump nuclear energy plan could reopen areas near the Grand Canyon to uranium mining." *The Arizona Republic*, April 24, 2020. https://www.azcentral.com/story/news/local/arizona-environment/2020/04/24/donald-trump-nuclear-plan-could-reopen-grand-canyon-uranium-mining/3012935001/.

58   Egan, Matt. "Trump's push to save coal is failing. Coal demand to plunge to 42-year low." CNN Business, CNN, October 10, 2019. https://www.cnn.com/2019/10/10/business/coal-power-trump/index.html.

59   "Prevalence of Black Lung Continues to Increase Among U.S. Coal Miners." National Institute for Occupational Safety and Health, Centers for Disease Control, updated July 20, 2018. https://www.cdc.gov/niosh/updates/upd-07-20-18.html.

60   Warren, Beth. "Kentucky coal mine officials charged with cheating on key safety tests." *Courier-Journal*, July 11, 2018, updated July 13, 2018. https://www.courier-journal.com/story/news/crime/2018/07/11/kentucky-coal-officials-face-federal-charges-coal-safety-test-scandal/756323002/.

61   Fritsch, David. "U.S. coal production employment has fallen 42% since (blog), US Energy Information Administration (EIA), December 11, 2019, accessed September 18, 2020. https://www.eia.gov/todayinenergy/detail.php?id=42275.

62 "Appalachian Region - Coal-Mining Employment 2018."
Statista, accessed September 18, 2020. https://www.statista.com/
statistics/215789/coal-mining-employment-in-the-appalachian-
region-by-mine-type/.

63 Walsh, Mary Williams. "Congress Saves Coal Miner Pensions,
but What About Others?" *The New York Times*, December 24,
2019. https://www.nytimes.com/2019/12/24/business/coal-miner-
pensions-bailout.html.

64 Dumain, Emma, and Will Wright. "Could fix on coal miners'
pensions boost McConnell, even without black lung help?"
Lexington Herald-Leader, December 16, 2019. https://www.
kentucky.com/news/politics-government/article238282818.html.

65 "Which states produce the most coal?" Frequently Asked Questions
(FAQs), US Energy Information Administration, updated October
19, 2020. https://www.eia.gov/tools/faqs/faq.php?id=69&t=2.

66 "Which states."

67 Lipton, Eric. "'The Coal Industry Is Back,' Trump Proclaimed. It
Wasn't." *The New York Times*, October 5, 2020. https://www.
nytimes.com/2020/10/05/us/politics/trump-coal-industry.html.

68 Perry, Rick (@GovernorPerry). ".@JoeBiden & Barack Obama killed
the coal industry and if elected he will come after oil & gas!
@realDonaldTrump is a champion for ALL American energy https://
nypost.com/2020/10/24/why-pennsylvania-miners-are-voting-
trump-even-though-he-didnt-bring-jobs-back/... #KAG2020."
Twitter. October 24, 2020, 1:25 p.m. https://twitter.com/
GovernorPerry/status/1320053693534920706.

69 Bissett. Interview.

70 Bissett. Interview.

71 Matney. Interview.

72 James, Connor. "'Never be afraid to stand up': Miners who started
protest reflect on Blackjewel saga." WYMT News, August 13, 2019.
https://www.wymt.com/content/news/Never-be-afraid-to-stand-up-
Miners-who-started-protest-reflect-on-Blackjewel-saga-540531811.html.

73 Franklin, Sean. "Eastern Kentucky coal miners face struggle after
company's abrupt bankruptcy." WBIR, July 9, 2019. https://www.
wbir.com/article/news/local/eastern-kentucky-coal-miners-face-
struggle-after-companys-abrupt-bankruptcy/51-b517fde7-d078-
4c22-b859-4dc128976905.

74 Browning. Interview.

CHAPTER 3

1 "Transcript: Clinton Addresses Poverty Issue in Appalachia Speech: July 5, 1999." CNN, July 6, 1999. https://www.cnn.com/ ALLPOLITICS/stories/1999/07/06/clinton.visit/transcript.html.

2 Streitfeld, David. "A Town's Future Is Leaving the Country." *Los Angeles Times*, March 28, 2004, Newspapers.com. https://www. newspapers.com/image/192892899/.

3 Maimon, Alan. "Patton video promotes E. Kentucky." *Courier-Journal*, January 9, 2001, Newspapers.com. https://www. newspapers.com/image/111503752/.

4 Maimon. "Patton video."

5 Drake, Richard B. *A History of Appalachia* (Lexington, Kentucky: The University Press of Kentucky, 2001). 73.

6 Greene, Rebecca Dayle. "Language, Ideology and Identity in Rural Eastern Kentucky" (PhD diss., Stanford University, 2010). https://stacks.stanford.edu/file/druid:fh361zh5489/RGreene%20 dissertation-augmented.pdf.

7 Maimon, Alan. "Some job seekers must shed their distinct way of speaking." *Courier-Journal*, April 9, 2001, Newspapers.com. https://www.newspapers.com/image/361481206/.

8 Medaris, Tyler. Interview by Alan Maimon, June 16, 2020.

9 Medaris. Interview.

10 Karl, Jonathan, and Sarah Netter. "'Prince of Pork' Hal Rogers Will Chair House Appropriations Committee." ABC News, December 8, 2010. https://abcnews.go.com/Politics/house-gop-appoints-prince-pork-hal-rogers-chair/story?id=12343673.

11 Clines, Francis X. "Backwoods Image Gone, Kentucky Town Revels in Hillbilly Roots." *The New York Times*, April 1, 2001. https://www.nytimes.com/2001/04/01/us/backwoods-image-gone-kentucky-town-revels-in-hillbilly-roots.html.

12 Clines. "Backwoods Image."

13 Maimon, Alan. "Letcher Fiscal Court rejects bottle bill, cites concerns about cost." *Courier-Journal*, October 9, 2001, Newspapers.com. https://www.newspapers.com/image/361869207/.

14 Mueller, John. Email to Alan Maimon, October 10, 2001.

15 Maimon, Alan. "Kentucky suffers more than its neighbors."
Courier-Journal, November 5, 2001, Newspapers.com. https://
www.newspapers.com/image/361823033/.

16 "Ten Year Summary: Fire and Acres Burned 2010–2019." Kentucky
Energy and Environmental Cabinet, accessed November 2020.
https://eec.ky.gov/Natural-Resources/Forestry/Documents/10-
Year%20Summary%20of%20Number%20of%20Fires%20
and%20Acres%20Burned.pdf.

17 "Kentucky Drug Threat Assessment." National Drug Intelligence
Center, US Department of Justice, July 2002, accessed January 9,
2020. https://www.justice.gov/archive/ndic/pubs1/1540/marijuan.
htm.

18 Barton, Shane. Interview by Alan Maimon, May 6, 2020.

19 Katers, Nicholas. "Tourist Attractions in Eastern Kentucky." *USA
Today,* accessed November 2020. https://traveltips.usatoday.com/
places-eastern-kentucky-area-26608.html.

20 Maimon, Alan. "Where the ELK run free." *Courier-Journal,*
July 31, 2005, Newspapers.com. https://www.newspapers.com/
image/180258223/.

21 Novelly, Thomas. "Donald Trump Jr. makes a stop at Applebee's in
Eastern Kentucky." *Courier-Journal,* September 30, 2018. https://
www.courier-journal.com/story/news/politics/2018/09/30/donald-
trump-jr-visits-applebees-eastern-kentucky/1480959002/.

22 Novelly. "Donald Trump Jr."

23 WKYT News Staff. "Fazoli's says Hazard restaurant opening most
successful in company history." WKYT, April 18, 2018. https://
www.wkyt.com/content/news/Fazolis-says-Hazard-opening-most-
successful-in-company-history-480131063.html.

24 "Visitation Numbers." About Us, National Park Service, updated
March 10, 2020. https://www.nps.gov/aboutus/visitation-numbers.
htm.

25 Sargent, Emily. "Boone's Ridge CEO gives update at chamber
meeting." *Harlan Enterprise,* March 13, 2020. https://www.
harlanenterprise.net/2020/03/13/boones-ridge-ceo-gives-update-at-
chamber-meeting/.

26 Noe, Caleb. "Appalachian Wildlife Center in Bell County receives $12.5 million grant." WYMT News, November 1, 2016. https://www.wymt.com/content/news/Appalachian-Wildlife-Center-in-Bell-County-receives-125-million-grant-399524751.html.

27 Estep, Bill. "Foundation plans to convert empty Eastern Kentucky industrial park into wildlife tourism attraction." *Lexington Herald-Leader*, May 20, 2015. https://www.kentucky.com/news/state/kentucky/article44600607.html.

28 Reynolds, Hannah. "The Appalachian Wildlife Foundation announces plans for additions to wildlife reserve, including zoo." WYMT News, April 2, 2019. https://www.wymt.com/content/news/The-Appalachian-Wildlife-Foundation-announces-plans-for-additions-to-wildlife-reserve-including-zoo-508026681.html?ref=681.

29 Sargent. "Boone's Ridge CEO."

30 Cheves, John. "State using coal taxes for Rupp Arena project, upsetting coal-county leaders." *Lexington Herald-Leader*, June 11, 2013. https://www.kentucky.com/sports/college/kentucky-sports/uk-basketball-men/article44428773.html.

31 Barton. Interview.

32 Dunlop, R. G. "The Elk, the Tourists and the Missing Coal Country Jobs." Kentucky Center for Investigative Reporting, October 22, 2020. https://kycir.org/2020/10/22/the-elk-the-tourists-and-the-missing-coal-country-jobs/.

33 Barton. Interview.

34 Barton. Interview.

35 Staff. "Census shows sharp population decline in Kentucky's rural areas, big bump around Lexington." WDKY, Fox Lexington, April 18, 2019. https://foxlexington.com/news/local/census-shows-sharp-population-decline-in-kentuckys-rural-areas-big-bump-around-lexington.

36 Barton. Interview.

37 "SOAR Blueprint." Shaping Our Appalachian Region, May 29, 2018, accessed September 20, 2020. https://www.soar-ky.org/blueprint.

38 Miller, Alfred, "They Were Promised Broadband and High-Tech Jobs. They're Still Waiting." ProPublica, January 15, 2020. https://www.propublica.org/article/they-were-promised-broadband-and-high-tech-jobs-theyre-still-waiting.

39 Arnett, Jared. "Creating a future now in Appalachia. 'A shining example of what is right.'" *Lexington Herald-Leader*, December 27, 2019. https://www.kentucky.com/opinion/op-ed/article238749513.html.

40 Marema, Tim. "Top 100 Counties, SNAP Participants as Percent of Population." *The Daily Yonder*, May 7, 2018. https://dailyyonder.com/top-100-counties-snap-participants-percent-population/2018/05/07/.

41 The Crittenden Press. "Kentucky report: 1 in 9 on disability." *Kentucky New Era*, November 17, 2017. https://www.kentuckynewera.com/news/ap/article_eb6e2e80-cbf6-11e7-8871-97ea4db5c5c9.html.

42 "Education – High School and College Completion Rates, 2014–2018." Appalachian Regional Commission, accessed September 20, 2020. https://data.arc.gov/reports/custom_report.asp?REPORT_ID=83.

43 Ravitz, Jessica. "Forget abortion: What women in Appalachian Kentucky really want." CNN Health, CNN, December 13, 2017. https://www.cnn.com/2017/12/13/health/kentucky-appalachia-women-eprise/index.html.

44 Khazan, Olga. "Kentucky Is Home to the Greatest Declines in Life Expectancy." *The Atlantic*, May 8, 2017. https://www.theatlantic.com/health/archive/2017/05/kentucky/525777/.

45 Mandell, Tim. "Eastern Kentucky has some of the nation's highest cancer mortality rates, study finds." Kentucky Health News, University of Kentucky, January 25, 2017. http://ci.uky.edu/kentuckyhealthnews/2017/01/25/eastern-kentucky-has-some-of-nations/.

CHAPTER 4

1 Mann, Thomas. *The Magic Mountain*, trans. John E. Woods (London: Vintage, 1996).

2 Bradlee, Ben, Jr. "Conviction splits 'Bloody Harlan.'" *The Boston Globe*, December 28, 1982, Newspapers.com. https://www.newspapers.com/image/437260934/.

3   Bradlee. "Conviction."

4   Bradlee. "Conviction."

5   Bradlee. "Conviction."

6   Bradlee. "Conviction."

7   Associated Press. "Sheriff convicted in plot runs again in Kentucky." *Courier-Journal*, January 21, 2002, Newspapers.com. https://www. newspapers.com/image/361890798/.

8   Browning, Paul III. Interview by Alan Maimon, December 27, 2019.

9   Alford, Roger. "Alleged dealer paid ex-sheriff." Associated Press, *The Messenger*, April 11, 2002, Newspapers.com." https://www. newspapers.com/image/530395238/.

10 Maimon, Alan. "Sheriff: Slain candidate faced investigation." *Courier-Journal*, May 24, 2002, Newspapers.com. https://www. newspapers.com/image/364576537/.

11 Maimon. "Sheriff: Slain."

12 Maimon. "Sheriff: Slain."

13 Gerth, Joseph, and Alan Maimon. "Drug investigation targeted suspect in sheriff's death." *Courier-Journal*, April 17, 2002, Newspapers.com. https://www.newspapers.com/image/361752065/.

14 Maimon, Alan. "3,000 mourn slain Pulaski sheriff at funeral." *Courier-Journal*, April 19, 2002, Newspapers.com. https://www. newspapers.com/image/361760014/.

15 *The St. Louis Republic*. "Kentucky Mountaineers: Feuds have existed for two hundred years." *The Des Moines Register*, July 2, 1899, Newspapers.com, posted by JaneMarieHoward1954, November 16, 2017. https://www.newspapers.com/clip/15168157/.

16 *The St. Louis Republic*. "Kentucky Mountaineers."

17 Maimon, Alan. "Ex-Jackson clerk had 'faith in the justice system.'" *Courier-Journal*, February 25, 2004, Newspapers.com. https:// www.newspapers.com/image/180435663/.

18 Gerth, Joseph, and Alan Maimon. "Clay clerk sued by two election workers." *Courier-Journal*, May 25, 2002, Newspapers.com. https://www.newspapers.com/image/364576816/.

19 Gerth and Maimon. "Clay clerk sued."

20 Maimon, Alan. "Jury finds pair guilty in election fraud case." *Courier-Journal*, September 17, 2004, Newspapers.com. https://www.newspapers.com/image/180726544/.

21 Maimon, Alan, and Mark Pitsch. "Clay clerk defeated; Wood wins in Pulaski." *Courier-Journal*, May 29, 2002, Newspapers.com. https://www.newspapers.com/image/364579987/.

22 Maimon, Alan. "Life sentence closes Catron case." *Courier-Journal*, December 20, 2003, Newspapers.com. https://www.newspapers.com/image/361806894/.

23 The Associated Press. "Ex-Harlan County deputy enters plea in murder." *Courier-Journal*, September 29, 2009, Newspapers.com. https://www.newspapers.com/image/181818407/.

24 Browning. Interview.

25 Browning. Interview.

26 Estep, Bill. "Final four defendants sentenced to time served in Clay County corruption case." *Lexington Herald-Leader*, April 23, 2014. https://www.kentucky.com/news/local/watchdog/article44486202.html.

27 Estep. "Final four defendants."

28 Gladwell, Malcolm. *Outliers: The Story of Success* (New York: Back Bay Books, 2008). 166.

29 Gladwell. *Outliers*. 167.

30 Editorial. "Eastern Kentucky can't soar while public corruption thrives." *Lexington Herald-Leader*, December 8, 2013. https://www.kentucky.com/opinion/editorials/article44459160.html.

31 Loftus, Tom. "Richie Farmer sentenced to 27 months in prison." *Courier-Journal*, January 14, 2014. https://www.courier-journal.com/story/news/local/2014/01/14/richie-farmer-to-find-out-his-sentence-tuesday/4472115/.

32 WYMT Staff. "Former Judge-Executive avoids jail time." WYMT, May 18, 2018. https://www.wymt.com/content/news/Former-Judge-Executive-avoids-jail-time--483085221.html.

33 Johnson, Johnny. Interview by Alan Maimon, August 28, 2020.

34 Estep, Bill. "Harlan County sheriff arrests judge-executive on more than dozen charges." *Lexington Herald-Leader*, June 4, 2013. https://www.kentucky.com/news/local/crime/article44427441.html.

35 Mosley, Dan. Interview by Alan Maimon, December 26, 2019.

36 Mosley. Interview.

37 Wigler, Josh. "The 37 Greatest 'Justified' Villains, Ranked." MTV News, January 20, 2015. http://www.mtv.com/news/2053465/ justified-villains-ranked/.

38 Browning. Interview.

CHAPTER 5

1 Maimon, Alan. "U.S. judge seeks compromise on commandments." *Courier-Journal*, March 31, 2001, Newspapers.com. https://www. newspapers.com/image/361498052/.

2 Maimon. "U.S. judge seeks."

3 Quinlan, Michael. "Patton signs bill on Commandments." *Courier-Journal*, April 22, 2000, Newspapers.com. https://www.newspapers. com/image/110513911/.

4 "Schools, not chapels." Editorial, *Courier-Journal*, April 19, 2001, Newspapers.com. https://www.newspapers.com/image/361511272/.

5 Maimon, Alan. "Cumberland High School chapel is reopened." *Courier-Journal*, April 26, 2001, Newspapers.com. https://www. newspapers.com/image/361478612/.

6 Caldwell, Alicia. "Religious liberty group takes part in case." *Tampa Bay Times*, December 4, 2000, Newspapers.com. https:// www.newspapers.com/image/328208907/.

7 "Liberty Counsel." Southern Poverty Law Center, accessed September 21, 2020. https://www.splcenter.org/fighting-hate/ extremist-files/group/liberty-counsel.

8 Maimon, Alan. "Judge: Ten Commandments displays must come down." *Courier-Journal*, June 23, 2001, Newspapers.com. https:// www.newspapers.com/image/361788324/.

9 Maimon. "Judge: Ten Commandments."

10 Forbes, Buddy. "'It's just somebody taking a blessing away': Organization demands Pike County schools to remove prayer lockers." WYMT, October 4, 2019. https://www.wymt.com/ content/news/Its-just-somebody-taking-a-blessing-away-Organization-demands-Pike-County-Schools-to-remove-prayer-lockers-562219971.html.

11 Estep, Bill. "Pulaski pays $230,000 in fees in 10 Commandments case." *Lexington Herald-Leader*, February 23, 2011. https://www.kentucky.com/news/local/crime/article44125044.html.

12 American Civil Liberties Union. "Unsuccessful Bid to Promote Religion Costly for Counties." Press release, September 9, 2011. https://www.aclu.org/press-releases/unsuccessful-bid-promote-religion-costly-counties.

13 Maimon, Alan. "ACLU seeks to reopen Boyd suit." *Courier-Journal*, July 7, 2005, Newspapers.com. https://www.newspapers.com/image/180247684/.

14 Savage, David G. "Justices to Hear Social Issue Cases." *Los Angeles Times*, January 7, 2000. https://www.latimes.com/archives/la-xpm-2000-jan-07-mn-51645-story.html.

15 Graham, Billy. "Billy Graham on the Sanctity of Life." *Blog from the Billy Graham Library* (blog), The Billy Graham Library, January 24, 2020. https://billygrahamlibrary.org/blog-billy-graham-on-the-sanctity-of-life/.

16 Estep, Bill. "Police officers lead prayer meeting to combat Eastern Kentucky drug problem." *Lexington Herald-Leader*, June 14, 2011. https://www.kentucky.com/news/local/crime/article44103216.html.

17 Fugate, Chris. Interview by Alan Maimon, November 8, 2020.

18 Maimon, Alan. "The female anatomy gets lots of attention." *Courier-Journal*, May 6, 2001, Newspapers.com. https://www.newspapers.com/image/361502400.

19 Maimon, Alan. "Eastern Kentuckians follow heart to crusade." *Courier-Journal*, June 22, 2001, Newspapers.com. https://www.newspapers.com/image/361787870/.

20 Smith, Peter. "'The only answer to the race problem is love.'" *Courier-Journal*, June 22, 2001, Newspapers.com. https://www.newspapers.com/image/361787870/.

21 Smith. "The only answer."

22 Maimon. "Eastern Kentuckians."

23 Goodstein, Laurie. "AFTER THE ATTACKS: FINDING FAULT; Falwell's Finger-Pointing Inappropriate, Bush Says." *The New York Times*, September 15, 2001. https://www.nytimes.com/2001/09/15/us/after-attacks-finding-fault-falwell-s-finger-pointing-inappropriate-bush-says.html.

24 Goodstein. "AFTER THE ATTACKS."

25 Associated Press. "THREATS AND RESPONSES; Muhammad a Terrorist to Falwell." *The New York Times*, October 4, 2002. https://www.nytimes.com/2002/10/04/us/threats-and-responses-muhammad-a-terrorist-to-falwell.html.

26 Kristof, Nicholas D. " Giving God a Break." *The New York Times*, June 10, 2003. https://www.nytimes.com/2003/06/10/opinion/giving-god-a-break.html.

27 "Franklin Graham calls Islam a 'wicked and evil' religion." BowersMediaGroup, video, 41:07, September 23, 2015. https://www.youtube.com/watch?v=I5VF_oMhE54.

28 Bailey, Sarah Pulliam, Susan Svrluga, and Michelle Boorstein. "Jerry Falwell Jr. resigns as head of Liberty University, will get $10.5 million in compensation." *The Washington Post*, August 25, 2020. https://www.washingtonpost.com/education/2020/08/25/falwell-resigns-confirmed/.

29 Galli, Mark. "Trump Should Be Removed from Office." *Christianity Today*, December 19, 2019. https://www.christianitytoday.com/ct/2019/december-web-only/trump-should-be-removed-from-office.html.

30 Halon, Yael. "Christianity Today's call for Trump's removal would have 'disappointed' Billy Graham, his son says." Fox News, December 23, 2019. https://www.foxnews.com/media/rev-graham-father-would-be-disappointed-in-christianity-today-after-paper-calls-for-trumps-removal.

31 Prothero, Stephen. "Billy Graham Built a Movement. Now His Son Is Dismantling It." *Politico Magazine*, February 24, 2018, accessed September 22, 2020. https://www.politico.com/magazine/story/2018/02/24/billy-graham-evangelical-decline-franklin-graham-217077.

32 McCarty, Winston. Interview by Alan Maimon, July 7, 2020.

33 King, Steven. Interview by Alan Maimon, July 9, 2020.

34 McCarty. Interview.

CHAPTER 6

1 Malone, James, Megan Woolhouse, Alan Maimon, and Deborah Yetter. "Fort Campbell lockdown brings traffic jam." *Courier-Journal*, September 12, 2001, Newspapers.com. https://www.newspapers.com/image/361757766/.

2 Maimon, Alan. "Mountain spirit: Law office readies New York trip to help in clean-up." *Courier-Journal*, September 12, 2001, Newspapers.com. https://www.newspapers.com/image/361764148/.

3 Maimon. "Mountain spirit."

4 Maimon, Alan. "Kentuckian honored in emotional ceremony." *Courier-Journal*, September 24, 2001, Newspapers.com. https://www.newspapers.com/image/361829862/.

5 Maimon, Alan. "A negligent death in Iraq." *Courier-Journal*, October 11, 2005, Newspapers.com. https://www.newspapers.com/image/180670288/.

6 Tackett, Sam. Interview by Alan Maimon, August 14, 2020.

7 Jaffe-Walt, Chana. "Unfit for Work: The Startling Rise of Disability in America." NPR, accessed October 9, 2020. https://apps.npr.org/unfit-for-work/.

8 Social Security disability statistics:

https://www.ssa.gov/policy/docs/quickfacts/stat_snapshot/

https://www.ssa.gov/policy/docs/statcomps/di_asr/2018/di_asr18.pdf

https://www.ssa.gov/policy/docs/statcomps/supplement/2016/5j.pdf

https://www.ssa.gov/policy/docs/statcomps/ssi_asr/2019/sect01.pdf

https://www.ssa.gov/budget/FY21Files/2021BST.pdf

Picchi, Aimee. "Social Security: Here's What Trump's proposed budget could mean for your benefits." *USA Today*, February 12, 2020. https://www.usatoday.com/story/money/2020/02/12/social-security-trump-budget-aims-cuts-disabled-workers-program/4738795002/.

9 *Social Security Disability in Kentucky: The Evolution of Dependence, 1980–2015* (Frankfort: Kentucky Cabinet for Health and Family Services, 2017). http://www.uky.edu/CommInfoStudies/IRJCI/SSDIinKy.pdf.

10 *Social Security Disability in Kentucky.*

11 Roller, Emma. "This Congressional District Ranks Dead Last for Well-Being." *The Atlantic*, March 25, 2014. https://www.theatlantic.com/politics/archive/2014/03/this-congressional-district-ranks-dead-last-for-well-being/455913/.

12 Sluka, Jeffrey. "Living on Their Nerves: Nervous Debility in Northern Ireland." *Health Care for Women International* 10, no. 2–3 (February 1989): 219–243.

13 Reynolds, Karen. "Fear, Medication and Black Mental Health: A Physician's View from the Front Lines." The Root, May 29, 2019. https://www.theroot.com/fear-medication-and-black-mental-health-a-physician-s-1835075765.

14 Gerth, Joseph. "'Mr. Social Security' campaigning." *Courier-Journal*, January 18, 2011, Newspapers.com. https://www.newspapers.com/image/181801363/.

15 Gerth. "'Mr. Social Security.'"

16 United States Senate Committee on Homeland Security and Governmental Affairs. *How Some Legal, Medical, and Judicial Professionals Abused Social Security Disability Programs for the Country's Most Vulnerable: A Case Study of the Conn Law Firm* (Washington, D.C.: United States Senate Committee on Homeland Security and Governmental Affairs, October 7, 2013). https://www.govexec.com/media/gbc/docs/pdfs_edit/100713cc1.pdf.

17 United States Senate. *How Some Legal.*

18 United States Senate. *How Some Legal.*

19 United States Senate. *How Some Legal.*

20 United States Senate. *How Some Legal.*

21 United States Senate. *How Some Legal.*

22 United States Senate. *How Some Legal.*

23 Paletta, Damian. "Disability-Claim Judge Has Trouble Saying 'No.'" *The Wall Street Journal*, May 19, 2011. https://www.wsj.com/articles/SB10001424052748704681904576319163605918524.

24 United States Senate. *How Some Legal.*

25 Coburn, Tom. "Social Security Disability Benefits: Did a Group of Judges, Doctors and Lawyers Abuse Programs for the Country's Most Vulnerable?" Prepared remarks, US Senate Homeland Security and Governmental Affairs Committee hearing, October 7, 2013. https://www.hsgac.senate.gov/imo/media/doc/Opening%20Statement-Coburn-2013-10-07.pdf.

26 Pillersdorf, Ned. Facebook photo, May 31, 2015. https://www.facebook.com/photo?fbid=10200496567373287&set=a.2207908653822.

27 Estep, Bill. "Lawsuit blames two suicides on move to cut disability benefits." *Lexington Herald-Leader*, January 21, 2016. https://www.kentucky.com/news/state/article55898210.html.

28 Pillersdorf, Ned. Interview by Alan Maimon, December 28, 2019.

29 Estep. "Lawsuit."

30 Rogers, Hal. Letter from Congressman Hal Rogers to Social Security Administration Commissioner Andrew Saul. October 17, 2019. https://halrogers.house.gov/_cache/files/4/6/46off5e8-295e-479c-92d4-0fe089544fc9/79AF69CA09F6E71432C75F6BDEBE 0E87.letter-to-ssa-saul-re-conn-10.17.19.pdf.

31 Estep, Bill. "The cost of helping Eric Conn in a massive disability Fraud? 25 years in prison." *Lexington Herald-Leader*, September 22, 2017. https://www.kentucky.com/news/state/article174868001. html.

32 Estep. "The cost."

33 "Fugitive Lawyer Involved in Largest Social Security Fraud Scheme Sentenced to 15 Years in Prison for His Escape and Related Crimes." Press release, US Department of Justice, September 7, 2018. https://www.justice.gov/opa/pr/fugitive-lawyer-involved-largest-social-security-fraud-scheme-sentenced-15-years-prison-his.

34 Estep, Bill. "Update: Person claiming to be fugitive Eric Conn offers terms of surrender in emails." *Lexington Herald-Leader*, June 10, 2017. https://www.kentucky.com/news/state/article155553529.html.

35 Estep. "Update."

36 Beam, Adam. "Kentucky lawyer behind disability fraud given 15 more years." Associated Press, September 7, 2018. https://apnews. com/f88882ebb6b54719808984b0dc0a1e02/Kentucky-lawyer-behind-disability-fraud-given-15-more-years.

37 Frost, Krista. "Man who helped Eric C. Conn escape gets jail time." WYMT, June 29, 2018. https://www.wymt.com/content/news/Man-who-helped-Eric-C-Conn-escape-gets-jail-time-486986951.html.

38 WYMT/WKYT. "Abraham Lincoln statue among Eric C. Conn items heading to auction." WYMT, August 10, 2018. https://www.wymt.com/content/news/Abraham-Lincoln-statue-among-Eric-C-Conn-items-heading-to-auction-490602561.html.

39 Pillersdorf, Ned. Interview by Alan Maimon, November 7, 2020.

40 Pillersdorf, Ned. Facebook video. February 15, 2018. https://www. facebook.com/ned.pillersdorf/posts/10204202509659528.

CHAPTER 7

1   *Occupational Air Quality Tests in Coal Mines, Before the Senate.*
    105th Cong. S8891–S8893 (July 23, 1998) (statement of Paul
    Wellstone, Senator from Minnesota). https://www.congress.gov/
    congressional-record/1998/7/23/senate-section/article/s8891-1.

2   Oppegard, Tony. "Paul Wellstone: In Memoriam." *The Mountain
    Eagle*, October 30, 2002.

3   Mongiardo, Vincent J. "Interview with Vincent J. Mongiardo, June
    17, 1986." Interview by Doug Cantrell, Appalachia: Immigrants
    in the Coal Fields Oral History Project, Louie B. Nunn Center
    for Oral History, University of Kentucky Libraries, June 17, 1986.
    https://kentuckyoralhistory.org/ark:/16417/xt7g7940tq7m.

4   Mongiardo, V. "Interview."

5   Mongiardo, Daniel. Interview by Alan Maimon, August 12, 2020.

6   Mongiardo, D. Interview.

7   Mongiardo, D. Interview.

8   Yetter, Deborah. "Senator might win new seat, keep old one."
    Courier-Journal, November 1, 2002, Newspapers.com. https://
    www.newspapers.com/image/362038520/.

9   Mongiardo, D. Interview.

10 Maimon, Alan, and Al Cross. "Candidate slams TV ad using 9/11
    images." *Courier-Journal*, October 11, 2002, Newspapers.com.
    https://www.newspapers.com/image/362116256/.

11 Mongiardo, D. Interview.

12 Huber, Tim, and Roger Alford. "Raucous pro-coal crowds pack
    mining hearings." Associated Press, *Hartford Courant*, October
    13, 2009. https://www.courant.com/sdut-us-mountaintop-mining-
    101309-20090ct13-story.html.

13 Mongiardo, D. Interview.

14 Cross, Al. "Conner indicted on mail fraud charge." *Courier-
    Journal*, July 10, 2003, Newspapers.com. https://www.newspapers.
    com/image/361917615/.

15 Mongiardo, D. Interview.

16 Loftus, Tom. "Failings of health care have spurred Mongiardo."
    Courier-Journal, May 23, 2004, Newspapers.com. https://www.
    newspapers.com/image/180093913/.

17 Schreiner, Bruce. "Bunning sets fund record in Senate race." Associated Press, *Courier-Journal*, August 7, 2004, Newspapers. com. https://www.newspapers.com/image/180289362/.

18 Cross, Al. "Bunning apologizes for 'joke' about political rival." *Courier-Journal*, April 1, 2004, Newspapers.com. https://www. newspapers.com/image/180451655/.

19 Cross, Al. Interview by Alan Maimon, July 8, 2020.

20 "Bunning's fitness." Editorial, *Courier-Journal*, October 14, 2004, Newspapers.com. https://www.newspapers.com/image/180731418/.

21 Lindenberger, Michael A., and Tom Loftus. "Mongiardo says Bunning allies' remarks out of line." *Courier-Journal*, October 29, 2004, Newspapers.com. https://www.newspapers.com/ image/180741550/.

22 Cross. Interview.

23 Mongiardo, D. Interview.

24 Loftus, Tom. "Bunning holds off challenge." *Courier-Journal*, November 3, 2004, Newspapers.com. https://www.newspapers. com/image/181149143/.

25 "Religion and the Presidential Vote." US Politics and Policy, Pew Research Center, December 6, 2004. https://www.pewresearch.org/ politics/2004/12/06/religion-and-the-presidential-vote/.

26 Ayers, John W. "Changing Sides: 9/11 and the American Muslim Voter." Review of Religious Research 49, no. 2 (December 2007): 187–198. https://www.jstor.org/stable/20447488.

27 Hawpe, David. "Heroes' tales underscore the paltriness of our politics." *Courier-Journal*, November 7, 2004, Newspapers.com." https://www.newspapers.com/image/181169500/.

28 Kentucky election data since 2000 can be found below:

https://elect.ky.gov/SiteCollectionDocuments/Election%20 Results/2000-2009/2000/00Gen_Statewidebycounty.txt

https://elect.ky.gov/SiteCollectionDocuments/ Election%20Results/2000-2009/2004/General%20 Election/2004statebyCOUNTY.txt

https://elect.ky.gov/SiteCollectionDocuments/Election%20 Results/2000-2009/2008/General%20Election/STATEwide%20 by%20candidate%20by%20county%20gen%202008.txt

https://elect.ky.gov/SiteCollectionDocuments/Election%20
Results/2010-2019/2012/2012genresults.pdf

https://elect.ky.gov/results/2010-2019/Documents/2016%20
General%20Election%20Results.pdf

https://elect.ky.gov/results/2020-2029/Documents/2020%20
General%20Election%20Results.pdf

29 Cross. Interview.

30 Brosi, George. "This Side of the Mountain." *Appalachian Heritage* 36, no. 4 (Fall 2008): 7. https://search.proquest.com/openview/15eab9352ac56d71e59c8d9bd02e3167/1.

31 "Hate Map." Southern Poverty Law Center, accessed September 24, 2020. https://www.splcenter.org/hate-map.

32 Smith, Ben. "Obama on small-town Pa.: Clinging to religion, guns, xenophobia." *Politico*, April 11, 2008. https://www.politico.com/blogs/ben-smith/2008/04/obama-on-small-town-pa-clinging-to-religion-guns-xenophobia-007737.

33 Matney, Paul. Interview by Alan Maimon, August 10, 2020.

34 Ornstein, Norman Jay. "Introduction." *Daedalus*, Spring 2013. https://www.amacad.org/publication/introduction-democracy-common-good.

35 Grunwald, Michael. "First Lady to Stump with Fists Up." *The Washington Post*, July 6, 1999. https://www.washingtonpost.com/wp-srv/politics/campaigns/keyraces2000/stories/hillary070699.htm.

36 Grunwald. "First Lady."

37 Bissett, Bill. Interview by Alan Maimon, July 15, 2020.

38 Barton, Shane. Interview by Alan Maimon, May 6, 2020.

39 Williams, Joan C. "What So Many People Don't Get About the U.S. Working Class." *Harvard Business Review*, November 10, 2016. https://hbr.org/2016/11/what-so-many-people-dont-get-about-the-u-s-working-class.

40 Williams. "What So Many."

41 Long, Heather. "Trump gives America's 'poorest white town' hope." CNN Business, CNN, February 6, 2017. https://money.cnn.com/2017/02/06/news/economy/donald-trump-beattyville-kentucky/.

42   Grimes, Alison Lundergan. "Official 2016 General Election
Results." Commonwealth of Kentucky, November 8, 2016. https://
elect.ky.gov/results/2010-2019/Documents/2016%20General%20
Election%20Results.pdf.

Grimes, Alison Lundergan. "Official 2012 General Election
Results." Commonwealth of Kentucky, November 6, 2012. https://
elect.ky.gov/SiteCollectionDocuments/Election%20Results/2010-
2019/2012/2012genresults.pdf.

43   Mayer, Jane. "How Mitch McConnell Became Trump's Enabler-in-
Chief." *The New Yorker,* April 20, 2020. https://www.newyorker.
com/magazine/2020/04/20/how-mitch-mcconnell-became-trumps-
enabler-in-chief.

44   Cross. Interview.

45   Massoglia, Anna. "Senate GOP 'dark money' group passing
millions to super PAC, avoiding disclosure." Center for Responsive
Politics, Opensecrets.org, October 21, 2020. https://www.
opensecrets.org/news/2020/10/senate-gop-dark-money/

46   McConnell, Mitch. "My record shows I'm a friend of coal families."
Louisville Courier-Journal, October 2, 2019.

47   Mongiardo, D. Interview.

48   Mongiardo, D. Interview.

49   Mongiardo, D. Interview.

CHAPTER 8

1   Ahrens, Frank. "A Newspaper Chain Sees Its Future, and It's
Online and Hyper-Local." *The Washington Post,* December
4, 2006. https://www.washingtonpost.com/wp-dyn/content/
article/2006/12/03/AR2006120301037.html.

2   Myron, Chuck. Interview by Alan Maimon, June 5, 2020.

3   "Finalist: Staff of *Courier-Journal*, Louisville, KY." The 2004
Pulitzer Prize Finalist in Public Service, The Pulitzer Prizes,
accessed September 26, 2020. https://www.pulitzer.org/finalists/
staff-132.

4   "The Wire - It's a Bad Time for Newspapers." *The Wire,*
Season 5, Episode 3, "Not for Attribution," video, 3:40, posted
by WireLover2, May 19, 2009. https://www.youtube.com/
watch?v=gKM34ijnhzI.

5   Maimon, Alan. "Judge lets some defendants attend worship as sentencing option." *Courier-Journal*, May 31, 2005, Newspapers. com. https://www.newspapers.com/image/180183308/.

6   Folkenflik, David. "Katrina Marked Turning Point for 'Times-Picayune.'" NPR, September 1, 2007. https://www.npr.org/templates/story/story.php?storyId=13984564.

7   Robertson, Campbell. "How a Newspaper War in New Orleans Ended: With a Baked Alaska and Layoffs." *The New York Times*, May 12, 2019. https://www.nytimes.com/2019/05/12/us/new-orleans-advocate-times-picayune.html.

8   Ungar, Laura. "C-J will close three Kentucky bureaus in '06." *Courier-Journal*, December 14, 2005, Newspapers.com. https://www.newspapers.com/image/180701173/.

9   Seelye, Katharine Q. "The Day the News Left Town." *The New York Times*, January 30, 2006, sec. Business. https://www.nytimes.com/2006/01/30/business/media/the-day-the-news-left-town.html.

10 Seelye. "The Day."

11 Maimon, Alan. "Fletcher wants stronger mine enforcement." *Courier-Journal*, January 12, 2006, Newspapers.com. https://www.newspapers.com/image/180651583/.

12 Maimon, Alan. "East Kentucky poverty dashes industrial hopes." *Courier-Journal*, December 22, 2005, Newspapers.com. https://www.newspapers.com/image/180719572/.

13 Halpern, Sue. "The One-Traffic-Light Town with Some of the Fastest Internet in the U.S." *The New Yorker*, December 3, 2019. https://www.newyorker.com/tech/annals-of-technology/the-one-traffic-light-town-with-some-of-the-fastest-internet-in-the-us.

14 Smith, Ben. "Bail Out Journalists. Let Newspaper Chains Die." *The New York Times*, March 29, 2020. https://www.nytimes.com/2020/03/29/business/coronavirus-journalists-newspapers.html.

    Rivera Brooks, Nancy. "Gannett Acquires Louisville Papers for $300 Million." *Los Angeles Times*, May 20, 1986. https://www.latimes.com/archives/la-xpm-1986-05-20-fi-6849-story.html.

15 Hall, Kevin G. "McClatchy files bankruptcy to shed costs of print legacy and speed shift to digital." McClatchy Washington Bureau, updated February 14, 2020. https://www.mcclatchydc.com/article240139933.html.

16   Anderson, Mark. "Bee journalists, newspaper guild say they're fighting McClatchy proposal to tie pay to clicks." *Sacramento Business Journal*, October 19, 2020. https://www.bizjournals.com/sacramento/news/2020/10/19/mcclatchy-tie-pay-to-clicks.html.

17   Hall. "McClatchy."

18   Rich, Steven, María Sánchez Díez, and Kanyakrit Vongkiatkajorn. "How to download and use the DEA pain pills database." *The Washington Post*, July 18, 2019. https://www.washingtonpost.com/national/2019/07/18/how-download-use-dea-pain-pills-database/.

19   "Hazard Physician and Wife Sentenced for Unlawful Distribution of Prescription Opioids and Health Care Fraud." Press release, The US Attorney's Office, Eastern District of Kentucky, US Department of Justice, September 29, 2017. https://www.justice.gov/usao-edky/pr/hazard-physician-and-wife-sentenced-unlawful-distribution-prescription-opioids-and.

20   "Big Sandy News closes its doors that were first opened in 1885 by 2 teenage owners." On Second Thought, Kentucky Press Association, May 3, 2019. https://members.kypress.com/articles/big-sandy-news-closes-its-doors-that-were-first-opened-in-1885-by-2-teenage-owners/.

21   Alba, Davey, and Jack Nicas. "As Local News Dies, a Pay-for-Play Network Rises in Its Place." *The New York Times*, updated October 20, 2020. https://www.nytimes.com/2020/10/18/technology/timpone-local-news-metric-media.html.

22   Moos, Julie. "How 2 twentysomething journalists brought down a corrupt Kentucky sheriff." Poynter, May 7, 2012. https://www.poynter.org/reporting-editing/2012/how-2-twentysomething-journalists-brought-down-a-corrupt-kentucky-sheriff/.

23   Tani, Maxwell. "Gannett Announces Pay Cuts and Furloughs Across Entire Media Company." *The Daily Beast*, March 30, 2020. https://www.thedailybeast.com/gannett-announces-pay-cuts-and-furloughs-across-entire-media-company.

24   Klein, Charlotte. "Can the News Industry Survive Coronavirus?" *Vanity Fair*, March 30, 2020. https://www.vanityfair.com/news/2020/03/can-the-news-industry-survive-coronavirus.

25 Sullivan, Margaret. "Local journalism needs a coronavirus stimulus plan, too." *The Washington Post*, March 26, 2020. https://www.washingtonpost.com/lifestyle/media/local-journalism-needs-a-coronavirus-stimulus-plan-too/2020/03/25/08358062-6ec6-11ea-b148-e4ce3fbd85b5_story.html.

26 Sonka, Joe (@joesonka). "I'm now on my third round of furloughs this week and will return June 8 — assuming I don't explode from not being allowed to report or comment on what's happening in Louisville right now. Please subscribe/pledge to your local newspaper/news source. Be safe and speak up." Twitter. June 1, 2020, 12:35 p.m. https://twitter.com/joesonka/status/1267494907993821192.

27 Fischer, Sara. "Newsroom layoffs will be brutal in 2020." Axios, July 21, 2020. https://www.axios.com/newsroom-layoffs-2020-c509fb2d-ef58-4fcf-bcdd-3d40022a7a39.html.

<h2 style="text-align:center">CHAPTER 9</h2>

1 Harnsberger, Daniel. Interview by Alan Maimon, May 30, 2020.

2 Harnsberger. Interview.

3 Harnsberger. Interview.

4 Trump, Donald. Twitter, December 20, 2019, 7:12 a.m. https://twitter.com/realDonaldTrump/status/1207997319821615105.

5 Reynolds, Hannah. "Harlan County becomes 2nd Amendment Sanctuary." WYMT, December 17, 2019. https://www.wymt.com/content/news/Harlan-County-becomes-2nd-Amendment-Sanctuary-566282321.html.

6 Whitaker, Jordan. "KSP: Investigation underway into Harlan County shooting." WYMT, December 14, 2019. https://www.wymt.com/content/news/KSP-Investigation-underway-into-Harlan-County-shooting-566216591.html.

Cooney, Lynnette, and T. J. Caudill. "Update: Police identify man shot in head in Harlan County, suspect arrested." WYMT, December 13, 2014. https://www.wymt.com/content/news/Man-shot-in-head-in-Harlan-County-no-arrest-made--566174941.html.

7 Lavoie, Denise. "Second Amendment Sanctuary push aims to defy new gun laws." Associated Press, December 21, 2019. https://apnews.com/article/b83c6654e4a618aec1e88a2ca2eea07a.

8 Schouten, Fredreka. "First on CNN: How a Bloomberg-funded gun-control group helped turn Virginia blue Tuesday." CNN, November 6, 2019. https://www.cnn.com/2019/11/06/politics/bloomberg-everytown-for-gun-safety-virginia-elections/index.html.

9 Sargent, Emily. "County declared a Second Amendment Sanctuary." *Harlan Enterprise*, December 17, 2019. https://www.harlanenterprise.net/2019/12/17/county-declared-a-second-amendment-sanctuary/.

10 Mosley, Dan. Interview by Alan Maimon, December 26, 2019.

11 Staff Reports. "Mosley wins second term as Judge-Executive." *Harlan Enterprise*, November 6, 2018. https://www.harlanenterprise.net/2018/11/06/mosley-wins-second-term-as-judge-executive/.

12 Alford, Roger. "Sex shop turned Bible store is up for sale." Associated Press. *Courier-Journal*, July 1, 2005, Newspapers.com. https://www.newspapers.com/image/180247004/.

13 Paul, Rand. Twitter, April 10, 2020, 8:48 p.m. https://twitter.com/RandPaul/status/1248774960992137217.

14 Mosley, Dan. Facebook post, April 11, 2020. https://www.facebook.com/dan.mosley.14/posts/2863846827030918.

15 Ladd, Sarah. "Easter churchgoers defiant after Kentucky troopers write down their license plate numbers." *Courier-Journal*, April 12, 2020. https://www.courier-journal.com/story/news/2020/04/12/kentucky-churches-hold-in-person-easter-services-despite-order/5127260002/.

16 "Trump posts a video of himself pummeling a man with CNN logo on his face." *Politico*, July 2, 2017. https://www.politico.com/story/2017/07/02/trump-posts-a-video-of-himself-pummeling-a-man-with-cnn-logo-on-his-face-240182.

17 Frum, David. "The Kentucky Governor's Race Is a Warning to Republicans." *The Atlantic*, November 6, 2019. https://www.theatlantic.com/ideas/archive/2019/11/andy-beshears-win-kentucky-warning-trump/601516/.

18 Pergrem, Madison. "Booker and McGrath spend last day campaigning in Eastern Kentucky." WYMT, June 22, 2020. https://www.wymt.com/2020/06/22/booker-and-mcgrath-spend-last-day-campaigning-in-eastern-kentucky/.

19 Mongiardo, Daniel. Interview by Alan Maimon, August 12, 2020.

20 Adams, Michael G. "Official 2020 PRIMARY ELECTION results." Commonwealth of Kentucky, June 23, 2020, accessed September 29, 2020. https://elect.ky.gov/results/2020-2029/Documents/2020%20Primary%20Election%20Results.pdf.

21 Booker, Charles. Interview by Alan Maimon, September 2, 2020.

22 Webb, James. "Secret GOP Weapon: The Scots-Irish Vote." *The Wall Street Journal*, October 19, 2004. https://www.wsj.com/articles/SB109814129391148708.

23 Booker. Interview.

24 Easley, Jonathan. "Trump condemns rioting, doesn't mention Blake in convention address." *The Hill*, August 27, 2020. https://thehill.com/homenews/administration/514092-trump-condemns-rioting-doesnt-mention-blake-in-convention-address.

25 Trump, Donald. Twitter, September 10, 2020, 10:14 a.m. https://twitter.com/realDonaldTrump/status/1304060630656311296.

26 Palumbo, Joe. Interview by Alan Maimon, November 7, 2020.

27 Blevins, Jerod. Interview by Alan Maimon, November 30, 2020.

28 Fugate, Chris. "Why I Love America," Sermon, Hazard, KY, November 8, 2020.

Index

About the Author

ALAN MAIMON is an award-winning journalist and author. As a reporter with The *Louisville Courier-Journal*, he was a finalist for the 2004 Pulitzer Prize in Public Service for a series about gaping holes in Kentucky's justice system. His work for the *Las Vegas Review-Journal* on police shootings and the court system garnered national awards and acclaim. He started his professional writing career in the Berlin bureau of *The New York Times*. Maimon is a former Fulbright fellow, and currently lives with his family in Hopewell, New Jersey.